940

F5

The New Europe

The New Europe

An Introduction to Its Political Geography

By Walter Fitzgerald

Professor of Geography in the Victoria University of Manchester

Published by
Harper & Brothers, New York and London

THE NEW EUROPE

COPYRIGHT, 1945, 1946, BY WALTER FITZGERALD

PRINTED IN THE UNITED STATES OF AMERICA

D-V

TO RUTH

Contents

Maps

Preface

British students of political geography discover, not without surprise, at the outset of their investigations, that little has been done in this country to define the scope and content of the subject. It is less than half a century ago that all humanistic aspects of geography—whether social, economic, or political—were grouped together under the label "political" to distinguish them from "physical" geography. This primitive stage in the organization of geographical study has passed away, partly because of autonomous developments in the subject in Britain itself, and partly in response to the advanced schools of geography on the continent of Europe. Systematization is still, however, rather backward in our country, with geographers somewhat reluctant to define and justify their methods.

In the English language there are several valuable treatises devoted exclusively to political geography. They are the applications to the study of the modern world of certain principles, the exact nature of which is tacitly regarded as established without the necessity for considerable, much less exhaustive, definition. Similar gaps in the presentation of geographical studies to audiences in Britain occur also in the historical and economic branches, particularly the former: and such deficiencies suggest that geography as a whole is as yet in the early stages of its career, as a part of British education. The contrast is certainly strongly emphasized with the stage reached in both the United States and Germany.

In view of the above-mentioned need for clearer definition and systematization in the handling of political geography the essay which follows begins with a short statement of the concepts and discipline of political geography in its application to the European continent.

Historical and economic investigations of European society are quite prolific. On the other hand, the relation of European peoples

xi

to their physical environments is considered much more rarely. The particular characteristics of the European environment and the response of population to the opportunities, as well as restrictions, which "place" provides or imposes, are matters on which the geographer is able to guide economic and political administration. It is hoped that this essay may make a small contribution to the solution of problems which, left disregarded or handled without objective purpose, are likely to continue to endanger the peace of Europe and of the entire world. The Second World War is not yet at an end, but the geographical realities with which this book is concerned will endure long after Peace is restored. Completion of the text was accomplished several months before the end of 1944, and it will be appreciated that no attempt has been made to forecast the dramatic events of 1945.

The reader should have easy access to a good atlas. Of those available, The Times Atlas is still by far the best. The sketch-maps included in this essay will, it is hoped, give additional help on particular points.

To many who have helped in various ways I extend my warm appreciation. In particular I owe to my wife unfailing encouragement and advice.

W. F.

CHEADLE,
September 1944

Preface to Second Edition

The delays which, unfortunately, war-time conditions of 1944-45 rendered inevitable prevented the first edition from being published until many months after the completion of the manuscript. Bearing in mind the author's endeavour to interpret from a geographical stand-point the political pattern of Europe rather than to record contemporary events, the demand for a second edition, nevertheless, offers a welcome opportunity to modernise the volume in the light of post-war conditions. New developments in the political geography of Central Europe and the Balkans receive particular attention: on the other hand, there is little to add or to change where one or two of the chapters are concerned.

W. F.

December 1945

The New Europe

"The old Europe has gone. The map is being rolled up and a new map is unrolling before us. We shall have to do a great deal of fundamental thinking and scrapping of old points of view before we find our way through the new continent which now opens before us."

(General J. C. Smuts,
at a meeting of the Empire Parliamentary Association,
November 25, 1943)

1.

The Concept of Political Geography

Interest in geography's contribution to an understanding of the basis of civilization has been much stimulated by experience of war. In the recent world conflict our military effort had to be calculated on a careful estimate of the actual and potential resources of all the belligerents, friendly or hostile. Moreover, in the prevalent mood for national as well as international reconstruction the planning of community life in its proper relation to environment is now accepted as deserving serious study. The statesmen of post-war Europe are undertaking a great experiment in political geography. The framework of frontiers which they recommend will prove its worth in so far as it both satisfies local needs and promotes international equilibrium.

In the application of political geography to the study of international affairs the following arguments, briefly outlined, emerge:

1. Geography establishes a close relationship between types of human organization and their environments; and the particular objective of political geography is an investigation of the extent to which the nature of States, together with their organization and inter-relations, is influenced by, and adjusted to, conditions of geography.

2. The political pattern of the world is subject to ceaseless modification, and for two main reasons:

(a) The factors of physical environment, on which the pattern largely depends, are themselves subject to processes of change which are beyond man's control. Thus, to take an illustration from the Middle East of the Old World, desiccation of climate in past time had the effect of destroying the prosperity of

States and indeed of denuding whole regions of all organized life.

(b) In the political, as also in the social and economic evolution of mankind, the adjustment of life—in all its varied manifestations—to environment is itself in process of continuous change. This adjustment is, in part, a conscious selection by man of opportunities offered by Nature. It is not solely a matter of geographical influence, much less of geography acting as an agent of determinism. Man assists in designing his own environment, and does so in the light of experience and of his estimate of the opportunities which the physical environment has to offer. Thus the stage of civilization reached is a factor of primary importance in shaping the character of the adjustment. Moreover, the communities of mankind greatly vary in their methods of response to environment, although care is taken not to attempt a comparison between peoples in respect of their innate capacities. Such an investigation is certainly not for the geographer.

3. The inter-relations of States become ever closer—though not necessarily more sympathetic—as man surmounts the geographical difficulties of distance, climate, and terrain. Political isolation is impossible to-day, as all States have been brought to realize.

At times of political re-settlement such as the present post-war period, the geographical basis of frontiers and their justification receive unusually thorough investigation. It is then realized that the boundaries which divide the sovereign States of Europe are instruments of regional partition which have no sanction in geography. Frontiers in geography are rare, and almost everywhere there is transition from one set of environmental conditions of climate, land-form, and vegetation —summarized by Herbertson in the term "natural region"—to another of contrasted characteristics. Moreover, transition is not confined to the physical environment of man. As all his organized activities—in settlement, economic production, state-building, etc.—are influenced by physical geography, the characteristics of one type of civilization, associated with a particular region, merge with those of a neighbouring type. Such mergence is at times in defiance of political frontiers, which, over long periods, are unable to prevent—though they tend to hinder—the spread of cultural influences from one country to another.

As no sanction for frontiers is found in geography the term "natural frontier" cannot claim geographical validity. It is most commonly employed in a military context, and to the soldier signifies a boundary which, of those available, is the most likely to provide an adequate line of defence.[1] Until the advent of air warfare the crest of a mountain-range was considered to be the ideal "natural frontier"; but configuration is not the only environmental feature which might be the basis of "natural" divisions. Equally "natural" would be a line defining the limits of nationality. Similarly, the limit of a coal-field or some other industrial zone is entitled to be termed "natural." Obviously, any such line is selected for, and justified by, the particular end which the boundary commissioners have in view, but that is not to say that it is endorsed by geography.

In earlier times, when man's ability to convert geographical features to his own use was more limited than now, a river-course was normally favoured as a line of frontier. It was an obvious and permanent division which obviated the necessity of selecting some more arbitrary and, therefore, disputable boundary. Moreover, taking into account both the urgent need for security and also the contemporary standards of military science and equipment, the river-banks, together with neighbouring marshy ground, might well provide the basis of an adequate defensive system. So, for example, before the Norman Conquest the line of the middle and upper Thames was for long the common frontier of Mercia and Wessex, and the present-day county boundaries within the same basin bear witness to the ancient partition.

No longer in war is a river-line dependable for defensive purposes. Moreover, as an international boundary it is open to very serious geographical objections. Unlike the mountain system which may divide from each other regions of geographical contrast, a river normally traverses a basin whose parts are drawn together and integrated into a regional entity; and the river, if navigable and therefore commercially useful, may assist in the process of regional integration. So we find, for example, that the Central Danubian Basin, centring

[1] Vide Holdich (Sir T. H.): *Political Frontiers and Boundary Making*, London, 1916.

on the Hungarian Plain, is one of the most clearly integrated regions of Europe. To split the Hungarian Plain politically has been termed "a geographical crime," yet, after the First World War, the unity of this region was disrupted by a complicated partition.

The search for satisfactory lines of defence is one of the most fruitless to which national statesmen are still committed. It is inevitable under existing conditions that every State will demand for its own security a frontier which nature has made defensible, the assumption being, almost invariably, that the neighbouring State is potentially hostile, and liable at a time convenient to itself to go to war. Yet it must be obvious that no one State can acquire a frontier advantageous for defence without at the same time placing its neighbour at a corresponding strategic disadvantage.

Political history offers very few instances of a frontier, drawn with such equity of purpose that neither of the States affected has received an unfair strategic advantage, but one outstanding example of the kind deserves special mention.

In 1880, after more than a quarter of a century of disturbed relations arising out of hostile contacts in the Andes, the prospects of a peaceful solution of the dispute between Chile and the Argentine seemed very remote. Yet, in the following year, the two Powers agreed to demarcate a common frontier, which should extend for approximately 1,700 miles along the crests of the Southern Andes. It was expected that the boundary would, by following the highest ridge, coincide with the watershed of the Cordillera; but, as was later discovered, there were many districts within the boundary zone where there was no such coincidence of crest-line and hydrographic "divide."

To the everlasting credit of the two nations, they agreed, in the event of negotiations reaching an *impasse*, to accept a decision by arbitration. This was the more commendable in that the desire for a strategically favourable frontier was at first, if not later, the dominant consideration of each Government. In 1896, the British Government was invited to appoint a frontier commission and to arbitrate on the basis of its findings. The compromise award, which Great Britain recommended in 1902, was readily accepted by both countries which, moreover, solemnly declared their determination to maintain good neighbourly relations for all time on the basis of the new frontier. The erection of the massive statue of the "Christ of the Andes" at the Uspallata Pass (11,000 feet above sea-level) is the impressive symbol of a compact[2] from which European Powers, much older in political experience than either Chile or Argentina, have something to learn.

As the world is a whole made up of inter-related parts, political frontiers—however "natural"—are artificial lines of division which obstruct inter-regional co-operation, their purpose being to partition what to Nature is indivisible. Through their influence adjacent peoples are turned away from association with each other, and are led to exaggerate the usually small ethnological and cultural differences which distinguish them. Moreover, as they correspond more with political ideals than with geographical realities they may be opposed to a satisfactory economic and social adjustment of the community to its environment.

In a Europe of rival sovereignties devotion to frontiers arises mainly through lack of confidence in any safeguard of social and political security other than military defence; and the defence of frontiers is intended to be a guarantee, both of the inviolability of individual States and of the stability of the political balance as a whole. There is, however, no possibility of dividing from each other the peoples of the great middle zone of Europe by frontiers which exactly define their limits. The widespread intermingling of populations of various ethnic and cultural origins, which is characteristic of European society, had already occurred before the partition of Europe into nation-states fixed the population of the continent, by restricting inter-regional migration. So has been created the hitherto insoluble problem of the "minority" groups of East-Central Europe. Detached from the parent body and set down amongst peoples of alien culture and nationality, each minority has resisted absorption by the nation within which it is geographically inset, and has kept alive the hope of ultimate reunion with its kinsmen.

If ever the European system of sovereign States should be replaced by the United States of Europe the nations would relinquish much of their individual claim to sovereignty, whilst retaining cultural and administrative autonomy. Boundaries would still be required, but merely for the convenience of local administration, as they are required, for example, in the federations of the Dominion of Canada

---

[2] The inscription (in translation) on the statue reads: "Sooner shall these mountains crumble into dust than the people of Argentina and Chile break the peace, which, at the foot of Christ, the Redeemer, they have sworn to maintain."

and the Union of South Africa. Once national sovereignty is removed from the concept of frontiers they cease to be the main source of international dispute, and changes affecting them become matters of comparatively simple local adjustment. The principles on which boundary demarcation would then depend would have more to do with the economic and social welfare of mankind than with the claims of nationalism.

The welfare of Europe depends on the economic integration of its regions, similar to the economic integration which the United States have attained; but, at the same time, the autonomy of Europe's many nationally conscious communities must be preserved. Only on such a basis does European equilibrium seem possible.

Naturally enough, wherever nationally conscious Europeans have migrated overseas they have carried with them respect for the sanctity of frontiers. Boundaries in Africa and South America were, in the first place, drawn hurriedly, in the scramble for territory, without surveys of the territories through which they were to pass. Several West and East African dependencies, annexed by European Powers during the nineteenth century, are still bounded by straight lines. Such frontiers obviously bear little or no relation to physical geography or to the distribution, either of population density or of tribal or other social and political groupings.[3]

It might have been expected that, after the opening-up of Africa and the immense accumulation of geographical knowledge then acquired, wholesale rectification of frontiers would have been inevitable. But rectifications have been rare, and on a very minor scale, whilst, with the passage of time, the unchanged original boundaries have increased, rather than lost, their rigidity. To alter a colonial frontier after it has remained fixed for a long period becomes virtually impossible, without disturbing international peace; for the cession of territory, which rectification would involve, is closely bound up with imperial prestige. The voluntary cession of colonial, as of national territory, without corresponding compensation elsewhere, is so rare in the history of international affairs as to be virtually unknown.

Not only Africa, but the Americas and Australia also—in aggregate nearly one-half the land surface of the inhabited earth—are so partitioned that the national or administrative units of which they

[3] The frontiers of South-West Africa, Angola, Tanganyika Territory, Kenya, and the Gold Coast illustrate the point particularly well.

are composed form patterns bearing little, if any, ascertainable relation to geographical or ethnological realities. It is, however, true in the cases of the U.S.A., Canada, and Australia, that their internal frontiers, not being international, are of secondary importance in the political and economic life of the communities concerned. The States of Australia and of the U.S.A., like the Provinces of Canada and of the Union of South Africa, relinquished their individual claims to sovereign independence when they accepted federation. Thus throughout these great sub-continental areas internal frontiers bounding States or Provinces are no longer able to provoke international disputes. Their re-delimitation, if rectification should be required, is now a mere domestic issue. It is notable that, although the majority of these frontiers have remained unaltered since they were first established, there has been little demand for their rectification. Many of them are purely artificial, and appear—on the Mercator cylindrical map-projection—as vertical or horizontal lines, so drawn as to be regardless of the facts of either physical or humanistic geography.

Within their arbitrarily-drawn boundaries, the communities of Australia, Canada, and the United States, respectively, evince strong local patriotism. The internal boundaries have acquired prestige by virtue of resistance to change over a long period, even though they may be unsuited to modern economic and administrative conditions. At the same time, the citizens of the Australian and North American federations fully recognize that their nationality is co-extensive with the limits of Commonwealth or of Union.

It should not be assumed, in this connexion, that the forty-eight States of the American Union are necessarily less significant individually, both as regards size of population and of territory and as regards international influence, than the sovereign States of Europe, west of Russia. In fact, they compare favourably in such ways with the European nationality-states. In world affairs their individual influence is very considerable, though expressed through the medium of the federal authority.

As previously indicated, respect for old-established frontiers tends to remain, even though their *raison d'être* no longer exists, because of changes in the distribution of population and of modifications in geographical conditions. Long and fortunate experience of national self-determination within inviolate outer frontiers, defined and guarded by the sea, renders the British point of view in these matters perfectly natural. Britain is a small country, which has prospered greatly under nationalism, and its influence in European affairs has favoured the promotion and preservation of national States, almost irrespective of their size in area and population. It may well be that Britain will continue to support a political plan for Europe based on a multiplicity of sovereign national States. West of the Russian frontier, all the States which have been familiar to us since 1920 reappeared on the political map after the Second World War, their existence confirmed, though each altered in territory or in authority according to military fortune.

Sympathy with small States of homogeneous nationality which characterizes Britain's attitude to Europe is due, in some measure, to a close association of the two concepts—"nationality" and "race." They are interchangeable terms in much that is written and spoken on the subject of the British people: yet our national genius has evolved as the outcome of the effective fusion within Great Britain of diverse communities of widely different ethnic and cultural origins.

Other great Powers, equally concerned in the future of Europe, are less committed than is Great Britain to a policy which would extend political sovereignty almost automatically to the individual national groups of Central and South-Eastern Europe. Both the United States of America and the Soviet Union are Powers on a scale much greater than that of peninsular Europe,[4] and their foreign policies are necessarily influenced by the vast geographical dimensions on which their own political planning has been conceived. A detailed partition of the continent of Europe based on the sovereign independence of national communities is a development in political geography for which they, with the experience of their own continents to guide them, show little enthusiasm. Yet they are quick to recognize the value and importance of the cultural contributions made by members of the many nationalities represented within their respective frontiers. Indeed, as federations of peoples, they acknowledge that their strength lies in the variety of the ethnic and cultural types which they incorporate. Turning away from the most narrow interpretation of nationalism, they focus attention on the need for a wide and varied economic basis, a basis which shall override nationality frontiers whenever the latter stand in the way of the integration of the economic life of the federation as a whole.

[4] The respective areas in square miles are approximately as follows: the U.S.S.R., 8,312,000; the U.S.A., 3,088,000; Europe without Russia, 1,637,000.

Germany for long based her imperial policy on the conception of the "super-state," involving hegemony over tributary lands and sub-ject-peoples.

Full rights of citizenship were to be restricted to the "master race," so that there was to be no question of national self-determination for those who were not German; whilst the economic resources of the super-state as a whole were organized primarily in the interests of the racially superior community. The rights of politically and economi-cally weak communities to sovereign independence were frankly, even brutally, denied, and there was similar denial of equity in the enjoy-ment of economic wealth by the subject-peoples.

The contrasts which have been drawn between certain of the great Powers in their politico-geographical conceptions are sufficient to indicate that the shape of the world to be will depend on the ability of mankind to reconcile profound differences of political thought which still divide the governments of the peoples. The age-old ques-tion of the relation of the community to environment, which is of the essence of political geography, remains as critical to society as ever. Europe, where the question is in its most acute form, threatens the peace of the world more menacingly than any other of the con-tinents. And it is in Europe where the promise of international reconstruction will be most severely tested in these post-war years.

Some form of federation of European peoples is generally con-ceded as essential to continued civilized life, but its concomitant, namely, the abolition of national sovereignty, has not yet been accepted by the majority of the national States of the continent. The suspicions and hatred which have bedevilled all attempts to secure international reconciliation are older, deeper, and more widespread than those of other continents. They can be allayed only by the appli-cation of impartial justice to the claims of the various national groups for territorial rights; but it would be advisable not to expect impartial justice from a peace conference limited to Powers whose individual interests are deeply involved in the territorial problems which await solution.

The need of the world is not a new partition of territories between the Powers, according to this or that formula, but an ordered redis-tribution of population within the habitable regions of the world. The present congestion of certain lands and the emptiness of others does not correspond to the distribution of the world's potential resources. There are vast areas within the temperate and tropical zones whose climate, soil, and vegetation are favourable to human life, but which still lie fallow. Their frontiers are closed to settlement for a variety of reasons, amongst them the desire for racial exclusiveness and the intention to protect certain economic standards against the intrusion of peoples of low material level.

On the other hand, there are large areas of the Old World, where densities exceed 1,000 persons to the square mile, and where standards of life are greatly depressed by extreme pressure on the available land. Such pressure is, in many instances, increasing because of a prolific birth-rate. In countries where congestion is very acute, not only internal administration, but foreign policy also, is affected, and the harmony of international society is endangered. Efforts on the part of individual States to ease the situation within their own borders cannot be more than partially effective, and the normal outflow of emigrants in search of new homes is prevented by frontier restrictions which had become increasingly prohibitive before the War.

The settlement of the empty, or half empty, but habitable lands, and a corresponding reduction of density in the congested areas, constitute the supreme task of planning now confronting the world. It is a problem to which the geographer should pay continuous attention.

In these introductory pages certain of the ideas which permeate the subject of political geography have been briefly outlined. Their interest and value will be measured by their ability to elucidate those tendencies in national and international affairs which preceded the greatest catastrophe in human history, and to contribute to the political reshaping of the world of to-morrow. In the pages that follow, Europe, the continent of most complex political geography, will be our main, though not exclusive, concern.

SELECTED BIBLIOGRAPHY

ADAMI, V.: *National Frontiers in Relation to International Law*, London, 1927.

ANCEL, J.: "Les Frontières: étude de géographie politique," *Hague Academy of International Law, Recueil des cours*, vol. 55 (1936), pp. 207-97.

BOGGS, S. W.: *International Boundaries*, New York, 1940.

BRIGHAM, A. P.: "Principles in the Determination of Boundaries," *Geog. Review*, vol. 7 (1919), pp. 201-19.

DAVIS, J. W.: "The Unguarded Boundary," *Geog. Review*, New York, vol. 12 (1922), pp. 585-601.

FAWCETT, C. B.: *Frontiers: a study in Political Geography*, Oxford, 1918.

FITZGERALD, W.: "Geography and International Settlement," *Nature*, vol. 152, 1943.

HARTSHORNE, R.: "The Nature of Geography," *Ann. Assoc. Amer. Geogr.*, vol. 29 (September and December 1939), pp. 173-658.

HARTSHORNE, R.: "Recent Developments in Political Geography," *Amer. Pol. Sci. Rev.*, vol. 29, 1935, pp. 785-804, 943-66.

HOLDICH, SIR T. H.: *The Countries of the King's Award*, London, 1904.

HOLDICH, SIR T. H.: *Political Frontiers and Boundary Making*, London, 1916.

JOHNSON, D. W.: "The Rôle of Political Boundaries," *Geog. Review*, New York, vol. 4 (September 1917), pp. 208-13.

LAPRADELLE, P. DE: *La Frontière; étude de droit international*, Paris, 1928.

McMAHON, SIR A. H.: "International Boundaries," *Jour. Roy. Soc. Arts*, vol. 84 (1935), pp. 2-16.

MAULL, O.: *Politische Geographie*, Berlin, 1925.

RATZEL, F.: *Politische Geographie*, Munich, 1903.

ROSE, W. J.: "The Sociology of Frontiers," *Soc. Rev.*, vol. 27, 1935, pp. 201-19.

ROXBY, P. M.: "The Scope and Aims of Human Geography," *Proc. Brit. Assoc.* (Bristol Meeting), 1930.

RUSSELL, I. C.: "Geography and International Boundaries," *Amer. Geog. Soc. of N.Y.*, Bull., vol. 35, pp. 147-59.

SAUER, C. O.: "The Prospect for Redistribution of Population," in *Limits of Land Settlement* (Council on Foreign Relations), 1937.

SEMPLE, E. C.: "Geographical Boundaries," *Amer. Geog. Soc. of N.Y.*, Bull., vol. 39 (1907), pp. 385-97; 1907, pp. 449-63.

SIEGER, R.: "Die Grenze in der Politischen Geographie," *Zeitschrift für Geopolitik*, Jahrgang 2, 1925, pp. 661-71.

VALLAUX, C.: *Le Sol et l'Etat: Géographie Sociale*, Paris, 1911.

VIDAL DE LA BLACHE, P.: *Etats et Nations de l'Europe*, Paris, 1889.

VOGEL, W.: *Politische Geographie*, Leipzig und Berlin, 1922.

WHITTLESEY, D.: *The Earth and the State: a study of Political Geography*, New York, 1939.

2.

The Nation-States of Western Europe: Their Evolution in Relation to Geography

In a survey of the political geography of Europe the middle zone is clearly to be distinguished from the western fringe of maritime countries. From the former, where German and Slav meet, there emerge a high proportion of the urgent international questions of our time. Our attention will be directed first to the Atlantic-facing countries, where, in striking contrast to the fluidity of the politico-geographical position characteristic of the continental lands farther east, there is, and has been for two or three centuries, a relatively stable order. Although protracted disputes preceded the final decisions regarding their alignments, the majority of the frontiers have long been confirmed by international consent, and their impressive antiquity is perhaps some guarantee of their future permanence.

The States of Western Europe are associated by reason of the strength and endurance of their national foundations. Belgium is the exceptional case of a State, built in modern times, in which a sense of national cohesion has not yet fully matured. Save for this one instance, all the Western European countries have experienced a slow natural growth of national consciousness, and, although the ingredients of nationality may vary to some extent, the foundations are similar throughout. Language everywhere plays its very important part as a unifying influence, although there are instances—Spain and Britain being notable—where nationality is found to cover linguistic diversities. Generally throughout the western lands, religion means less than language as a basis of nationality, but its influence is formidable, as, for example, in Ireland where it largely determines the national allegiance of two politically distinct communities. Where divergencies of language and of religious belief exist within a State they are not wholly explicable without recourse to geography.

The conception of communal solidarity, upon which the strength of national sentiment depends, involves more than a political association of people bound together by ties of culture and tradition. Attachment to a particular physical environment, within which the "personality" of the national group has grown and matured, is also an essential factor. Nationality is a phenomenon of slow growth, and the influence of "place" makes itself felt through long contact with a particular area, whose landscape is an essential part of the national heritage. Devotion to a familiar territory is not only a factor of strength in national life: it is a guarantee of the continuance of national culture and tradition, and therefore of the nation itself. In Central Europe there is not an equally definite relationship between "nationality" and "place." The German nation in particular has, in the course of long-persistent colonization within the Slavonic realm of Europe, lost much of its geographical compactness, and depends to a considerable degree on the idea of blood kinship.

The frontiers which define the nation-states of Western Europe seem in many cases to be suggested by geography. Quite commonly we find that the national homeland approximates fairly closely to a region of strongly-marked characteristics, whose limits can be stated in terms of physical geography. This is not, however, true of all the western nations, and the Kingdom of the Netherlands is an instance. It is to be remembered, however, that in former centuries, during the formative stages of nation-building, geographical conditions in many districts of the North European Plain were different from those of to-day, especially in respect of vegetation-cover and the distribution of land and sea. The modern map does not reveal the former existence of zones of forest and marsh, yet, surrounded by such natural defences, certain European communities grew to national consciousness. Throughout the medieval period isolated situation and difficult geographical conditions saved some lands of the Atlantic fringe from the social and political upheaval which repeated irruptions from Western Asia produced in Eastern and Central Europe.

Before we pass to the countries in turn there are two further matters of general application. In every instance the evolution of nationality followed, and was a consequence of, the establishment of political authority (i.e., the State) over an area whose limits were in the first place determined largely by situation and unattractive geographical considerations. Normally, the State expanded slowly by incorporating territories and their populations; but slow though the process of state-building may have been, the evolution of nationality was even more leisurely.

Before their incorporation within the State, the various petty kingdoms or tribal entities were, to a greater or lesser degree, independent and inspired by patriotic ideals based on traditions of land occupancy within well-recognized geographical limits. It was the first task of the State to break the power of regional particularism and to extend the authority of one government throughout the incorporated lands.

Secondly, the State strengthened its internal authority by joining, in effective partnership, the various communities which conquest had brought within its frontiers. Improvements in transportation, the clearing away of forest and marsh, and a more intensive utilization of the resources of the land, were some of the means by which inter-regional co-operation within the State was made possible.

So a wider loyalty was evolved, together with a body of tradition common to all inhabitants within the State. Local patriotism, based on ancient association with some provincial unit or region, has usually survived, and has done much to enrich and vitalize national development; and, so long as the State is sympathetic to its existence, there is usually little danger of its political expression becoming a threat to national integrity.

The process of national evolution in Western Europe was little affected by the ethnic origins of the peoples concerned. Diversity of racial composition is far more common than purity of stock, and within the same nation may be found individuals so strongly contrasted in their physical build that they might well be drawn from opposite extremities of the continent. Because "nationality" and "race" are terms so frequently confused in discussions of national development, it has been thought advisable to include here brief mention of the ethnic composition of the national groups of Western Europe. The importance of the geographical factor in the distribution of ethnic types will naturally enough not be overlooked.

BRITAIN AND IRELAND

During several millennia, ending about the eleventh century A.D., the ingredients of the modern population were supplied by a series of migrations which reached our shores from the neighbouring coasts of the continent. The process of ethnic fusion was continuous, though most active in recent centuries as a result of the increased intermingling of population which improved communications have made possible. In the course of the prehistoric and early historic periods, representatives of each of the main race-types of Europe—usually designated "Mediterranean," "Alpine," and "Nordic"—settled in both Britain and Ireland. It is of the first importance to appreciate that the modern Briton is, in the ethnic sense, a blend of most of the stocks which have populated Western and Central Europe since the retreat of the Quaternary glaciation. Both "Mediterranean" and "Nordic" types—or reasonably close approximations to these idealized primary stocks—are widely found, and each has its particular regional distribution. On the other hand, indications of the settlement of "Alpine" man are relatively scarce, as well as much more localized than is the evidence of the other stocks.

By the close of the Neolithic Age in Britain (placed usually c. 2000 B.C.), the greater part of the British Isles was occupied by successive migrations of "Mediterranean" man from the western basin of the Mediterranean. No subsequent occupation of other racial types has completely displaced the "Mediterranean" elements from their strongholds, and it is generally held that they constitute a large, if not the larger, part of the modern population, not only in Britain, but in Ireland also. In England, it may be true that the "Mediterranean" strain is proportionately weaker than in the other three countries, but even so it seems to predominate in most parts, except on the eastern side.

Long before the Christian era, immigrants from the North European Plain, usually west of the Elbe, came in by the eastern and south-eastern coasts. There were many waves in a long succession, and characteristic of the majority were physical traits showing a fusion of "Nordic" and "Alpine" characters. It was at this time that peoples speaking one or other of the Celtic languages entered Britain and Ireland. Many were, no doubt, of mixed "Nordic" and "Alpine" ancestry, with the first predominating. They included the Belgae, who were politically dominant in Southern Britain at the time of Caesar's invasions.

It is unfortunate that the term "Celtic" is generally and loosely used in an ethnic sense. Its cultural, and especially philological, significance is very real in the British Isles to-day, but if there ever was, as seems doubtful, a Celtic stock of fairly uniform racial characters, the term is certainly without meaning to-day for the purpose of ethnic identification. A geographical survey of the Celtic peoples of modern times reveals clearly how heterogeneous they are from the physical standpoint. They include such groups as the broad-headed and stocky Bretons, the agile, long-headed and markedly brunet valley-populations of Glamorganshire, and also the mixed peoples of Ireland, ranging from the short, dark type found in parts of Connaught to the blond and tall "Nordic" of the Wexford coastlands.

The period of nearly four centuries during which Britain, south of Hadrian's Wall, formed a province of the Roman Empire has mattered little in the racial history of the British people. Both the civilization and the personnel which came from Rome retreated, or were completely lost in the Anglo-Saxon irruptions of the fifth and sixth centuries; and there is no ethnic trace of an occupation which lasted longer than the period separating Tudor times from the present century. Similarly, India after two centuries of British rule is unaffected in its racial composition.

The Anglo-Saxons penetrated the heart of England from the eastern and southern coasts, utilizing every accessible and navigable river. In the process, some, but by no means all, of the earlier peoples—mainly of "Mediterranean" type—were displaced and forced westwards towards the Cambrian and Devonian peninsulas. Most of lowland England was forested, and there was, in addition, much marshland, including the fen of the Wash. Under pressure, exerted by the aggressive newcomers, the older population took refuge in forest clearings and on "islands" enclosed within marsh, whilst the open land fell to their supplanters. This partial segregation of population, which occurred over a thousand years ago, is still recorded in the existing distribution of ethnic traits within the eastern half of England. Over this area, as a whole, the index of nigrescence of the population is low, in response to the strong influence of a predominantly "Nordic" Anglo-Saxon ancestry, but where dense forest existed, as for example in Hertfordshire, the older stock persists and greatly increases the index.[1]

The Scandinavian occupation of the coastal districts of Northern Britain[2] and the succeeding invasion of the Normans—themselves a very mixed people, though originally Norse—added smaller contributions to the human stock of England than did the Anglo-Saxon. Such influence as they had, however, lay in the direction of increasing the proportion of tall, blond folk in the population. It has been estimated by one authority that, as late as the reign of Edward I, not more than one-fifth of the English were even partially of Norman descent.[3]

Largely because of its geographical situation on the extreme edge of Western Europe, Ireland was free from both Roman and Anglo-Saxon intrusion. The sea-power of the Norsemen in the ninth and tenth centuries, however, facilitated Norwegian and Danish settlement at almost every natural harbour along the Irish coast. Dublin and Wexford were founded as Norwegian colonies, and Limerick began as a garrison of the Danes. There was no Scandinavian settlement far distant from tidal water, so that it is in the ports of to-day that the traits of Viking ancestry are revealed. In the tenth century, the inhabitants of Scandinavian origin were a larger proportion of the population of Ireland than were the settlers of Danish stock in the population of England at that time. Later invasions of Ireland, including the Anglo-Norman (beginning in the twelfth century), together with the "plantations" of Ulster and other parts in almost modern times, have tended to increase the tall blond element in the eastern half of the country. The elevated, and usually infertile, lands of the west, notably Connaught, remain, as they always have been, the strongholds of the folk of "Mediterranean" ancestry: they have been little affected by successive waves of invasion from the neighbouring island. A similar distribution is true of Britain: the eastern and midland districts, wide open to the continent, were repeatedly overrun,

[1] Illustrating the variation within Britain of the index of nigrescence (where a low index indicates a tendency to blondness, and a high index a tendency to dark complexion) are the following: East Anglia 10, Hertfordshire 30, South Wales 62.

[2] In Yorkshire and farther south most of the Norsemen were of Danish origin, but in Northern and Western Scotland, as well as in Ireland, most of the Scandinavians came from Norway.

[3] v. W. Z. Ripley: The Races of Europe. Chapter 12—The British Isles—is specially to be noted.

but the western highlands, of Wales particularly, retain with little change the characteristics of the ancient brunet folk.

To summarize—the racial composition of the British and Irish peoples illustrates the falsity of any theory that nationality is derived from community of race. In both islands the dominant stock remains —as it was before the dawn of history—the dark-complexioned, rather long-headed type which made its way northwards from the Mediterranean before and during the Neolithic culture period. On this ethnic substratum were superimposed, at different times, peoples of Nordic-Alpine and Nordic traits, who settled the eastern parts of both countries and there remain prominent, if not dominant, to this day.

How often is the Irish nationality differentiated from the English on grounds of racial divergence! Such a view results from a complete lack of appreciation of the very similar racial histories of the two peoples. "Mediterranean," "Alpine," and "Nordic" types are common to both, but because fusion has occurred everywhere, and yet has varied in degree from one district to another, there is no race-type which can be regarded as embodying the ideal characteristics of either Englishman or Irishman. The ethnic dissimilarities to be found amongst the nationals of either country are as easily perceptible to the eye as they are to anthropometry.

The geographical detachment of Ireland from Britain has hindered easy intercourse between the two peoples. Their ways of life have continued to diverge, despite the improvements in marine transport which have facilitated communication between the two islands. English and Irish cultural achievements have not always promoted mutual understanding, and the limitations which geography has imposed on Ireland are partly responsible: its people have not yet, for good or ill, felt the full influence of modern industrialism.

The Irish attained the status of nationhood very early in the Christian era, and claims based on the antiquity of national sentiment and achievement have figured prominently on all occasions of political negotiation with England. Long before the English occupation, Ireland's contacts with continental Europe were direct, across the sea, to France and Spain, and the close cultural link with the southern lands of the continent was preserved throughout the dark centuries— the sixth and seventh in particular—when civilized life in North-Western Europe was rare.

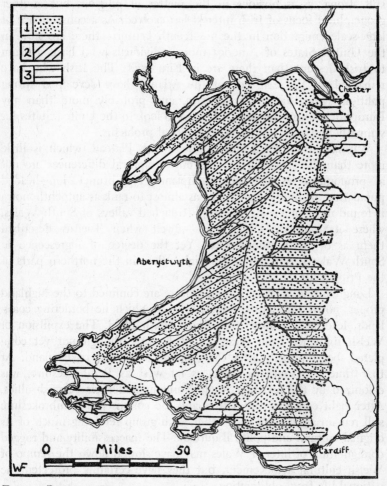

Fig. 1.—Principal Welsh-speaking and English-speaking Parts of Wales

1. Land (in Wales) above 500 feet.
2. Areas where more than 90 per cent of the population speak Welsh as their first language.
3. Areas where more than 50 per cent of the population speak English only.

The attachment of Ireland to Latin of Mediterranean culture is still strong, as is obvious in the matter of religion, but another geographical focus of Irish interest has evolved. As a consequence of large-scale emigration in the nineteenth century, there are now in the United States of America more individuals who have a claim to Irish descent than there are in Eire itself. The Irish who have remained on the east side of the Atlantic have developed strong political sympathies with America, and probably more than any European country Ireland has tended to look to the United States for sympathetic consideration of its political problems.

Within the confined area of the Welsh Plateau, which is little more than the size of Yorkshire, ethnographical differences are not as pronounced as they are in Ireland. The brunet, long-headed population, of lineage so ancient as almost to rank as autochthonous, is found most purely in the deeply-trenched valleys of South Wales, where its ancestors—the Silures—dwelt when Tacitus described them as of "dark complexion." Yet the degree of nigrescence in South Wales is not very much higher than in the northern parts of the Principality.

Long continuity of breed and culture are confined to the highland proper, north and south, respectively, of which lie bordering coast-lands, leading westwards from the English Plain. The expulsion of Welsh influence from these marginal strips, though not yet completed, began shortly after the Norman Conquest of England. At that time the southern coast, as far west as Pembrokeshire, was colonized by the invading Anglo-Normans and their Flemish allies. After eight centuries the natives and the colonists of Pembrokeshire still remain aloof from each other, each group retaining much of its original cultural and political outlook. The inaccessibility and rugged configuration of interior Wales may have slowed down the tempo of Welsh cultural achievement, but they have certainly protected the national life from obliteration.

It is generally admitted that the Scottish nation embraces as wide a range of ethnic types as appears in England. The same elements that occur in South Britain are repeated, but fusion has produced at least one unusual type. Brunet features are pronounced in the west, as is usual in Britain as a whole, and their frequency culminates in Argyllshire and neighbouring parts of Inverness-shire. The population of the south-western peninsula—Galloway—is dark-complexioned, but quite remarkably tall—a combination of traits rare in Western Europe. On the east, both north and south of the Firth of Forth, blondness is widespread, and the influence of Anglian settlement in Midlothian during the Anglo-Saxon period is thus attested. As in the case of Ireland, Norwegian influence has affected a very long coast-line, and the counties north of Inverness-shire, together with the Hebrides, are Old Norse colonies, in race and culture more true to Scandinavian tradition than is any part of the British Isles.

In Scotland, as also in Ireland and Wales, nationalism grew in cohesion and vigour during the centuries of struggle with England. Yet as late as the middle years of the eighteenth century the political influence of powerful clans, each within its own territory, was so considerable as to hinder that unity of national direction which alone would have rendered possible successful resistance to English hegemony. Scotland at the time of union with England was a country of divided loyalties. The ancient Celtic-speaking stock was already confined to the highland areas north of the Midland Valley, whilst the eastern coastal plain and Midland Valley had long been the strongholds of immigrants—descendants of Angles, Normans, Danes, and other North Europeans—who were unsympathetic to the preservation of Celtic traditions. The former dualism is strongly reminiscent of present-day Ireland, with however this difference—that, whereas in Scotland fusion has prevented the evolution of two distinct and unfriendly nationalities, in Ireland the native and the immigrant continue to face each other with hostility, with a political frontier between them to confirm and, unfortunately, to perpetuate the dualism.

Scotland is fortunate in the degree of autonomy which she enjoys. Union with England in 1707 did not deprive her of her code of law, and, at the same time, her religion was safeguarded. These and other concessions satisfied in general the aspirations of her nationals. Yet Gaelic, the old language, has all but disappeared, as was true of Ireland also prior to rather artificial stimulation in recent years. There could be no better illustration of the endurance of a strong sense of nationality long after the language with which it was originally associated has virtually disappeared.[4] The survival of the ancient language

---

[4] Gaelic was recognized as the "official" language of Scotland as late as the fourteenth century, and down to that time the speech of the Lowlanders (largely of Anglo-Saxon origin) was known as "Inglis" or English. When the population of

of Wales is not only the most remarkable achievement of Welsh culture: it is the greatest obstacle to the extension of English ways of
life throughout the Principality. We cannot think of Welsh nationality apart from its language, and devotion to the native tongue alone
makes possible the survival of nationalism as a vital experience in
the life of the Welsh people. The position is entirely different, as we
have seen, in Ireland, where anglicization of language has left unimpaired the political aspirations of her nationals.

We return to England to indicate quite briefly the stages by which
nationhood was attained. Before the Danish invasions of the eighth
century the widespread settlement of the Anglo-Saxons had been
completed. Widely extending areas of impenetrable forest and marsh
separated, and largely isolated, the main centres of settlement. Thus
the forbidding Forest of Andreada, covering most of the Weald,
detached the South Saxons from the main body of the Saxons in the
valley of the Thames and from the Jutish colony of Kent east of the
Medway. Not for many centuries were the intervening stretches of
"no man's land" cleared and settled, and long before that time local
tradition and patriotism (associated with each regional unit) were
already firmly established. When, under the direction of the Kingdom of Wessex, the political consolidation of England began, certain
of the former entities which had had the rank of kingdoms were not
forgotten, and as units of local administration were transformed,
geographically intact, into counties. Thus the fullest use was made
of local tradition and experience, whilst at the same time regional
sentiment, so important a factor in English administration, was
encouraged.

Certain early and interesting features of the geography of the
ancient kingdoms are still retained. Sussex, for example, is for purposes of administration not one but two counties. The partition
runs northwards from the coast, a little to the west of Brighton.
Without doubt, it records a dualism in the Kingdom of Sussex. The
main South Saxon colony lay on the coastal plain behind and to the
east of Selsey Bill, whilst a second nucleus of settlement, at first

---

the Lowlands greatly increased, during the fifteenth and sixteenth centuries, its
language was more widely spoken than the Gaelic of the Highlands. To continue
to call it "English" became a slur on the nationality of the Lowlanders: consequently, in the sixteenth century, the Lowlands' speech came to be known officially,
as "Scottish."

completely detached from the former by a shallow extension of the sea covering the present Pevensey Levels, was situated on the higher land in the neighbourhood of Hastings. In a similar way Suffolk,

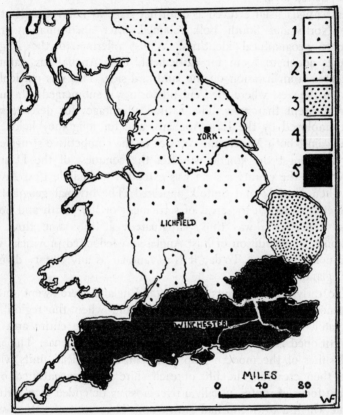

FIG. 2.—THE MAIN POLITICAL DIVISIONS OF ENGLAND IN THE EIGHTH CENTURY
1. Mercia.   2. Northumbria.   3. East Anglia.
4. Celtic areas outside Anglo-Saxon authority.
5. Wessex; including the annexed kingdoms of Essex, Kent and Sussex.

representing the union of two geographically separate Anglian communities, was, in the period of county building, divided into two—West Suffolk and East Suffolk. This partition, which persists in county geography, recalls an original dual settlement: one colony lay around the estuarine reaches of the Orwell, Deben and Stour: the other was on the sandy tracts in the district of the upper Lark (north-western Suffolk) as a result of penetration up the navigable Ouse. Between the two settlements lay a heavily forested and, at first, unpopulated area.

East Anglia itself evolved as a further stage in political federation. The North and South Folk retained, after amalgamation, their separate geographical identities. Whilst offering to the Anglian peoples adequate room for settlement, East Anglia was naturally protected from invasion on the landward side. This was particularly true on the west where the Fenland basin was submerged to a much greater extent than now. The natural advantages for defence were well employed by the East Anglians, and for long they held their own against both Mercia and Wessex in the competitive struggle for power amongst the kingdoms. After the conquest of the Danelaw by Wessex the county system was extended to include East Anglia, and then Norfolk and Suffolk appeared. The original geographical distinction between the areas of settlement of the North and South Folk, respectively, was thus perpetuated: at the same time, the suitability and tradition of East Anglia as a federated provincial unit were not overlooked. To-day it is as familiar as any county division of England.

The early political units of Central England were swept out of existence during the Danish invasions, and when the region was ultimately conquered by the Kings of Wessex the entire area was re-partitioned for purposes of administrative convenience. The mid-land shires of the modern map represent the artificial units which were then created. The life of each shire was concentrated on a natural focus of routes, usually a river-crossing defended by a fortress, round which a township had grown up.[5] The county frontiers were devised to make direct administration not only feasible but efficient, having regard to the difficulties of regional inter-communication. Consequently, the Midland shires were made fairly uniform in size as well as small—smaller, that is to say, than the counties of the south-east. As an experiment in frontier-drawing the system had the merit of preserving, as far as possible, the unity of the "natural" divisions of the Midlands. Frequently, the line of separation was along

[5] Nottingham, Bedford, Huntingdon, and Warwick are typical of such bridge-head towns.

a water-parting, where, conveniently enough, settlement was usually sparse.

In Norman times the extension of the county system to Northern England obliterated those political units which had evolved slowly in distinctive regions during the time of Anglo-Saxon settlement. Yet, certain of the old regional units, older by far than the counties in which they were incorporated, still retain some geographical meaning for their inhabitants. The broad acres of Yorkshire stretch across the boundaries of Holderness, Craven, Cleveland, Hallamshire, and Richmondshire, and these regional names come down from an ancient past.

The origins of Irish county geography show an interesting comparison: indeed, to a greater extent than in the case of England, the county map reproduces the frontiers of the "kingdoms" of pre-Conquest days. This is the more notable in that the process of county building continued intermittently until the sixteenth century. It seems that there was a wise intention, on the part of the English Government in Ireland, to utilize as local government areas those ancient clan units which still retained, even after conquest had destroyed the authority of native institutions, some meaning in the regional life of the country. Instances of approximate coincidence of county and "kingdom" are numerous, and include County Donegal, which corresponds almost exactly to the ancient limits of Tirconnel; County Waterford, which replaced the clan domain of the Deisi (Decies); and County Kilkenny, whose prototype was the Leinster sub-kingdom of Ossory. The County of Dublin has an unusual origin; it is a geographical reproduction of the Scandinavian Kingdom of Dublin—*Dyflinarskirri*—which was the territory of Norwegian kings during the ninth and tenth centuries.

In Britain the disappearance of the regional kingdoms was the necessary preliminary to the evolution of the English State and of those closer inter-regional contacts by which alone the sense of nationality could develop. With the establishment of Norman rule the power of a strong central government was soon able to unify the entire area of the English Plain as far north as the Humber, and westwards as far as the Welsh Marches. Such delay as occurred was due more to the difficulties of transport than to the effectiveness of military opposition, and, long after political unification, the obstacles to communication continued to hinder direct contacts between one region and another, and between the capital and the outlying provinces. Wide-spreading forest and marshland were major hindrances to settlement and movement until the close of medieval times, after which more than three centuries elapsed before the country was provided with adequate roads. The Roman system of highways was not maintained, and the lost art of the road-builder did not reappear until the nineteenth century.

The political incorporation of Wales within England was conceived by Edward I as one stage in a programme which was to culminate in the unification of Great Britain, as a whole. Difficulties of terrain, in North Wales particularly, prolonged and made arduous the campaign of Edward I, but he gained his main objective, which was to contain the Welsh within their highland and to open to traffic the coastal plain between Chester and Anglesey. Down to his time all communication between London and the English Pale (in Ireland), based on Dublin, was by way of the more open coastal plain of South Wales, thence by the sea-crossing between Pembrokeshire and either Waterford or Wexford. The direct approach to Dublin, by way of Chester and North Wales, was quite impracticable until the Welsh hillsmen were subdued.

Following the unification of England came the need and opportunity to organize the economic life of the young State. In the days of Edward III, England was the foremost wool exporter of North-Western Europe, and trade with the textile manufacturing towns of Flanders (especially Bruges and Ghent) was greatly encouraged. But the organization of wool export at that time was in foreign hands, especially those of the "Hansa of London," an association of merchants from Rheims and Amiens. Edward III initiated the change-over from the large-scale export of raw wool to the manufacture of woollens within England itself, so that from the fourteenth century onwards the export of raw wool progressively declined. At the same time the desire increased to liberate England from the financial control of those merchant communities—the Hanseatic League, Lombards, Venetians, especially—whose aid had been, in the first place, essential to her commercial apprenticeship. In a similar way to-day, nations, backward in the development of their resources, are striving to establish a wide basis of manufactures and to free themselves from the financial domination of the Great Powers.

By Tudor times England had gained her economic freedom, and

had gone far along the road towards self-sufficiency in the supply of food, raw materials and manufactured products for the home market. Further, her people were by then fully conscious of their common interests, so that when Spain threatened, the response came from a united community.

The abandonment of Latin and French as "official" languages assisted the development of English nationhood, and was itself a tribute to the endurance of the vernacular. English had become the language of Parliament by the second half of the fourteenth century, when, as recorded by Froissart, French was very little understood by the great mass of the people. It is geographically notable that the East Midland variety of Anglo-Saxon was accepted as the standard, for between East Anglia and Northamptonshire lay, in the fourteenth century, the centre of gravity of the English population.[6] The attraction of continental trade, with which the East and East-Midlands were actively concerned, helped to draw population towards the east.

It has been argued that the ultimate political mergence of Scotland with England was assured, once the geographical nucleus of Great Britain, namely the English Plain, was wholly under one authority, it being held that the resources of Scotland in material wealth and man-power could not indefinitely challenge those of England. Yet with equal cogency it might be suggested that the geographical build of Great Britain favoured, not political unification, but rather a federation of separate units, of which the Midland Valley—the geographical pivot of Scotland—is one. The vigorous national outlook of the Scots is still possible because of their geographical separation from the main centre of English influence, some three or four hundred miles away to the south. Again, in the case of Ireland, there can be no doubt that it is geography which has preserved for the inhabitants their national customs, and has enabled them to establish their claim to political independence.

With the example of Great Britain before us, we have traced the stages by which the State has grown through the coalescence, first of small, then of larger, political aggregations, to the final stage of unification. Within rather miniature geographical limits, the incorporation of regional units to form the State has not obliterated

---

[6] Density was about 65 persons per square mile in East Anglia, and rather less in other East Midland districts; which is lower than the modern density for any English county.

the reality of local sentiment and tradition. It is reasonable to expect that geography will always exert opposition to those political systems which endeavour to reduce to uniformity the regional variety existing within all countries. From the case of Britain may be learned the possibility and desirability of retaining those values which derive from local loyalties, whilst accepting the implications of a wider and fuller citizenship.

FRANCE

As a nation-state, France is built on ancient foundations, and the ideals and other more material expressions of its civilization have had a profound influence in helping to shape the social and political life of the Old and New World. Alone of European countries, it forms a bridge between the northern and southern marginal seas, so that the commingling of blond and brunet strains is a not-unexpected feature of its ethnic history. From the north the way across France lies open to the extreme south-west, whilst inland from the Mediterranean a natural line of advance is afforded by the continuous valley of the Rhône-Saône—either towards the Rhineland centres of German life, or across the easy gradients of the Langres Plateau to the gates of Paris.

Of equal importance, throughout the national experience of France, has been the influence of the long eastern frontier-zone which, though generally formidable in a strategic sense, is breached at several points by easy lowland passageways. The Sambre-Meuse corridor, narrowly skirting the massif of the wooded Ardennes, and the Burgundian Gate, opening between the Rhine and Rhône-Saône basins, have, from time to time, permitted the cultural influence of France to extend eastwards at the expense of Germanic ways of life; but, less happily, they provide the routes by which the embattled strength of the Teuton has moved in to strike repeatedly, with unexpected suddenness, at the very heart of France.

There is strong suggestion that French national genius owes much to a harmonious blend of human stocks. Racial composition is nicely balanced, and the representation of the three main ethnic groups of Europe is in better proportion than in any other country of the continent. Although intermixture of strongly contrasted types has been widespread and continuous, the dominant characteristics of each stand out prominently in those areas where, because of geographical isolation, fusion has been difficult.

Three regions, widely separated from each other and from the main internal passageways of France, have sheltered the broad-headed "Alpine" peoples, who, conceivably, represent the oldest in lineage of the primary ethnic groups. The *Auvergnats* of the *Massif Central,* highest and most inaccessible land of interior France, the *Savoyards* of the Alpine margins of the south-east, and, to a less extent—because of the only partial isolation of their domain—the *Bretons,* have been able to resist racial change. After the passage of millennia they still approximate closely to the ideal type of the broad-headed or round-headed "Alpine." Long-headedness, whether it be of "Nordic" or "Mediterranean" origin, is a general characteristic of the lowlanders of France, wherever they occur. Those of the north and of the Paris Basin show pronounced "Nordic" affinities; and comparatively tall stature, dolichocephaly and blondness there culminate. At the opposite side of France, brunet traits of "Mediterranean" man came in early along the littoral, between the Pyrenean outposts and the Alps, and spread far up the lower valley of the Rhône.

Thus we see that ethnic complexity is a factor to be considered in a study of French population, but it is noteworthy that, despite their very mixed racial origins, the French as a whole have fused into one of the most coherent of European nations. Their varied ethnic composition may help to explain the rarity of racial prejudice amongst them, when they are brought into contact with other peoples. Skin colour has been a much less serious hindrance to social and political harmony in the overseas territories of France than it has been within those tropical and sub-tropical lands where the Anglo-Saxons rule.

The Roman tradition in law and government did not disappear from Gaul, but remained an important factor in the shaping of French civilization. In their penetration of Gaul the legions first occupied the lower valley of the Rhône, where was established the earliest Roman province (cf. Provence) outside Italy. All France, as we know it, lay under Roman authority, and the civilization then founded was sufficiently virile to survive the destruction wrought by the barbarian hordes of the early medieval centuries. From the same point of penetration the centralizing power of the Roman Church spread northwards and westwards, losing, however, in influence as distance from the Mediterranean coast increased. Other events of real significance for the later political evolution of France affected the northern half of the country mainly. Early in the Christian period the Germanic peoples entered from the east, and their largest group, the Franks, closely settled the Paris Basin. Later, in the tenth century, Norsemen colonized the shores of the Seine estuary, succeeded in expelling a large proportion of the older population of Normandy, and brought to that province a more considerable infusion of "Nordic" characteristics than it had previously known.

The Paris Basin, dominant as a region in most aspects of the life of France, and headquarters of government for close on ten centuries, is the classical instance of a national cradle. Yet its advantages as the geographical nucleus of the State are not as complete as is often supposed. True, it encloses the richest and broadest plains of France with the most varied possibilities of cultivation, and with easy access to the heart of Europe. But it is placed by Nature too far north to be readily accessible from all parts of the country, e.g., the distance to Paris from the nearest point on the Mediterranean coast is 400 miles, much of it across difficult terrain.

Of more serious consequence, Paris lies only 100 miles from the nearest point on the eastern frontier, a fact which has enabled Germany on three occasions during the last seventy-five years to threaten the capital, immediately after invading France.[7]

Within its own region, Paris undoubtedly occupies both a central and a dominating position. It is near the hydrographic focus of the Seine Basin, and the earliest settlement was on a naturally-protected island within the middle reaches of the Seine. Here was the nucleus of the Duchy of France,[8] still remembered in the regional term—Ile de France. It is of interest that the boundaries of that regional unit approximate to those of the domain of Hugh Capet who, in 987, was proclaimed King of France. The authority of Capet and his successors rarely extended beyond the limits of the Paris Basin, but control of the balance between Northern and Southern France facilitated their ultimate supremacy. It was fortunate that, in their claim to leadership, the Counts of Paris were able, because of geographical position, to hinder the military union of their greatest rivals, the Dukes of Normandy and Burgundy.

The process of accretion, by which the kingdom of France grew,

[7] The predecessors of Hugh Capet held the titles "Duke of France" and "Count of Paris."

[8] Orléans is more central and more easy of access to all parts of the country than Paris. It was, indeed, regarded as the French capital until the close of the twelfth century.

was inevitably delayed so long as claims to suzerainty, made by English monarchs, divided the country in war. In the twelfth century, Henry II, already Duke of Normandy and of Anjou and suzerain lord of Brittany, Count of Maine and of Touraine, acquired

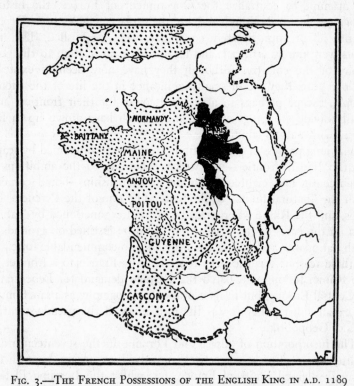

FIG. 3.—THE FRENCH POSSESSIONS OF THE ENGLISH KING IN A.D. 1189

Territories held by the English King shown by stipple
Territories held by the French King, as his personal domain, shown in black
Frontier of 12th-century France shown by double, broken lines

by marriage the lands of Guienne, Poitou, and Gascony, and thereby held nearly all parts of Western France which English sea-power could reach directly. Not for another three centuries was the English overseas empire completely reduced by a French Government, able at last to rely on a nationally-awakened population.

So did national cohesion, consequent on political unification, slowly replace a variety of regional loyalties, whilst the area of the

State of France continued further to expand. Until the close of the eighteenth century, however, the Provinces, such as Brittany and Normandy, retained a limited authority in local administration. This concession to regional sentiment was withdrawn in 1790 when, in an attempt to centralize the Government of France, the historic Provinces were abolished and, in their place, eighty-three Departments, all of approximately equal size, were established. The new units were purely artificial, and had little or no relation to the geography of the country. Although they have now been in existence for 150 years they are of small significance in the life of the French people, except perhaps in a negative sense, for their frontiers arbitrarily divide groupings of population which have grown up in harmony with natural conditions.

The long process of political unification was accompanied by search for the "ideal" frontier—one which, according to the ambitions of seventeenth- and eighteenth-century statesmanship, should coincide with the "natural limits" of the State. The line of the Pyrenees, the Alps, and the Rhine was regarded as a frontier sanctioned by Nature; and, in the cases of the first two, it could be justified on grounds of both nationality and military strategy. Not so commendable for either of these reasons was the persistent claim by France to a frontier on the Rhine. It long ante-dated the German demand for *Lebensraum* in Central Europe, but in its evocation of geography as a sanction for an expansionist policy it was the forerunner of the pseudo-scientific idea of *Geopolitik*.

The incorporation of Alsace and Lorraine in the seventeenth and eighteenth centuries, respectively, involved expansion beyond the naturally-defined limits of France, for, whilst the Lorraine Plateau is intermediate to the Paris Basin and the Rhineland, Alsace turns away from France and is an essential part of the Rhine Basin. By their inclusion within political France the two provinces were prevented from working out an independent life, as at one time seemed possible, on the basis of the long-held traditions of the Duchy of Lorraine.

There can be little doubt that the political allegiance of both Alsace and Lorraine will continue to be a European problem of the first magnitude until the relations of France and Germany reach a basis of mutual understanding. Meanwhile, there is no sound geographical argument for continuing to regard Alsace-Lorraine as one unit rather than two. Alsace is sharply separated from France by the north-south axis of the Vosges *massif*, and is in easy contact with Baden, of similar structure, on the opposite bank of the Rhine. Be-

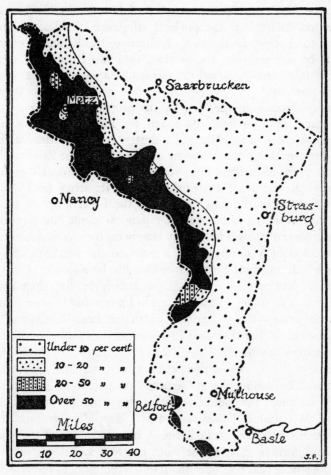

FIG. 4.—THE PROPORTIONS OF FRENCH-SPEAKING INHABITANTS IN THE POPU-
LATION OF ALSACE AND LORRAINE (YEAR 1919)

cause its geographical aspect is eastwards, German influence has pene-trated deeply and is strongly established. It is not denied that a clear majority of the population of Alsace are of German speech and that the

German claim to the province is so based. But language is only one of several tests that might be applied to an analysis of Alsatian community life, and the desires of the Alsatians regarding their national and political future have never been satisfactorily ascertained by either Germany or France. It is one of the tragedies of Europe that *force majeure* alone has determined the political allegiance of Alsace from one period to another. In the case of Lorraine, the Franco-German linguistic boundary divides the province into two fairly equal areas, so making it culturally, as well as physically, a marcher-zone between the two nations.

Franco-German competition for the province of Lorraine intensified when methods were discovered for the utilization of its extensive iron-ores in metallurgical industry. It was a fortunate chance for Germany that her annexation of part of Lorraine in 1871 almost synchronized with these discoveries, though Bismarck's geologists unknowingly defined the ore-field short of its actual limits, so that about one-half of the iron was left on the French side of the new frontier. Germany's vast industrial expansion in the late years of the nineteenth century was based very largely on the closely inter-locking organization of Westphalian coal and Lorraine iron. Western Lorraine, which remained French, was found to be also rich in iron, and extensive development followed, particularly in the Briey-Longwy district. It is of strategic disadvantage to France that her two principal industrial zones—the coal-mining district of Lens-Valenciennes and the ore-field of Lorraine—are in close proximity to the vulnerable north-eastern frontier.

Alsace and Lorraine in their entirety were regained by France in 1919, and, by adding the ex-German iron reserves to her own, she greatly increased her industrial potential; yet, owing to the absence of coal in Lorraine, France was still as dependent as ever on the high-grade coal of the Ruhr Basin. A big proportion of the *minette* ores continued to move to the Ruhr furnaces, and it was not, therefore, surprising that the industrialists on either side, in full realization of their interdependence, co-operated more thoroughly than before in the organization of the Ruhr-Lorraine heavy industry. Such co-operation, which was not without its sinister aspect, had much to do in certain quarters of France, with the weakening of resistance to Nazi Germany.

Farther north than Lorraine, the plateau is continued in the Ardennes, and, on grounds of physical geography alone, there would be little criticism if the French frontier were to include the southern third of Belgium. The Walloons of this region speak French of a rather archaic form, and their cultural relations with France are closer and more sympathetic than they are with the Flemish zone to the north. Nevertheless, the Walloons regard themselves as a community of independent traditions, and are opposed to union with France. The Ardennes *massif* comes down to the North European Plain, well beyond the corridor of the Sambre-Meuse valley; and close to the orographical junction lies the boundary between (i) Walloon and Flemish speech, and (ii) Nordic and Alpine racial characters. The political frontiers of Belgium—probably more arbitrary than those of any European State—show that no respect was paid in 1831, when Belgium became a kingdom, to linguistic, racial, or geographical considerations.

Unity of outlook which the conception of nationhood demands, is not yet widespread throughout Belgium. It seems likely, however, that the loyalty of Walloons and Flemings to their respective groups will ultimately be enlarged to a truly national allegiance. Much will depend on sufficient time being given for the nation to evolve, in freedom from those international entanglements, which, arising out of its intermediate situation—between France and Germany and between Germany and Great Britain—have endangered its very existence.

From the experience of both England and France, which we have outlined, we know that the evolution of national consciousness is a slow progress, occupying the time of centuries. Not only has Belgium had brief opportunity for its task: it has not been provided by geography with a natural birthplace of nationality, as have Britain and France—its political foster-parents.

The numbers of Walloons and Flemings are fairly evenly matched, with the latter a majority and particularly strongly represented in the lower and lower-middle classes. The Flemings have long complained that their share of the higher appointments under the State is inadequate and unrepresented, and that, excepting Ghent, the universities are still French cultural centres, as they have always been.[9] In the middle provinces, notably Brabant, where the two peoples are in fair numerical balance, the upper class is predominantly French-speaking.

Social unrest has for long helped to keep alive a Flemish national movement which, before the Second World War, had strong German support. The Belgian Labour Party, one of the few organizations in which Walloons and Flemings have amicably co-operated, is a powerful force working for national consolidation, though it was unable, down to the Second World War, to obtain a majority in the Belgian Parliament.

THE NETHERLANDS

The Kingdom of the Netherlands has been more fortunate in its national life. Yet in certain respects, notably religion, there is marked cultural divergence between certain of its provinces.

The nation, which has maintained the Protestant tradition as firmly as any in Europe, contains a proportion of about one-third who are Catholic. This large religious minority was added to the original Protestant nucleus during the seventeenth century, after the establishment of the federal republic (the United Provinces of the Netherlands) and at an advanced stage in the evolution of national consciousness. The Catholic areas lie to the south of the east-west line of the River Waal (principal outlet of the Rhine delta), and within those provinces which were under Spain during the sixteenth century. They include part of the original province of Brabant, known as North Brabant, together with that part of the mainland which lies to the south of the islands of Zeeland and on the left bank of the lower course of the Scheldt. It is highly creditable to the Protestant religionists that their tolerance of outlook made it possible for the newcomers to merge themselves with the nation. In the hands of lesser men than the Dutch there might well have developed a minority question which even time would not have been able to solve.

Religious unity, strengthened in war with a ruthless enemy, was certainly a factor of profound significance in the welding of the Dutch nation. Yet organized life in the Netherlands could hardly have survived the Spanish onslaught, but for the defensive advantages of a terrain which was to a large extent inundated.

In the beginning, Holland—a maze of low-lying islands and shallow

[9] There are universities at Brussels, Liége, and Louvain, in addition to Ghent.

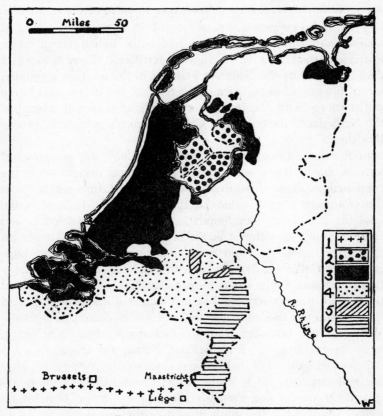

FIG. 5.—THE LOW COUNTRIES

(International frontiers shown by broken lines)

1. Linguistic boundary between Walloon and Flemish zones of Central and Eastern Belgium.
2. Reclaimed territory of the Zuyder Zee.
3. Other land below sea-level.
4. Territory conquered by the Dutch in the seventeenth century.
5. Territory acquired by Holland from the Duchy of Cleves in the eighteenth century.
6. Territory acquired by Holland in 1839.

sea-channels, situated to the south-west of the Zuyder Zee—was a
marcher-zone under the authority of the Count of Holland, whose
duty it was to ward off raiding Norsemen. From this time (tenth century), Holland grew by a slow process of accretion, the accession of
each new province being the result of either military conquest or
marriage alliance. One of the annexed territories, the archipelago of
Zeeland, ceded by the Count of Flanders in the fourteenth century,
was of the utmost importance to the political and commercial future
of the young State, for, together with Holland proper, it assured to
the Netherlands the control of Central Europe's greatest gateway—
the Rhine.

In the sixteenth century the federal republic[10] was composed of
territory largely below sea-level, the geographical nucleus being the
combined provinces of North and South Holland, from which comes
the customary English name for the Netherlands. Holland is the
low-lying land kept from inundation by massive sea-defences and
constant pumping; within it lie the main centres of the Netherlands.

After the inclusion within the Netherlands of the southern provinces with Catholic majorities, the principal factor in the preservation of national unity was a common language. Early in medieval
times three tongues were spoken in different districts, although, of
these, Saxon was limited to the confined area of Eastern Gelderland.
Within a zone extending from the German province of Schleswig
as far westwards as the River Scheldt, Frisian was at one time the
dominant language, but its territorial range steadily diminished, until
finally it was restricted to a small district immediately to the north-
east of the Zuyder Zee. Frankish, the language of the Teutonic invaders, who entered the southern part of the Low Countries, gradually prevailed over Frisian and expelled it from the heart of the
Netherlands, i.e., from Zeeland, North and South Holland. It is from
Frankish that both modern Dutch and also literary Flemish of
Northern Belgium have evolved.

It will be seen that as a formative factor in the evolution of the
nation-state of the Netherlands the rôle of geography was considerable. The unity of the nation was achieved—and in view of the forces
dominating the North European Plain, between France and Germany, could only have been achieved—within a natural refuge, such
as Holland's partially sea-girt and half-inundated lands.

[10] The seven provinces, united in 1578, were Holland, Zeeland, Utrecht, Gelderland, Over-Ijssel, Frisia, and Groningen.

SCANDINAVIA

The sympathetic inter-relations of the Scandinavian States rest firmly on close affinities of both race and culture. Yet a triune federation is not acceptable to them, and each is intent on the preservation of its sovereign independence.

Taken as a whole the Scandinavians are, in their ethnic composition, the most purely "Nordic" of all Europeans. Their blond, tall and usually dolichocephalic characteristics have not remained entirely unmixed with alien strains, but only in Denmark is there any considerable departure from the idealized type. This phenomenon of a highly individualized human stock, geographically associated with the peninsulas of Northern Europe, is, in the main, a consequence of its remoteness from the chief currents of European life, including its complete detachment from the Slavonic zone. The early "Nordic" peoples seem to have penetrated to Norway after first reaching Sweden, and, since that prehistoric event, no considerable intrusion of other ethnic elements has affected either country. Contrary to what might perhaps be expected in view of the association of the Norsemen with the western fjord coast, in Norway the inhabitants who are closest to the ideal "Nordic" type are to be found in the interior valleys, of which that of the Glommen River is an outstanding instance.

Commonly classed as "Nordic," the Danes are considerably mixed with broad-headed and dark-complexioned elements, although the "Nordic" strain is frequently visible. Racial differences between Danes and Norwegians certainly go back to a fairly remote time, and in the ninth century A.D. they were already well known. Perhaps nowhere in Europe was the ethnic dissimilarity more clearly recognized than in Ireland, whose inhabitants distinguished the *Finn Ghoill* (Fair Strangers)—that is, the Norwegians, whose settlement in Ireland was very extensive—from the *Dubh Ghoill* (Dark Strangers), in whom colonists from Denmark were identified.

In the political development of the Scandinavian communities the influence of geography has tended to produce segregation. The Swedes are gathered most densely within the well-farmed and industrially-important lowland which extends without break from the neighbourhood of Gothenburg to Stockholm. The remainder of Sweden, save for the small southerly province of Scania, whose traditions are naturally linked with those of neighbouring Denmark, is incapable of supporting a density higher than fifty persons per square mile. Climatic severity in the north and the vast extent of the lofty and infertile plateau which dominates the entire peninsula combine to reduce the settled area of Sweden to a mere southern and eastern fringe.

The population of Norway, excessively scattered as it is, attains a fair density only in two localities, which are themselves separated by the highest summits, exceeding 6,000 ft., of the Scandinavian Plateau. Around Oslo, and thence along the northern shore of the Skager Rak, settlement is more highly concentrated than elsewhere, and is based on the only considerable lowland of the country; but there is a second nucleus, this time along the Atlantic coast from the Stavanger to the Varanger Fjord, to which Bergen, second city of Norway, is intermediate. The maintenance and improvement of communications across the high plateau, between the Oslo nucleus and the Atlantic coast, has been one of the most difficult problems of Norwegian national life, although enterprise has exploited to the full the circuitous route by sea.

There could be no more complete physiographical contrast than that of the rugged fjord environment of Atlantic Scandinavia and the rolling farm-land of the Danes. In Denmark, population distribution is determined by the intermittent fertility of a lowland which is a miniature extension of the great plain of North Germany. Jutland is less intensively tilled than the islands of Fuen and Sjaelland, and the centre of gravity of Danish population lies towards the Baltic approaches, where stands Copenhagen with one-fifth of the national population.

Passing reference has already been made to the geographical affinities of Scania (southernmost Sweden) and the Danish Isles, and it might be added that intimate associations have gone far to produce a cultural life which is common to both. It was not until the middle years of the seventeenth century that political encroachment by Sweden was able to detach Scania from Denmark, and even then the continuity of culture was little affected. Geographically considered, the main bases of Danish national life, whilst fairly remote from the main centres of Swedish and Norwegian civilization, are precariously near the very heart of the Teutonic zone; and the consequent necessity for Denmark to regard her political relations with her powerful neighbour as more immediately urgent than those with any other

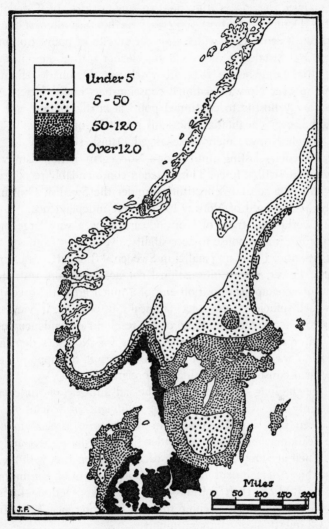

Fig. 6.—Scandinavia: Distribution of Population Density. (Year 1931)
(Inhabitants per square mile)

European State should be considered sympathetically by her friends.

Sea-power, based on the prestige and wealth of Copenhagen, granted Denmark political supremacy within Scandinavia until the seventeenth century, by which time the growth of population in both Prussia and Sweden rendered impossible her further supremacy over the Baltic. Long before 1814, in which year Denmark relinquished dominion over Norway, national consciousness in the latter country was strongly hostile to continued political amalgamation with Denmark, however equalitarian the basis might be or become.

Although Norway merely exchanged Danish suzerainty for union under Sweden—lasting until 1905—Norwegian nationalism was already an irresistible force. This, Sweden commendably recognized by the grant of a separate constitution under the Swedish Crown, and, finally, by the right of Norway to complete independence.

The world-wide trade of Norway, carried by a very large mercantile marine, is a response to accessibility, over a long frontage, to the open Atlantic. It has no parallel in Sweden.[11] The latter is essentially a Baltic Power, whose international contacts are more restricted by reason of geographical position and of a much greater degree of economic self-sufficiency. It is geographically interesting, in view of the poverty of her environment and of her resultant dependence on maritime enterprise, that one of the reasons for Norway's demand for separation was the refusal of Sweden to permit the appointment of Norwegian consuls in the principal foreign cities.

Although long experience of the advantages of independent sovereignty has worked against the fulfilment of federation, there have been few sinister episodes in the historic association of the three Scandinavian Powers to hinder their mutual respect and tolerance. Their age-long contacts with each other, together with a certain geographical detachment from the main currents of European life, and, in addition, their cultural—not to speak of ethnic—affinities, have encouraged them to come together in conference, from time to time, on questions of common import.

Geography provides an impressive illustration of the sanity of

[11] Norway, with only three million inhabitants, possessed five million tons (gross) of shipping in 1939. This total was greater than Germany's in the same year, and nearly four times greater than that of Sweden, whose population is twice that of Norway.

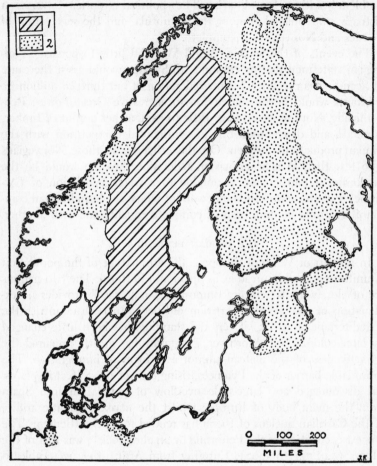

FIG. 7.—MAXIMUM EXTENT OF THE SWEDISH EMPIRE

1. Modern Sweden.   2. Swedish annexations of the seventeenth century.

Scandinavian life: it is to be found in the 1,000-mile frontier between Sweden and Norway. By agreement, at the time when Norway gained independence, the common boundary of the two countries was left unfortified and unguarded, a settlement which is unique in Europe and reminiscent of the contemporary Andean agreement between Chile and the Argentine. Certainly one of the factors which has helped to promote good relations is the absence of a "minority problem" within Scandinavia. The political frontier traverses a virtually unpopulated zone of the Peninsula, and the segregation of Swedes and Norwegians is complete.

The events of the Second World War did little to persuade Norwegian statesmen that federation with Sweden would assist the cause of Scandinavian security. Such a federation of but thirteen million inhabitants would be no match for an aggressive Great Power. Economically, Norway would have little to gain, as her output of timber, minerals, and dairy produce is in commercial competition with the similar products of Sweden. On the other hand, those Norwegians who fear that, in a Scandinavian federation, Sweden would be the predominant partner, are favourable to a wider association of (Atlantic) Powers, within the framework of which the Scandinavian communities would be on a basis of complete equality one with another.

THE IBERIAN PENINSULA

In no part of Western Europe is the ethnic type of the population as uniform and widespread as in Spain and Portugal. The two nations are of closely-similar ethnic composition, and "race" provides no explanation of the political partition of Iberia. In both countries the "Mediterranean" stock, of very old standing, has been little changed by later colonization. Moreover, geography has greatly impaired the attractiveness of the plateau-interior as a focus of immigration. The formidable barrier of the Pyrenees, rising to over 10,000 feet in places, has discouraged any large-scale overflow of population into Spain from the main body of Europe: whilst the marked climatic aridity of the Castilian nucleus of Iberia has tended to repel settlement. The longest occupation of the Peninsula by an alien society was that of the Moors (A.D. 711 to 1492). Entering from Africa, they were able to utilize the easy route to the heart of Spain by way of Andalusia, whose great valley (of the River Guadalquivir) opens widely towards Morocco. Accustomed to climatic aridity, they found favourable conditions for their mode of life in Andalusia, and made it their headquarters.

The ancient and compact plateau-block—the *Meseta*—is ribbed by high ridges (*sierras*) which, in parallel arrangement, extend east and west, and sub-divide the interior into a series of river-basins. Beyond the western edge of the *Meseta* there is sharp descent to the moist and generally fertile plains which constitute Portugal. Both the nationality boundary and inter-state frontier—for the limits of nation and state coincide—follow closely, for a considerable distance, the geological and geographical line of separation between the *Meseta* and the western plains. They run south, cutting the valley of the Tagus, close to its descent from the plateau.[12]

The Atlantic-ward orientation of Portugal, the navigability of the estuarine reaches of the Douro and Tagus, and the complete orographical and climatic contrast between Portugal and Castile, have helped to promote those differences of outlook which are reflected in their separate nationalisms. Without invoking geographical determinism, the historic association of the Portuguese with oceanic enterprise seems entirely natural. As in the Scandinavian Peninsula, so also in Iberia, political partition has left no heritage of frontier disputes. No "minority" enclaves have been isolated from the parent nation on either side.

The evolution of mature nationhood within Spain has not yet reached its final phase. Certain of the difficulties which remain are due to the natural tendency of certain communities to retain their separatist aspirations within the partial isolation which geography makes possible. Catalonia is the outstanding problem. In point of race, the Catalans are true representatives of the "Mediterranean" stock, to which the great majority of Spaniards belong. The slight advantage of stature which they possess over the majority of their countrymen is believed to be due, not to racial inheritance, but to the higher material standard of life which their generally fertile region makes possible.

The approximate limits of the ancient principality of Catalonia are still remembered, and accord with the distribution of the modern population, which is concentrated along the narrow coastal plain, between the outlet of the Ebro and the abrupt termination of the Pyrenean Folds.[13] Here there is a physiographical link with Provençal

[12] The juxtaposition of the *Meseta* and plain of Portugal is clearly shown to the east of Coimbra, the ancient university city of Portugal. North of Coimbra the edge of the *Meseta* approaches the coast, leaving the international frontier well to the east.

[13] For administrative purposes, Catalonia is sub-divided into the "provinces" of Gerona, Barcelona, and Tarragona, all of them situated along the Mediterranean fringe, together with Lerida within the middle basin of the Ebro. Lerida lies beyond the true physical limits of Catalonia, for it is to the west of the folded range, rising to over 4,000 feet, which runs parallel to the coast and detaches the main centres of Catalan life from the Ebro basin of Aragon.

France. The eastern end of the Pyrenees lies back from the Mediterranean, leaving a narrow strip of lowland littoral, by which, in the eighth and ninth centuries, Frankish influence penetrated southwards over the Catalan plain. The modern dialect is derived from Frankish, and indeed is more closely akin to Provençal than to Castilian, the official language of all Spain. Alliance by marriage brought Catalonia into close association with the neighbouring kingdom of Aragon and so with Castile, after the marriage of Ferdinand and Isabella in 1469. It has never been, however, fully merged with Spain. The Catalan demand for full autonomy has persisted, and as recently as 1932 a statute, guaranteeing self-government and the official recognition of the language, was accepted by the Cortes.

Energetic Catalan response to the opportunities afforded by an environment more hospitable than that of the Meseta has long distinguished the region from all others in the economic life of Spain. In manufacturing industry, including textiles of cotton, silk, and wool the "province" of Barcelona is easily supreme. This position, illustrated by the commercial pre-eminence of Barcelona—largest city of Spain, with more than one-third of the entire Catalan population—cannot be explained wholly in terms of geographical advantage. By contrast, Lerida, the inner province of Catalonia, shut off from the Mediterranean littoral by the Catalan ranges and geographically a part of Aragon, is economically backward and its limited resources undeveloped. Again, it is admitted that geography, although adverse to intensive settlement, is not the only factor involved.

Much more detached, even than Catalonia, from the life of metropolitan Spain is the country of the Basques. Throughout the western Pyrenees, on both flanks, but more particularly on the Spanish side, Basque society has maintained, in an environment favouring almost complete isolation, its ancient culture and language. The mountainous terrain, which has made this possible, extends farther westwards into the Cantabrian Mountains, where other communities, including the Gallegos of Galicia, have also preserved much of an earlier independence of social and political outlook. The influence of geography on the course of Spanish history is particularly well illustrated by the inability of the Moorish invaders, accustomed as they were to a parched landscape, such as Castile offered, to conquer the lofty and forested home of the Basques and other northern mountain people. In this region of Northern Spain, resistance to the Moorish occupa-

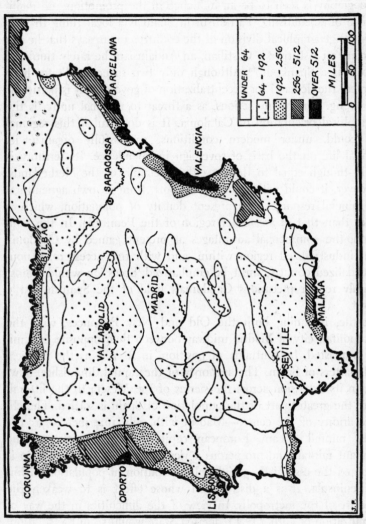

Fig. 8.—Distribution of Population Density in the Iberian Peninsula (Year 1931)
(Inhabitants per square mile)

UNDER 64

64 - 192

192 - 256

256 - 512

OVER 512

MILES

0   50   100

CORUNNA

OPORTO

LISBON

BILBAO

VALLADOLID

MADRID

SEVILLE

MALAGA

SARAGOSSA

BARCELONA

VALENCIA

tion was organized, and from it the tide of conquest was rolled back, southwards across both Spain and Portugal.

Geography is seen to be an influence in the promotion and maintenance of separatism. "Patriotism in Spain is a local thing that reflects the geographical division of the country; a man says that he is a Galician, an Asturian, a Castilian, an Andalusian; he rarely thinks of himself as a Spaniard."[14] Although only two sovereign States have emerged, the demand for decentralization of government is persistent and strong. Particularly serious, as a threat to national unity, is the geographical orientation of Catalonia. It is doubtful if this regional unit could, under modern conditions, successfully organize its national life on the basis of sovereign independence. Its territory is small—though equal to that of either Belgium or the Netherlands. Moreover, it could with difficulty support, from its own agricultural and mineral resources, the present density of population, which is higher than that of any other region of the Peninsula. In this connexion, the commercial advantages at present gained by Catalonia as an industrialized region within, and with free access to, a non-industrialized country, must be emphasized. Secession would almost certainly render precarious Catalonia's hold of the Spanish textile market.

Castile, including both the Old and New Provinces, with the metropolitan city of Madrid midway between their opposite extremities, is assisted, by centrality of position, in its rôle as the political headquarters of Spain. The authority of the capital diminishes, however, in its extension across the sierras of the Meseta to the littoral, where the greater part of the population of Spain is settled. The climatic aridity of the centre—Madrid with only 16.4 inches has the lowest rainfall of any European capital!—is in contrast to the abundant rainfall and prosperous agriculture of the coastlands. So is explained the essentially peripheral distribution of population within the Peninsula. It is a distribution whose effect is to weaken the authority of the metropolis. In view of the difficulties in the way of centralization of authority a federated State would seem the solution, but, at the time of writing, there is little expectation of policy moving in that direction.

14 I. Bowman: The New World, p. 215, 4th ed., London, 1928.

SELECTED BIBLIOGRAPHY

"L'Alsace-Lorraine, et la frontière du nord-est" (vol. 1, Travaux du Comité d'Études), Paris, 1918.

A Manual of Belgium and the Adjoining Territories (with atlas), H.M.S.O., n.d.

BARKER, E.: Ireland in the Last Fifty Years (1866-1918), 2nd ed., Oxford, 1919.

BLANCHARD, R.: La Flandre, Paris, 1906.

BRAUN, G.: Die nordischen Staaten: Norwegen, Schweden, Finnland: Eine soziologische Landerkunde, Breslau, 1924.

BOECKH, R.: "Die Sprachgrenze in Belgien," Zeits. für allgemeine Erdkunde, Berlin, vol. 3 (1882), pp. 80–97.

Cambridge Modern History, vol. XI, "The Growth of Nationalities," Cambridge, 1909.

CERECEDA, J. D.: Resumen fisiografica de la Peninsula iberica, Madrid, 1912.

CLAPHAM, J. H.: The Economic Development of France and Germany, 1815–1914, 4th ed., Cambridge, 1936.

COLE, GRENVILLE: Ireland, the Outpost, Oxford, 1917.

COON, C. S.: The Races of Europe, New York, 1939.

COUSSANGE, J.: La Scandinavie, le nationalisme scandinave, Paris, 1914.

DEL VILLAR, E. H.: El valor geografico de Espana: Ensayo de ecetica. Estudio comparativo de las condiciones naturales del pais para el desarrollo de la vida humana y la civilizacion, Madrid, 1921.

DEMANGEON, A.: "Belgique, Pays Bas, Luxembourg" (Tome 2, Géographie Universelle), Paris, 1927.

DEMANGEON, A.: Les Iles Britanniques, Paris, 1927.

DRACHMAN, P.: The Industrial Development and Commercial Policies of the Three Scandinavian Countries, Oxford, 1915.

EAST, G.: An Historical Geography of Europe, London, 1935.

FITZGERALD, W.: Historical Geography of Early Ireland, London, 1926.

FLACH, J.: Les Origines de l'Ancienne France, 4 vols., 1886–1917.

FLEURE, H. J.: The Peoples of Europe, London, 1922.

FREEMAN, E. A.: The Historical Geography of Europe, 2 vols., 3rd ed., by Bury, 1903.

FURTH, —.: La Frontière linguistique en Belgique, etc., 1896.

GALLOIS, L.: "Alsace-Lorraine and Europe," Geogr. Rev., vol. 6, 1918, pp. 89–115.

GOBLET, Y. M.: "La Frontière de l'Ulster," Ann. de Geogr., vol. 31, 1922, pp. 402–16.

GOOCH, G. P.: Nationalism, London, 1920.

HADDON, A. C., and HUXLEY, J. S.: We Europeans, London, 1935.

HOLLAND ROSE, J.: Nationality in Modern History, London, 1916.

JOHANNET, R.: Le Principe des Nationalités, Paris, 2nd ed., 1923.

JOSEPH, B.: Nationality: its Nature and Problems, London, 1929.

KNOWLES, L. C. A.: Economic Development in the Nineteenth Century, London, 1932.

"L'Alsace-Lorraine, et la frontière du nord-est" (vol. 1, Travaux du Comité d'Études), Paris, 1918.

LAVALLÉE, T.: Les Frontières de la France, Paris, 1864.

LE FUR, L.: Races, Nationalités, Etats, Paris, 1922.

LONGNON, A.: La Formation de l'Unité Française, 1922.

LOWE, M.: "La population de l'Espagne d'après le recensement de 1920," Ann. de Geogr., vol. 33, 1924, pp. 177–82.

MACKINDER, H. J.: Britain and the British Seas, Oxford, 1906.

MARVAUD, A.: Le Portugal et ses colonies, Paris, 1912.

MIROT, L.: Manuel de Géographie Historique de la France, 1930.

MORTILLET, G. DE: Formation de la Nation Française, 1897.

OAKESMITH, J.: Race and Nationality, London, 1919 (written with special reference to England).

REDSLOB, R.: Le Principe des Nationalités, Paris, 1930.

RENIER, G. J.: The Dutch Nation, London, 1944.

RIPLEY, W. Z.: The Races of Europe, New York, 1900.

ROBERTSON, J. M.: The Evolution of States, 1912.

SEIPEL, I.: Nation und Staat, Vienna, 1917.

VERMEYLEN, A.: Quelques aspects de la question des langues en Belgique, Brussels, 1919.

VIDAL DE LA BLACHE, P.: Etats et Nations de l'Europe, Paris, 1889.

VIDAL DE LA BLACHE, P.: La France, Tableau géographique, Paris, 1908.

WRIGHT, J. K.: The Geographical Basis of European History, New York, 1928.

YOUNG, G.: Portugal, Old and Young: an Historical Study, Oxford, 1917.

ZEEMAN, J.: Moderne Geographie van Nederland, 2nd ed., Amsterdam, 1917.

3.

Frontiers of Nationality in Central and Eastern Europe

(I) THE GEOGRAPHICAL SETTING

East and south of Germany the pattern of nationality distribution becomes intricate and can be comprehended only in the light of a highly diversified environment, with sharp contrasts of configuration, soil, and vegetation cover. Because of this necessity to take environmental conditions carefully into account, an outline of the main features of the geographical framework will provide the reader with a key to what otherwise would appear a confusion of peoples, varying widely in culture and maturity of national outlook.

THE RUSSIAN PLATFORM

In respect of physical as well as political geography, Russia dominates the entire eastern half of the continent. It is, indeed, the great continental base or platform from which Peninsular Europe extends, ever narrowing between bordering seas, towards the western ocean. Vast extent and simplicity of structure—with rock strata nearly horizontal over great distances—and approximate uniformity of surface relief are the first considerations. Although not strictly a plain, the altitude is everywhere modest, less than 1,000 feet, with much the greater part below 600 feet. The Valdai Hills towards the northwest of the Platform are the largest swelling on the surface within the limits set by the Ural and Caucasus ranges: but their elevation is not impressive, although sufficient to divide the drainage of the Baltic slope from the great Volga river-system.

European Russia is, therefore, despite its enormous bulk, without those sharp contrasts of relief which, whilst promoting variety of landscape, bring diversity to the economic and social activities of nations. Further, on account of the monotony of land-surface, local variations of climate are rare, and a gradual transition of temperature over immense distances is normal. Winter severity, to which all parts, excepting the sheltered south-eastern coast of the Crimea, are fully exposed, indicates the absence of an effective wind-break; and thus it is that the cold of January at Kazan is as extreme as at Archangel, not less than 500 miles farther north. Yet climate, expressed in terms of rain, snow, and summer heat, is responsible for the wide contrasts of vegetation-cover which determine the major regional divisions of Russia.

To the south of the Arctic fringe of cold desert (tundra) lies a vast zone of coniferous forest—the taiga—covering about one-third of the Platform and, beyond the Urals, extending even more widely in Siberia. On its southern side the great forest has no well-defined limits, but, in the latitude of Moscow, it is thinning out. Approximately as far south as this latitude, all settlement, including the one city of metropolitan size—Leningrad—has been, at one time or another, founded within forest clearings.

The grey forest-soils are generally poor, and agriculture is correspondingly meagre; so that density of population rarely exceeds an average of twenty per square mile, save in the neighbourhood of the few considerable towns. Western Russia, adjoining Poland, had formerly a rich reserve of timber in a mixed deciduous and coniferous zone, but, as in the case of the deciduous forest (oak, beech, etc.) of Western Europe, the greater part of the woodland has been cleared away. Agriculture and settlement are much more intensive than in the taiga, as indicated by an average population density, ranging from thirty to sixty per square mile, outside the towns.

Southwards from the latitude of Moscow, forest becomes intermittent, and finally gives place to steppe, which is grassland devoid of tree-growth. The transition occurs over a wide zone whose north-to-south extent may be measured by the distance between Moscow and Kiev. To the south of Kiev's latitude there is nothing but steppe, varying in its luxuriance according to the amount and duration of precipitation and to the quality of a series of soils. First comes the great band of fertile loess which, from the neighbourhood of Kiev, continues westwards across the heart of Europe, providing one of the major physical controls of organized life within the continent. Still farther south, closer to the Black Sea, are the similar but even richer "black earth" soils, abundant in humus, on which the great agricultural wealth of the Ukraine is based. On these soils agricultural settlement has been more intensive from early times than elsewhere in Russia, and rural densities exceeding 200 per square mile are not uncommon. To the east of the lower Don and particularly around the northern shores of the Caspian, the steppe is little better than semi-desert, for its saline soils receive scanty rainfall. Until very recently this land was the home of nomadic Turki-Tatar pastoralists, but irrigation and soil-improvement projects are changing the mode of life, and sedentary occupation is increasing.

We note that throughout European Russia the correspondence between soil fertility and population density is particularly close, and is little disturbed by the areas of industrial activity which occur. Moreover, the standard of agriculture is highest on the fertile and populous Ukrainian steppe which, by some scholars, is regarded as the cradle of Slavonic civilization. Unfortunately, Southern Russia is wide open to invasion, from the west as well as from the arid grasslands of Western Asia, and in earlier centuries suffered greatly from periodical incursions. Against the Turki-Tatar hordes of the twelfth and thirteenth centuries the broad rivers of Russia—Dnieper, Don, Donetz, and Volga—offered no satisfactory defence, because of the ease with which they could be crossed, especially when ice-bound.

LOWLAND CONNEXIONS OF THE RUSSIAN PLATFORM WITH CENTRAL EUROPE

Westwards from Russia the trunk of Europe narrows, at first abruptly, between the Baltic and Mediterranean coasts. The Platform is continued in the North European Plain which, as a gradually narrowing corridor, extends, uninterrupted by highland, as far as the Dover Straits. Almost immediately west of the Ukraine, the great bastion of the Carpathians lies astride the passage-way from Russia to the European midlands. It diverts all routes, either northwards to the North Europe Plain, or southwards through the much more restricted valley of the lower Danube which leads to the Plain of Hungary.

Although from the orographical map it would seem that the almost uniformly low relief north of the Carpathians offers no hindrance to east-west movement, there are in two zones wide areas of marsh which have played an influential, if negative, part in history; they have been barriers to settlement, and occasionally have acted as natural defences behind which a number of small though ancient communities have been protected from racial and cultural submergence. To the north of the latitude of Kiev and in the upper basin of the Dnieper—here known by its great west-to-east tributary, the Pripet—lies the most extensive marshland of all Europe. It may be traced eastwards within the basin of the Pripet from Brest Litovsk past Pinsk (from which it is sometimes named) as far as the junction with the Dnieper, and the area involved is equivalent to half of England. This great area of marsh forms a true boundary zone between the nationality domains of Russia and Poland, respectively. Elsewhere on the vast plain of East-Central Europe there is no natural "divide" between the two countries.

Again, much farther to the north, in the hinterland of the Baltic, there is an extensive but discontinuous series of shallow lakes and marshes, which may be followed from eastern Estonia, in the neighbourhood of Lake Peipus, southwards across the eastern halves of both Latvia and Lithuania, as far as the Masurian Lakes of East Prussia. This waterlogged strip of territory, acting as a moat, had in earlier times the effect of checking the movement of both Slavs and Germans into the lands immediately behind the East Baltic coast, so that a number of communities, long in residence, have been able to survive in partial isolation.

Between the two zones of marshland the Russian Platform projects westwards as a triangular wedge of higher ground, with its apex pointed towards Warsaw. Here surface drainage is adequate, so that main communications and towns are restricted to its limits, which are roughly defined by two main lines of railway—that from Warsaw to Leningrad, and—along the southern side of the wedge—that from Warsaw to Moscow. Certain of the towns which were in dispute between Russia, Poland, and Lithuania after the War of 1914-18 lie along this low upland; the best-known in the events of that time was Vilna, a Lithuanian outpost south of the marshes of the Baltic hinterland.

South of the Pripet Marshes the land slowly rises to a low fertile plateau, loess-covered, which lies in front, i.e., to the north, of the Carpathian arc of mountains, and has been well named the "Carpathian Foreland." The greater part of it is natural steppe, but, as on the platform of the Ukraine, with which it is continuous, much is cultivated, with wheat as the typical product of tillage. As already indicated, this low upland, capped with loess soils, is prolonged well beyond the limits of Eastern Europe: it extends west of the Ukraine into Eastern Galicia. The contrast between the well-drained, fertile loess of Galicia and the low-lying, poorly drained and indifferent farming-land of North-Central Poland is strongly emphasized. Farther to the west, the loess upland country continues without interruption, and occupies in turn much of Silesia and Saxony, where it fringes the outer ramparts of the diamond-shaped Bohemia.

Reference to the juxtaposition of the Pripet Marshes and the Carpathian Foreland invites attention to the position of Kiev, in its relation to the communication system of East-Central Europe. Situated on the great River Dnieper, below its junction with the Pripet, it focuses upon itself the river-traffic of numerous headstreams, and at the same time controls the east-west highway, which must here bridge the Dnieper in order to outflank the Pripet Marshes on their southern side.

THE LANDS WITHIN THE CARPATHIAN "CRESCENT"

With its bulge convex towards the South Russian Platform, the Carpathian mountain-system describes a great arc to enclose much of the Danube Basin. Not only is it one of the most clearly defined elements in the *physique* of Central Europe; it grants clear definition to the broad depression of the Hungarian grassland.

The lofty and well-wooded Carpathians have been a difficult obstacle in the way of the movement and settlement of peoples throughout history. Belonging to the same folded system as the Alps, they are of complicated structure, but for our purpose fall readily into three main divisions. Towards the west, in Slovakia, the landscape is that of a broad and greatly dissected plateau, maintaining an average elevation of 3,000 feet and culminating in one summit at rather more than 8,000 feet. This plateau—the Tatra—is bounded on the north by a series of folded ranges—the Western Beskids—which overlook the loess-covered foreland of Upper Silesia and Galicia. Throughout the Western Carpathians, population is concentrated in valleys which open southwards towards the Danube.

Eastwards from the Tatra, the Carpathians are narrowly compressed into a chain of folds—the Eastern Beskids—whose well-defined watershed corresponds closely to the southern limit of Polish nationality and language. Although a useful natural "divide," the chain is not a barrier to transmontane intercourse, and a number of passes, including the historically famous Jablonica, permit regular communication between Galicia and the Hungarian Plain. Here it was that the Magyar horsemen, coming from the Asiatic steppes in the eighth century, crossed from Galicia to establish themselves within the Danubian Basin.

The great crescent is completed by a partial encirclement of the Transylvanian plateau-basin. Its east- and south-facing flanks are sharply defined where, as the Transylvanian Alps, they overlook from high altitudes the trough-like depression of Wallachia and Moldavia. On their inner side the Transylvanian Alps merge gradually with the much lower altitudes of the Transylvanian plateau-basin, whose general slope is westward, towards the Plain of Hungary. The valley of the Maros River, forming the central corridor of Transylvania, gathers to itself the drainage of the region, and diverts it westwards to the Plain of Hungary.

Transylvania terminates abruptly along a north-south edge, overlooking the Alfold (or Greater Plain)—true home of the Magyar people. Budapest, the Magyar capital, at the western threshold of the Alfold, shelters under a rampart of hills. The Bakonyer Wald traverses Hungary diagonally from the Eastern Alps to the Danube, beyond which it is continued by the Matra Hills to the Carpathians. Upstream from the gap between the Matra and Bakonyer Wald, the lowland—under the name of the Little Hungarian Plain—again opens out. It is now more restricted, for the flanks of the Eastern Alps and of the Slovakian Plateau, respectively, close in to within 30 miles of the Danube on either side. Before Vienna is reached, the encirclement of the Little Hungarian Plain is completed by the diagonal ridge of the Little Carpathians—reminiscent, though on a smaller scale, of the Bakonyer Wald—which extends from the Western Beskids to the Danube, at a point opposite the outposts of the Eastern Alps. Bratislava (Pressburg), river-gateway to the Little Hungarian Plain, stands under the lee of the Little Carpathians in a situation analogous to that of Budapest, whose relation to the Bakonyer Wald has been indicated. Vienna, under the foot-hills of the Eastern Alps, looks across the Danube to a small lowland basin, the

Marchfeld, the farthest outlier of the Hungarian Plain and a factor in the supply of cereals to the Austrian capital.

THE BALKAN PENINSULA

Although of highly complex, mountainous structure, the Balkans are not shut off from the trunk of Europe by a continuous and lofty barrier, as are the comparable peninsulas of Iberia and Italy. In consequence of the compressed folding of the highlands, along axial lines trending generally from north, north-west to south, south-east, the region opens freely to the trunk of Europe. On this side, a series of longitudinal valleys—those of the Bosna, Drina, and Morava being typical—descend upon the long Danube-Sava river-frontage. Correspondingly, in the southern half of the quadrilateral, where the same axial lines of folding are continued, the trend of most valleys is south-eastwards towards the Aegean littoral.

Penetration of the Balkans from either the Danubian or the Aegean side always has been easily effected; but, because of the geographical "grain" of the Peninsula, there is no natural east-to-west passage-way, and communication between the longitudinal valleys has always been particularly difficult. The most critical feature of Balkan geography is the north-to-south "corridor" provided by the valleys of the Morava and Vardar Rivers. From their common watershed near the old fortress town of Skoplje (Uskub), they lead in opposite directions to the Danube (below Belgrade) and Aegean coast, respectively.

Within the Morava-Vardar "corridor" much of the tragic history of the Balkans has been enacted. Along it, from one end or the other, have moved a long succession of migrating peoples, of advancing or retreating armies. Without control of it—as the Ottoman Turks experienced—the maintenance of political authority throughout the Balkans proved impossible. Peoples have, from time to time, crowded into its narrow limits, so that cultural and ethnic complexity is to be expected. In war its inhabitants have been forced to abandon their farms and seek mountain refuge from aggressors entering the "corridor" behind them. As the main highway of South-Eastern Europe its record is one of almost unending population movement, conflict, and political instability.

To the east of the central corridor the physical "grain" of the Peninsula is transformed. From the Danubian defile of the Iron Gate the long range of the Balkan Mountains continues the great crescent of the Transylvanian Alps. It swings sharply along an east-to-west axis, avoiding the Rhodope Plateau of Southern Bulgaria. Impressive as they appear on the map, the Balkan Mountains have not proved to be a barrier to southward penetration from the lower Danube. True, a maximum altitude of 9,000 feet is attained, but the average level of the crest-line is 3,000 feet lower, and the entire range is traversed by convenient passes, which may be approached with ease, particularly from the Danubian side. This comparative facility of southward penetration was made evident by the Bulgar invasion of the seventh century.

In a region ill-provided with interior lowlands, the Basin of Rumelia offers unusual scope for settlement. It is, in terms of political geography, the nucleus of Bulgaria. Physically, it is the elongated depression followed by the Maritza River as far as the point where, diverted by capture, that river changes its course and swings south sharply to the Aegean. Rumelia is well sheltered on its northern edge for about 100 miles by the southern flank of the Balkan Mountains and on the south by the Rhodope Plateau. A more genial climate than is usual in the Balkans is a consequence of the seclusion provided by these highlands. Moreover, the soils of Rumelia are of rich fertility, and cultivation takes on a semi-tropical luxuriance. Sofia, the Bulgar capital—though better suited to the rôle of frontier fortress town— occupies a high upland basin above the Rumelian Plain. By means of the depression between the Balkan Mountains and Rhodope Plateau the way is comparatively easy across the watershed between the Maritza and Morava Rivers, by way of the Dragoman Pass (at 2,400 feet), down to Nis (Nish). By this route the transcontinental express traverses the Balkans between Istanbul and Belgrade.

There is no corresponding ease of access to the central "corridor," from the Adriatic, or western side, of the Peninsula. The entire north-western zone of the Balkans is a much dissected highland, patterned in a series of lofty and parallel mountain-folds, with whose north-west to south-east axes the trend of the Dalmatian coast is in harmony. Known comprehensively as the Dinaric Alps, these ranges of gaunt limestone offer a most formidable barrier to communication with the interior. Moreover, their arid slopes are practically devoid of settlement, so that the peoples of the confined Adriatic littoral are virtually debarred from contact with their compatriots beyond the mountains. So is explained the difficulty of co-operation between

the regions of Jugoslavia. The rock-bound Dalmatian coast, fes-
tooned with islands—themselves the partly submerged remnants of
outer Dinaric folds—is abundantly provided with deep and sheltered
anchorage. There are several ports which were affluent in medieval
times. Dubrovnik (Ragusa) and Split (Spalato) based their rich
commerce on wide Mediterranean contacts, and had comparatively
little to do with the primitive and inaccessible civilization of the
Balkan hinterland.

Most passage-ways between the Dalmatian coast and the interior
outflank the Dinaric ranges. To the east of the Istrian Peninsula,
however, a breach occurs through which Fiume, at the head of a
deeply penetrating gulf, makes easy contact with the Hungarian
Plain. At the southern extremity of the Dinaric ranges, where the
trend of the coast changes to an almost due north-south course, lies
the Albanian Gap. Here is a cleft, where the gorge-like and tortuous
valley of the Drin offers a difficult and indirect approach to the
central corridor of the Peninsula. Beyond the river, southwards, the
Albanian coastal plain is flat, ill-drained, and malarious; and, despite
its wide expanse—unequalled throughout the Western Balkans—
settlement is sparse. The main centres of Albanian culture, including
Tirana, are well behind the coast, at the junction of the foothills
and the plain.

The mainland of Greece is an appendage of the Balkan Peninsula
projecting far to the south, within a Mediterranean setting. The
severity of winter-cold, experienced throughout the Balkan interior,
gives place to the sub-tropical warmth of the Morea and innumerable
Aegean islands, where January temperatures almost equal those of
the North African coast. But there is another Greece, quite different
from this scattered array of sun-baked islands and peninsulas: it is
a large, compact quadrilateral, lying wholly to the north of the Gulf
of Corinth, whose climate is transitional to the normal Balkan severity
of winter. Both Epirus and Thessaly are dominated by the lofty
crest-line of the Pindus Mountains, but the plains of Thessaly,
though interrupted and encircled by highlands, are more extensive
than those of Mediterranean Greece. These lowlands with their
promise of successful plough-agriculture are left largely undeveloped.
Their bitter winds are hostile to the normal cultivation of the Greek
farmer—the production of Mediterranean fruits.

Also included within the domain of the Greek is the fringe of

Macedonia and Western Thrace, around the northern shore of the
Aegean. Macedonia cuts across the "grain" of the Balkan region,
and may be defined as a succession of restricted river-basins—those
of the lower Vardar and Struma, in particular—set within a matrix of
highlands. Western Thrace intervenes between the lofty summits
of the Rhodopian massif and the sea, and is, by tradition, limited
on its eastern flank by the north-to-south line of the lower Maritza.
Beyond, Eastern Thrace continues as an extensive triangle of lowland,
based on the northern shore of the Sea of Marmora. It commands
one of the great cross-roads of the Old World, and its geographical
significance has been critical throughout history. Here the land-bridge
between two continents crosses the oldest seaway of history—from
the Black Sea and the Narrows to the Western Ocean.

A north-to-south section across the trunk of Europe, from East
Prussia to the Morea (Greece) covers not less than 1,200 miles,
though it falls short, by 500 miles, of one drawn across the Russian
Platform from the Arctic to the Black Sea coast. Westwards from
the East Prussia-Morea line the European trunk becomes narrower
abruptly, as a result of the northerly projection of the western basin
of the Mediterranean; so that between Emden and Genoa, or between
Stettin and Trieste, the "waist" of Europe is not more than 600 miles
across. Yet, within these restricted limits, are three major structural
regions of the continental peninsula; they are: the North German
Plain; the Hercynian Uplands and Basins; the Alpine Highlands.

THE NORTH GERMAN PLAIN

From the Polish outlier of the Russian Platform to the Low
Countries, the European Plain narrows with fair regularity, so that,
whereas between Silesia and the Baltic coast the distance is not less
than 200 miles, from the Rhenish Plateau to the Friesland coast it is
but one-third of that extent.

The North German Plain is not remarkable for its attractiveness to
human settlement. Density of population remains comparatively low
throughout, save in close proximity to the arterial rivers, where
urban development is concentrated. Certainly, agricultural wealth
is much less than the area of the plain would suggest. There is the
climatic disadvantage of exposure, during one-half of the year, to
the severe winds of Eastern Europe. Spring comes late, and the
agricultural season is unduly short. At Berlin, fairly centrally placed

within the plain, April is the first month of the year whose mean temperature exceeds 40° F., and the same is true even as far west as Hanover, where more genial, Atlantic influences might be expected to have their effect.

More serious from the agricultural standpoint is the indifferent quality of the soils. Lowland Germany in Pleistocene times was heavily glaciated, and its present surface is witness to the erosion and deposition wrought by the glaciers, in their alternating advance and retreat across the plain. Glacial soils, including much sterile sand and heavy clay, are widely distributed; and morainic ridges, extending generally east and west, are a commonplace of the landscape. Relief is mildly diversified, though very rarely does the elevation reach 600 feet. Much of the better-drained country is forest-clothed, and a national policy of afforestation has done much to improve the poorer land. Depressions between the glacial hummocks and ridges are often lake-filled or encumbered by marsh. Such is the typical landscape of Mecklenburg. The latter's average population density is 128 per square mile, which suggests an indifferent standard of soil fertility, and is representative of Hanover and Pomerania also.

It is not, therefore, possible to think of Berlin as the nucleus of a rich agricultural region. The soils of its district are generally poor, and there is no other resource, such as mineral wealth, to help to explain the selection of its site. Moreover, Berlin has not been throughout history a natural focus of routes, and there are other cities of Germany—in particular Leipzig—which on geographical, as well as historical, grounds have a better title to metropolitan status. Yet Berlin has become, during the short period which has elapsed since the unification of Germany, the most populous city of peninsular Europe.

In considering the conditions for settlement within the North German Plain, the loess belt, which lies on the southern edge of the plain under the slopes of the Central European Uplands, deserves particular attention. We have already traced this narrow zone of fertility through Galicia to Silesia; and it may be followed thence through Saxony, where it covers the rich basin of Leipzig, and then under the northern edge of the Sauerland to the "bay" of Cologne. Wherever the loess extends, agricultural productivity and density of population are both high (cf. Saxony, with 880 per square mile and Mecklenburg, 128).

THE HERCYNIAN UPLANDS AND BASINS

The variety of land-forms in the Hercynian region helps to explain the complexity of its political map, as it was before the foundation of the German Empire (1871). The Hercynian lands are the relics of an ancient mountain-system, originally as lofty as the Alps of the present day. Mountain-building came at the end of the Palaeozoic Age and after the deposition of the Carboniferous strata; and it is of the greatest geographical importance that, within the basins formed by down-folding and faulting, have been preserved the rich coal seams on which depend the industrial fortunes of Europe.

The old Hercynian highlands extend widely across West-Central Europe, but their main mass covers the middle Rhineland, South Germany, and Bohemia, where their elevation is still considerable— from 3,000 to 5,000 feet. At first sight, the geographical confusion is complete, for the axial lines trend in various directions; yet the summit levels are usually gently rounded, as witnesses of age-long denudation. Relief is greatly complicated by crustal dislocations, dating from the Tertiary period of mountain-building, when the Alps were up-folded; but arbitrary as regional division must be to some extent in such orographical confusion, the geographical individuality of each of the following is unmistakable:

(i) The deeply dissected Rhineland *Massif* (Eifel, Hunsruch, Westerwald, Taunus), bisected by the Rhine in its northerly passage through the gorges between Bingen and Bonn; and further subdivided, by the deep valleys of the confluent Moselle and Lahn Rivers, into the plateau "blocks" above-named;

(ii) The Rift Valley of the Rhine—the only true lowland of South Germany—formed by subsidence along lines of fracture defined by the inner edges of the Vosges and Schwarzwald *massifs*. Baden, part of Hesse and Alsace are here included, and, despite the divergence of political allegiance, caused by the Franco-German frontier, it is obvious that here is a region of distinctive personality;

(iii) The broad plateau-basins of Southern Germany. They include the basin of Stuttgart—the nucleus of Württemberg—and the two basins of Bavaria. The latter, divided from each other by the Franconian Jura, are respectively, the basins of Nürnberg and of the Upper Danube-Isar (of which München is the regional capital);

(iv) The "Bohemian Diamond," a great plateau-block, with exceptionally well-developed ramparts—Bohmer Wald, Erz Gebirge, and Sudetes—and with the river-basin of the Elbe-Ultava, centred at Praha (Prague).

Further regional sub-division might be noted, but, for the purpose of this brief summary, enough evidence has been adduced for the argument that physical geography in no way determines, or even favours, the political fusion of Southern Germany with the North German Plain.

THE ALPINE HIGHLANDS

Bounding the Hercynian Uplands on the south, the Alps present themselves as a great barrier, made up of a succession of folds and over-folds, whose axial lines maintain the same general east-to-west direction. So highly compressed has been the folding that there is, save one, no naturally easy passage-way through the mountain-system between north and south, though several routes are practicable. Thus it is that defensive advantages of terrain, such as those which Nature grants to Switzerland, have been treated with respect, even by governments to whom the violation of frontiers is a matter of small account.

For Italy, France, and Germany the rôle of the Alps is that of a frontier-zone, but Austria and Switzerland are largely, or wholly, restricted to Alpine limits. It is perhaps not always appreciated that Austria, though of miniature size, even by European standards, is so extensive from east to west as to cover half the main axis of the Alps. Both Switzerland and Austria extend beyond the High Alps, and, in each case, a majority of the population lives below the 2,500-foot level.

The concentration of life in Switzerland is forced northwards by the great masses of the Bernese, Pennine, and Pontine Alps, which dominate the south and leave no room for considerable settlement. Between these High Alps and the Jura Mountains, which provide the frontier with France, is an elongated plateau, not more than 2,500 feet above sea-level, which extends, diagonally, between the frontier lakes of Geneva and Constance. This plateau is the true nucleus of Switzerland, with more than 70 per cent of the entire population, and it is notable that the great majority of the Swiss live their lives in an environment no more lofty than that of Spain. As this plateau nucleus is geographically continuous with the uplands of Bavaria, the historic spread of German speech southwards was effected without difficulty. On the other hand, when account is taken of the difficult approach to Switzerland from the southern side, the explanation of the small proportion of Italian linguists in the Swiss population is not far to seek.

Western Austria is of the same geographical texture as the Swiss High Alps, and the crest-line of the Tirol is maintained well above 9,000 feet. Yet it is here that the easiest, as well as the oldest, route across the Alps may be followed. Since the Bronze Age there has been traffic through the Brenner Pass (4,485 feet) which, from the Italian side, is approached by a long ascent of the Adige valley, in the long-disputed region of the Trentino. Easternmost Austria, beyond the Alps, is the merest fringe of lowland, but one-third of the Austrian population is there concentrated.

Vienna has for several centuries maintained its rank as the foremost seat of culture and commerce in Central Europe, partly by reason of its geographical accessibility and the remarkable variety and abundance of its contacts. Its situation and spatial relations, one aspect of which was indicated on an earlier page, deserve close attention, for they have had much to do with the political history of Europe. On the right bank of the Danube, under the sheltering foothills of the Eastern Alps, Vienna looks across to an outlier of the Hungarian Plain, upon which a number of extremely important natural avenues converge. The valley of the Upper Danube, beyond the city, is the most direct passage-way to Bavaria and the Rhineland. Commerce-centres that have grown along it—e.g., Linz and Passau— are, like the highway through the Brenner Pass, older than history itself. The navigability of the Danube is fully utilized as far up-river as Ulm, on the western frontier of Bavaria, but it is down-river from Vienna that the volume of river-traffic is especially high. Vienna functions as a transhipment centre for traffic changing over from barge or river-steamer to railway or road transport, and vice versa. The combination of land- and river-routes that converge on the Danube at Vienna is significant of the far-reaching contacts of the city.

At the centre of Czecho-Slovakia, between the eastern flanks of the Bohemian "diamond" and the Western Beskids, lies the Moravian "corridor" which links the North European Plain and the Danube. Vienna controls the southern approach to the "corridor," and much of its strategical and commercial importance is thereby explained.

From the standpoint of Czecho-Slovakia, concerned as it is with the problem of knitting together territories which are strung out from west to east, the north-to-south trend of the "corridor" is a serious inconvenience. Moreover, as it links two parts of Teutonic Europe, across the body of Czecho-Slovakia, it is a source of strategic weakness to the Slav Republic.

One other great and historic routeway, converging on the Danube at Vienna, starts from the head of the Adriatic Sea at Trieste. It finds its rather devious way eastwards by a series of gaps in the hill-country between the Julian and Dinaric Alps. Gathering a converging route from Fiume, it skirts the Eastern Alps in Austria until it strikes the convenient longitudinal groove of the Mur Thal and the low, easy Semmering Pass. From the Semmering, the approach to Vienna is northward and direct. And so, as the natural capital of Central Europe, Vienna provides the medium through which the interests and activities of several regions of varying and complementary resources are brought into effective relationship.

(II) THE NATIONALITIES IN THEIR GEOGRAPHICAL RELATIONS

The framework of Central and East Europe which has been outlined provides the setting for more than twenty nationalities, varying between themselves in their standards of culture and outlook, but all putting forward claims to political autonomy, if not to sovereignty. Until quite modern times, there was, throughout the region as a whole, ceaseless movement of population—directed along certain definite avenues by configuration and other surface conditions—which promoted both ethnic fusion and cultural interchange. This ebb and flow of population took the form both of considerable waves of migration and of more localized movement, a passing to and from highlands and other natural refuges, according to the security or insecurity of the time.

The expansion of the Slavs from the third to the seventh centuries of the Christian era, which set in motion the Germanic peoples to

their west, and was itself largely a response to the onward march of
Asiatic steppe nomads, constituted for continental Europe the main
episode of the Great Migrations. The Slavonic peoples, bound together by language and by similar agricultural economies, established
themselves throughout the greater part of the European land-mass and
became a majority of the population west of the Urals. On a similarly
vast scale was the Turki-Tatar onslaught upon Southern Russia and
the lower Danubian lands in the twelfth and thirteenth centuries, itself followed after an interval of little more than a century by the
Turkish conquest of the Balkan Peninsula. Yet, despite the widespread dislocations caused by these later movements of population
in Eastern and Balkan Europe, the distribution of the Slavonic
peoples was not greatly altered, if we except the displacements caused
by the Magyar entry into Hungary.

From their area of characterization in South-Western Russia and
Southern Poland[1] the Slavs moved outwards, adapting their culture
to the many different types of physical environment within Central
and Balkan Europe, and attaching themselves to the land they
occupied by a laborious husbandry. The directions they followed may
be traced. One was generally westwards, across the North European
Plain, and it is reasonable to suppose that the *loess* belt of Galicia
and Silesia offered opportunities for movement superior to those of the
forested land farther north. There was a certain amount of filtration
through the Carpathians on to the Plain of Hungary, whilst the lower
Danube valley offered itself as a corridor leading from the Russian
steppes.

The westward limit of the Slavonic advance across the North
European Plain can be placed fairly definitely along the approximately north-south river-line of the middle Elbe and Saale (its
tributary), in the vicinity of Magdeburg. For a time they compressed
the Germanic peoples within this frontier, until, in the twelfth

[1] History is vague and rather unreliable in regard to the geography of the original
Slavonic domain. According to the oldest tradition—set forth in the first Russian
chronicle of Pseudo-Nestor—the Slavs originated as a distinctive community
within the Danubian Basin, but this statement is not acceptable to historians. It
is generally held that the earliest home of the Slavs was to the north and north-
east of the Carpathians; and some would place it within the Pripet Basin, which,
because of its vast marshes, would seem to geographers a highly improbable basis
for settlement and cultural development. The open and fertile belt of *loess* farther
south was then, as now, infinitely more attractive.

century, the latter were able to expand eastwards into the zone of
Slavonic occupation. Thus, German expansionist policy, expressed
in more modern times by the term *Drang nach Osten,* is seen to
have a very respectable antiquity. Before the tide of German colonization began to flow there was a period of slack, during which the
Slavonic "front" was stationary; and along that "front" (within the
"bulge" of the lower middle Elbe) was established a fortified marcher-
zone—the "Altmark"—for the protection of Teutonic civilization.
In the Hercynian Uplands, to the south of the Elbe-Saale line, the
Slavonic westward penetration extended to the well-defined limits of
Bohemia, whilst the Slav groups that moved up the lower Danubian
corridor fanned out westwards and southwards, so as to occupy both
the Plain of Hungary and the greater part of the Balkan Peninsula.[2]
Subsequent invasion of the Hungarian Plain by non-Slavonic peoples
of Asiatic origins, including the Magyars—who alone retained their
identity of race and culture—forced the earlier Slav occupants to
abandon the lowland and take refuge in the Carpathians or in the
Balkan Highlands.

Another main stream of Slavonic settlement led from the Ukrainian
steppes into the forests of Central and Northern Russia; but this
was a particularly slow and difficult penetration, in no sense an
organized conquest, for the density of the *taiga* excluded all possibility of mass movement. Nevertheless, it resulted—after several
centuries—in a Slavonic spread as far northwards as the edge of the
cold wilderness of the *tundra.* Any considerable advance of the Slavs
eastwards from South Russia on to the grasslands of Turkestan and
South-Western Siberia belongs to a very modern phase. Because of
climatic aridity there was little incentive to agricultural expansion
in this direction and when, in the nineteenth century, Slav colonization began, it was organized by a Government, equipped with the
necessary capital and science for the rehabilitation of the drought-
ridden Asiatic steppes.

In respect of both ethnological and cultural characteristics the
Slavs were, prior to their migrations, much less differentiated than
they are to-day. The farther they moved from their original homeland, into contact with peoples and regions new to their experience,
the more differentiated they became, both in racial type and in the

---

[2] Mountainous Albania and the Mediterranean zone of southernmost Greece
alone lay beyond their occupation.

organization of life. In material culture, if not also in ethnology, the differentiation was most marked on the western frontiers of the Slavonic domain, where contact with Germanic genius for urban and industrial organization wrought an impressive change in the evolving life of Czechs and Poles. Those Slavs who penetrated the Russian forests in a northerly direction absorbed a scattered population of broad-headed Asiatic stock, whose physical type and culture (associated with the pre-Aryan Finno-Ugrian language) are still to be found within the East Baltic fringe of Russia.

THE RUSSIAN SLAVS

Accepting the view that the Slavonic peoples were cradled on the Dnieper steppes and on the grasslands farther west, it is reasonable to suppose that the modern Ukrainians—with their alternative names of Little Russians or Ruthenes[3]—are lineal descendants of the original, undifferentiated Slavs as they existed in the early centuries of the Christian era. As in the case of the whole body of Slavs the Ukrainians are associated with the "Alpine" racial type, which is stocky and of considerable breadth of face and head. They are taller than the average for Russia, but this is credited to advantages derived from occupation of a supremely fertile soil rather than to racial inheritance; and their supremacy within Russia in respect of cultural standards is similarly explained.

The Little Russians look back proudly to the days when Kiev, "the mother city" of Russia, was, after Byzantium, the most prosperous mart of South-Eastern Europe. In the early Middle Ages the city grew in intimate relation to a transcontinental trade route which, using the extensive navigability of the Dnieper for much of the way, linked the East Baltic lands by way of Novgorod with Byzantium. Yet its civilization was under constant threat from the West Asiatic steppes, and the catastrophic invasions of the Tatar hordes during the twelfth and thirteenth centuries well-nigh obliterated organized Ukrainian life. The Tatar occupation inevitably promoted intermixture of strains, yet its ethnic consequences were

[3] The term "Little Russia" was officially used by the Tsarist Government in order to enforce the doctrine that the Ukrainian language was not more than a mere local variation of standard Russian. "Ruthenes" is commonly applied to those Slavs of Ukrainian affinities who occupy Eastern Slovakia, Eastern Galicia, the Bukovina, and Bessarabia.

less than might be supposed, taking into account both the vigour and the duration of the invasions.

All told, the Little Russians, including those called Ruthenes, number about forty millions, whose distribution went far beyond the western frontier of the Ukrainian Soviet Republic, as it was in 1938. The Pripet Marshes have prevented their expansion beyond a point more than 80 miles to the north of Kiev, but south of the vast water-logged region they have spread westwards over the natural grasslands— now largely converted to cereal cultivation—of Bessarabia, the Bukovina, and Eastern Galicia, which, as parts of the Carpathian Fore-land, are continuous with one another.

Partially detached by mountain crests from the main body of the Little Russians are those Ruthenes whose ancestors climbed the thickly-wooded Central Carpathians by the Jablonica and other passes, and descended the southern slopes to the foothills overlooking the Plain of Hungary. The Carpathian Ruthenes form a compact group, exceeding half a million, within the easternmost extension of Czecho-Slovakia. They have lived for long in a highland refuge apart from the main currents of life crossing Central Europe, and it is not surprising that their civilization is comparatively primitive. Never-theless, national sentiment has been strongly awakened in recent years, and is a factor to be reckoned with in the re-shaping of the political geography of Central Europe.

Eastern Galicia, much of which comes within the upper basin of the Dniester, is limited, conventionally, on its western side, by the south-to-north course of the River San (Vistula tributary). Within it there are approximately five million Ruthenes who represent more than 60 per cent of the entire population. The remaining inhabitants are mainly Poles and Jews, who congregate in the towns (capital— Lwow), and are thus socially and geographically segregated from the Ruthenes, who are the peasantry. In addition to this distinction between Ruthenes and Pole, there is a sharp religious cleavage, for one is Orthodox and the other Roman Catholic. It is the geographical place of the Galician Ruthenes within the circle of Ukrainian influence which will, henceforth, determine their social and political future: similarly, recent decisions concerning the future of the Carpathian Ruthenes show appreciation of their affinities with the Little Rus-sians beyond the mountains, both in Galicia and in the Ukrainian Republic. The Ruthenes of Bessarabia and the Bukovina are not a majority of either province and their distribution will be considered in relation to that of Rumanian nationals at a later stage.

There is no fundamental distinction between the Ukrainians and the Great Russians, who form the main mass of the Slavonic population within the U.S.S.R. The explanation of the minor cultural dissimilarities that exist is that the two groups have evolved during the last millennium within environments characterized by wide differences of vegetation, and have inevitably developed different spatial relationships. Yet they are now, and have been for centuries, united under one government and—more important—they recognize a common ancestry. Thus there are safeguards of tradition which would oppose any tendency towards the political dissociation of Great and Little Russia. Ethnically, the resemblance is strong. Except for the slightly taller stature of the Little Russians, and for the somewhat lighter complexion of the Great Russians, they are virtually indistinguishable. The absorption of Tatar strains by the Ukrainians is matched by the Great Russians' incorporation of small, scattered groups of Finno-Ugrians whom they encountered in their colonization of the northern forest zone.

From the Slavonic base on the Dnieper steppes the ancestors of the modern Great Russians carried out a gradual settlement of the forest-lands of Central and North Russia. In the first of these two regions the greater part of the land was, during a thousand years of colonization, brought under cultivation; and the establishment of Moscow as the principal settlement of the Great Russians concluded the first stage of their great migration. As they passed on to penetrate the taiga, a colder and more inhospitable environment than that of Central Russia, their agricultural economy was abandoned. Recourse to hunting and fishing (in the great, northward-flowing rivers) became necessary. Until the twentieth century very little of the taiga was felled; but the forests of Central Europe were greatly reduced before the modern period, and, as means of transportation improved, contacts between the Little and Great Russians were strengthened.

When, in the fourteenth century, Tatar usurpation of South and South-Central Russia ended with the revival of Slavonic civilization, the Russian State was restored and organized, but from Moscow, not from Kiev. The central zone of the country was the first to be cleared of Tatar domination.

Definition of the frontiers of Great Russia on the Baltic side raises the question of the national independence of those non-Russian communities, formerly within the Russian Empire, which enjoyed sovereign rights in the period between the First and Second World Wars. It is notable that the Great Russians reach the Baltic shores at no point save Leningrad and its immediate neighbourhood. The isthmus which separates Europe's greatest lake—Ladoga—from the Gulf of Finland is occupied by a majority of Finnish people, except within a distance of 20 miles from Leningrad; whilst to the west of that city, along the southern shore of the Gulf of Finland, the non-Slavonic Esths are numerically dominant not more than 50 miles away. Leningrad is, therefore, despite its recent metropolitan status, essentially an outpost of the Great Russians. Its selection by Peter the Great as imperial capital in preference to Moscow diverted, to some extent, the natural development of the Russian State. To the north of Lake Ladoga, where population density is low—indeed, less than twenty per square mile!—the language frontier, dividing Great Russians from Finns, is difficult to determine. In this region, as fairly generally throughout Eastern Europe, language is the basis of nationality. The political frontier, drawn after the First World War, proved satisfactory to neither Russia nor Finland, yet it was an attempt to conform to the linguistic preferences of the border peoples. There seems little doubt that Finnish nationals form a majority on the plateau "divide" of Karelia, where drainage to the White Sea is diverted from that to the Baltic.

The expansion of the Great Russians beyond the Urals has been greatly expedited during the last twenty-five years in response to the phenomenal industrial development of Western and Central Siberia. As recruitment of Slavs for the new industries is on a vast scale, it is reasonable to suppose that the Great Russian population of Western Siberia, if not also of Russian Turkestan, is now as numerous as all the non-Slavs combined. Indeed, it seems inevitable that, ultimately, the Russian Slavs will be numerically dominant throughout Northern Asia. Their long history provides abundant evidence of their adaptability as colonists. Very notable is their ability to settle successfully within zones of greatly varying climatic characteristics,[4] and to co-operate with alien peoples.

In Tsarist days, the White Russians were the most oppressed of

[4] Slavonic settlers have adapted themselves to the most extreme climate of the world, that of north-eastern Siberia, where a mean temperature of 60° F. for July alternates with minus 59° for January.

FIG. 9.—THE PEOPLES OF THE EAST BALTIC LANDS

Peoples of Ugro-Finnic origin
{
1. Esths
2. Lapps
3. Finns
4. Karelians
}

Slavs
{
5. Great Russians
6. White Russians
}

Other East Baltic peoples
{
7. Letts
8. Lithuanians
}

Scandinavians
{
9. Norwegians
10. Swedes
}

(Areas of very sparse population are left blank)

the Russian Slav communities, and only since the Revolution have they been granted the privilege of national self-expression. They occupy territory, still largely forested, to the north of the Pripet Marshes, and this barrier to settlement has to some extent segregated them from the Little Russians who reach the southern confines of the Marshes. There is no corresponding geographical hiatus between the White Russians and their eastern neighbours—the Great Russians —to whom they are particularly close, in respect of both ethnic traits and language.[5]

On an earlier page reference was made to a wedge of low plateau, rarely over 600 feet, which extends westwards from the main mass of the Russian Platform between bordering zones of marsh. The White Russians are situated right athwart this wedge, within east to west limits which may be set at Smolensk and Grodno; and their concentration is greatest around Minsk which, by tradition and geographical situation, is their national centre. Their aggregate population is very difficult to determine as, until the War, they were dispersed between the four political units of Poland, White Russia, Lithuania, and Latvia. Five millions were known to be within the White Russian Republic, as it was in 1938, and the Soviet authorities then estimated that more than half as many again were under foreign domination.

Communication between them and the main current of Russian civilization has always been hindered by the inaccessibility of their marsh-enclosed forest home, which, nevertheless, has served them well as a refuge. Equally significant is their outpost position which has promoted contacts, as close with the Poles and Lithuanians as with the Great Russians. They represent an essentially rural population, and the towns which lie within their geographical range are largely made up of Polish, Jewish, and German communities. The White Russians endured for many centuries the lot of a serf-like peasantry, and, until the Revolution, more than half the territory where they formed a majority was held by Polish landlords. At the same time, commerce was near to being a monopoly of Jewish town-dwellers. Taking into account their long-depressed social condition, it is not surprising that the national renaissance of the White Russians was slow in its development down to 1917.

[5] The White Russians are the fairest of the Russian Slavs, but not quite as blond as the Poles.

THE EAST BALTIC NATIONALITIES

It has already been remarked that, with the exception of the
Leningrad neighbourhood, both the Great and White Russians
nowhere reach the Baltic coast. The littoral of Estonia, Latvia, and
Lithuania—in all a continuous zone of over 400 miles—together
with the south-western peninsula of Finland, is occupied by a series
of non-Slavic and non-German communities, whose sovereign independence was recognized for the first time in 1919.

In respect of race and language, the Finns and Esths show strong
affinities, though there is a dualism in the Finnish community which
complicates any ethnic or cultural definition of that people. Linguistically, the Esths and a majority of Finns are of the Ugro-Finnic
group, an outpost of which established itself very early in North-
Eastern Europe. Ethnically, the Esths and the Finns of interior Finland are, in the main, set apart from the tall, blond "Nordic" type
which is characteristic of Scandinavia. Outside its Baltic littoral, Finland is the home of broad-headed peoples of rather short stature—
both brachycephaly and inferior height being marked in the direction
of Lapland.

The presence of the "Nordic" type and of Swedish culture and
speech on the East Baltic shore is evidence of long-enduring contacts between Scandinavia and Finland. Indeed the Finnish lands
in close proximity to the Baltic are sometimes classified as part of
Scandinavia, for purposes of regional analysis. The Finnish coastal
plain is strongly contrasted to the much weathered plateau of the
interior; its climate and soils are more favourable to settlement than
those of any other part of the country and have attracted colonists
from Sweden, many of whom have congregated within the coastal
towns, to influence strongly the political and commercial life of Finland.[6] Since the twelfth century, when Swedish missionaries first
introduced Christianity to Finland, the influence of Swedish culture
has been strong if not predominant throughout the coastal belt.[7]
The forested hinterland supports a thinly-spread population, but its
inhabitants are nationally-conscious and resist the expansion of
Swedish cultural domination much as, formerly, they opposed the

[6] All towns of Finland—except Tampere—with populations of over 25,000, are
confined to the narrow coastal plain.

[7] Here is the explanation of the occasional inclusion of Finland as part of
Scandinavia.

political domination of Russia. They have retained their Finnic speech despite the six centuries of Swedish rule which preceded the hegemony of Russia. Moreover, even within the Baltic littoral belt the hold of the Swedish language does not go unchallenged. The two

FIG. 10.—THE EAST BALTIC LANDS: DENSITY OF POPULATION (YEAR 1931)

1. Under 25 inhabitants per square mile   3. 65–130 inhabitants per square mile
2. 25–65   ”   ”   ”   ”   4. Over 130   ”   ”   ”   ”

divisions of the Finnish population make their closest contacts, though without merging, in the coastal towns and particularly in Helsinki, the capital, where each represents a distinct stratum of society. Russian influence has been a further disturbing factor since the beginning of the nineteenth century; but, in recent years, a considerable number of Finns have been prepared, in their opposition

to Swedish influence, to consider some degree of political association
with the Soviet Union. It is undeniable that national unity will be
postponed so long as the two sections in the life of Finland remain
divided in purpose and outlook, as also in tradition.

When, subsequent to their early migration across Eurasia, the
ancestors of the Esths and Finns finally settled on opposite coasts of
the Gulf of Finland, geography deprived them of land contacts with
each other. Nevertheless, the ethnic and linguistic affinities of the
two peoples are still notable. The Esths speak a Ugro-Finnic language,
and their racial characteristics, though modified by long-continued
fusion with alien strains, are closely related to those of the non-
Nordic Finns. Within the forested and peat-encumbered peninsula
—outlined by the Gulfs of Riga and Finland and by the long moat of
Lakes Peipus and Pskov—the Esths have retained their identity as
a people, despite their diminutive numbers (1,126,000 in 1934) and
enforced submission to alien Powers. Widespread bog, marsh, and
forest have afforded them a refuge and so ensured their national
survival; but at the same time these geographical hindrances have
tended to isolate them from the main currents of Baltic civilization.
Moreover, the forest soils, where cleared of timber, are of indifferent
quality for agriculture, and impose rather narrow limits upon economic development.

Of recent advantage to Estonian welfare has been the elimination
of the landed estates and their replacement by peasant holdings. As
late as the second half of the nineteenth century the greater part of
the land was, despite Russian suzerainty, under German ownership.
German interest in East Baltic territory is traceable to the missionary
activities of the Order of the Teutonic Knights, whose members, in
late medieval times, took up residence between the lower Vistula
and the shore of the Gulf of Finland. Their successors became the
land-owning class—the Balts—and remained largely in control of
social and economic affairs even when Estonia passed under first
Sweden and then Tsarist Russia. In 1939, by agreement between
Russia and Germany, the Balts of Estonia, who numbered about 2
per cent of the total population, were repatriated. Only one considerable alien minority within Estonia now remains, namely, a Russian
population of about 90,000. The withdrawal of the German element
does not, however, eliminate German influence, which has left its

impress on Estonian civilization, notably in the widespread acceptance of the Lutheran religion.

Immediately to the south of Estonia the Letts represent a larger
but less homogeneous community in which, apart from several
considerable minorities, there is a certain cleavage of interest between
a large urban population and the peasantry. The Lettic language,
unlike Finnic and Estonian, is of Aryan origin and similar to
Lithuanian. Moreover, in addition to linguistic kinship with their
southern neighbours, the Letts, though mixed in ethnic composition,
resemble the Lithuanians more than they do the Esths. Fair complexion, a tendency to brachycephaly and stature taller than the
average of East Baltic peoples, are characteristic traits.

In its external contacts the Latvian community throughout its
history has been strongly influenced by proximity to the civilizations
of Poland, Germany, and Russia. As in Estonia, the legacy of the
Teutonic Order was the establishment of a German land-owning
caste, which was able to maintain its social and economic privileges
despite the nominal political supremacy of Sweden and, later, Russia.
The agrarian problem could not have been more acute than it was
when the First Great War occurred, and the Land Laws which
followed expressed the resentment of a peasantry for those who had
held them so long in serfdom. Most Letts bear witness to German
influence, particularly in their Faith, which is Lutheran. In the
south-eastern province of Latgale, however, Roman Catholicism
prevails, as a consequence of the early intrusion of Polish influence.

Until reunion with Russia in 1944, it was a disadvantage to the
Latvian nation that, compared with its small numbers—about two
millions only—the Russian minority of a quarter of a million was
so considerable. Another minority—of Jews—is much smaller and
almost entirely confined to the towns, where its place in commerce
is out of all proportion to its size. Latvia lies within the northern
limits of the broad belt of East-Central Europe, extending from the
Baltic shore to the Carpathian Foreland, where the Jews form a
large and influential element as town-dwellers. Despite the past
decade of tragedy it is this zone which is likely to remain, as it has
been for long, the world's main concentration of Jews.

The outstanding importance of Riga in the life of Latvia has no
parallel in any other Baltic country, save Denmark, where also a
great port-metropolis supports one-fifth of the national population.

Riga attained its commercial status, not merely as the port for the circumscribed hinterland of Latvia, but as one of the main Baltic gateways to the Russian Empire. Its inhabitants, as much concerned with manufacturing industry as with trade, are necessarily out of touch with the special agrarian problems affecting the Latvian peasantry. All alike, however, are dependent on the volume of trade flowing through the great port. The political events of the period between the two World Wars did not assist the continued development of Riga as a focus of continental commerce, and its prosperity has ebbed and flowed in response to the fluctuating state of Latvia's relations with the Soviet Union.

Lithuania, yet another East Baltic national community of rather diminutive size (approximately two millions) is keenly aware of its ancient military traditions. The conquering Order of the Teutonic Knights encountered a strong resistance when, in the thirteenth century, it attempted to extend eastwards from Memel-land up the valley of the Niemen. Yet Lithuanian resistance could not have continued, save for the difficulties which dense forest and wide areas of marsh placed in the way of the German colonists. As it was, the latter were able to make good their claim to Memel in their advance northwards into Courland (south-west Latvia), and the port remained, until the close of the Second World War, an essentially German town, with Lithuanian nationality dominant in its near neighbourhood.[8] The early Teutonic conquest of the coastal belt had the effect of frustrating Lithuanian efforts to obtain an independent Baltic outlet for their commerce. When, in 1793, Lithuania—previously united to Poland—was annexed by Russia, Memel-land was left to Prussia: but the re-born Lithuania has shown its intention of taking from German possession the maritime gateway of the country, and has based its claim on both commercial necessity and the numerical predominance of Lithuanian nationals within Memel-land.

Polish influence on the civilization of Lithuania is apparent in the Roman Catholic allegiance of all districts, save only Memel-land. Within the frontiers of the State, as it was defined in 1938, the number of Poles was inconsiderable, but Lithuania lays claim, on

[8] The coastal strip extending from the Niemen outlet (into the Kurisches Haff) as far as the Latvian frontier has a population of about 750,000 (1939), mostly Lithuanian; but included is the town of Memel whose population of 38,000 is almost entirely German.

the basis of the national allegiance of the inhabitants concerned, to territory much farther to the east, including the city of Vilna. The dispute with Poland over Vilna is complicated by the national allegiance of the inhabitants, both of the town itself and of the surrounding countryside. Poles and Jews together make up a high proportion of the urban population, and, in the cultural history of Poland, Vilna is remembered as the place of education of Mickiewicz, the national poet. The Lithuanians counter the Polish claim to the city by recourse to the history of the fourteenth and fifteenth centuries, when Vilna attained the status of capital of the Grand Duchy of Lithuania. It was a time of Lithuanian political supremacy over much of East-Central Europe between the Baltic and Black Seas. Better founded is the Lithuanian claim that in the district around Vilna their nationals considerably outnumber the Poles, although both nations are apt to overlook the presence of large numbers of White Russian peasants in the same vicinity.

THE WESTERN SLAVS

Despite the antiquity and magnificence of its national traditions, Poland, as a political unit, continues to be threatened by instability. It is not for the geographer to assert that the difficulties which have beset Polish national evolution are wholly due to environmental factors beyond human control: but at least there should be some estimate of the hindrances which impede a successful adjustment of national aspirations to the prevailing geographical conditions.

It is unfortunate that Poland cannot be defined in terms of geography with even approximate precision. The national nucleus is the basin of the middle Vistula, but there is no clearly marked boundary zone, except on the southern margin, where the crest-line of the Western and Central Carpathians marks the limit of Polish population. Only on this side can a frontier be drawn in accordance with national aspirations, without transgressing the rights of neighbours. Elsewhere around the periphery of the Polish national home it is virtually impossible to find a line which would serve as a satisfactory partition, and, without doubt, the indefiniteness of physical geography is at the root of the problem. Poland is essentially a land of the North European Plain. Relief is monotonous, marked accentuation being confined to the Carpathian south, so that the river-basins of the Upper Oder, Warthe, Vistula, and Bug, where Polish settlement congregates, merge into one another without easily discernible demarcation. Between the middle Vistula and the middle Oder—within the Germano-Polish marcher-zone—there is a complete absence of any outstanding feature of the landscape which might be utilized as a suitable frontier between the two countries.

Under such uniform conditions of physical geography, ethnic fusion of Germans and Poles along their common "fronts" has proceeded so far that, from the standpoint of race, there is now little to distinguish the peoples on either side of the nationality frontier. On the other hand there is a clear distinction between them on the grounds of culture, including both language and religion. Nevertheless, because of the ease of movement across the monotonous plain the two nationalities are intermingled in great geographical confusion. According to the ebb and flow of the political authority of Germany and Poland, respectively, so has the movement of their border populations fluctuated: for example, between 1920 and 1935, within the western frontiers of the new Poland the numbers of Germans steadily diminished as, by one means or another, this national minority was encouraged to leave the country. It is probably true that, on balance, in the period 1900-1939, the proportion of Poles within the border provinces of Pomorze and Poznan (Posen) increased at the expense of the German element. Until 1919 over a period of about three centuries, the Polish nation was slowly receding along its western front, largely as a result of the superior technique and organization of Teutonic settlers who took up land and entered towns farther and farther to the east. In the sixteenth century the population as far west as the middle and upper Oder was overwhelmingly Polish, and even as late as 1790 Breslau, the Silesian capital, was more Polish than German. The German advance not only forced back the Polish "front": it penetrated behind that "front" and, in the nineteenth century, was most notable wherever opportunities for mining and metallurgical industry offered, as, for example, on the coalfield of south-eastern Upper Silesia. We have remarked on the notable tendency for Poles to dominate the urban life of the Lithuanian, White Russian, and Little Russian territories, so that the numerical inferiority of Poles to Germans, in the larger towns of districts west of the Vistula Basin, was, until 1944, in striking contrast.

The geographical distribution of Polish nationals along their

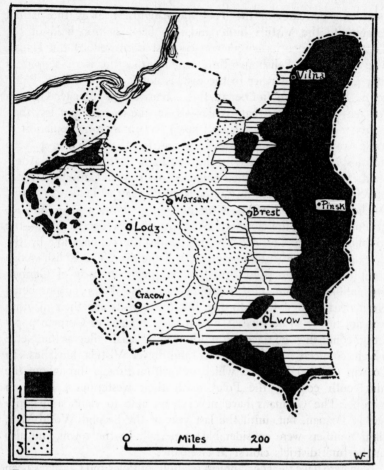

FIG. 11.—PROPORTIONS OF POLES IN POPULATION OF POLAND (YEAR 1920)
1. Areas where Poles were less than 25 per cent of the total population
2. Areas where Poles were 25–75 per cent of the total population
3. Areas where Poles exceeded 75 per cent of the total population

eastern "front" has already been outlined, and it remains to define
their limits over against Germany. The basin of the Vistula is
Polish in its entirety, save only where the great river has built its
delta on the Gulf of Danzig. Here, in the near neighbourhood of
the Baltic, from Danzig round to Königsberg and beyond, the
population is predominantly German and has been so since the

colonizing activities of the Teutonic Knights. Danzig, the natural gateway to the Vistula hinterland, has been a stronghold of the Teuton ever since its commerce was first organized by the Hansa. The obstacle to Polish maritime aspirations is the more serious in that East Prussia, farther to the east, is not merely a strip of Baltic coast. The southern frontier of this extensive and compact German enclave—rather larger than Wales—is, on the average, not less than eighty miles from the sea. East Prussia had in 1939 a population of some two and a quarter million Germans, together with over 400,000 Polish-speaking Masurians in the southern districts around Allenstein. The latter, despite their language and Roman Catholic religion, preferred to be regarded as Germans rather than as Poles.

The western coast of the Gulf of Danzig shows a predominance of Poles, and is the northern extremity of a wedge of Slavs—the so-called "Polish Corridor"—which marks the colonization by the Poles of the lower Vistula basin, west of the river. This Polish wedge completely detaches East Prussia from the main body of German population. Within the "Corridor" in 1938 Poles outnumbered Germans by about three to one, but thirty years ago their majority was not nearly so decisive. A west-to-east "bridge" of German population could then be traced along the wide, glacial valley of the Netze which connects the lower Oder and lower Vistula lowlands. In Poznan (Posen) Province, which was within Prussia throughout the nineteenth century, the Poles reach their westernmost limits in Europe. The Germans have never been able to claim a majority within Poznan, but, until the last year of the Second World War, their numbers were considerable,[9] especially in the towns and also in the rural districts closest to Germany.

Nowhere have the geographical relations of Poles and Germans been as intricate as in the extreme south-east of Upper Silesia where the presence of coal, iron, zinc and lead determines one of the foremost mining and metallurgical regions of Europe. Outside the close-clustered industrial towns, the Silesian loess soils are highly fertile, so that the region is economically attractive to both the Polish peasant and the German townsman. Although for several centuries the Province was dominated, first by Austria and later by Prussia, a large proportion of the population has retained its Polish speech. During the second half of the nineteenth century, penetration of the Polish-

[9] In 1913 the German inhabitants of Posen Province were about 35 per cent of the total population.

speaking part of Silesia by German industrial interests was greatly accelerated, until in the organization of mining and manufactures, as well as in capital investment and technical skill, economic development was almost exclusively German. But, although the life of the towns before 1919 was of a German pattern, most of the work-people on the Silesian coalfield were—and still are—Polish. Here, more than perhaps anywhere in Europe, the application of the ideals of extreme nationalism to the solution of boundary problems becomes an absurdity. There is no more striking example of the welfare of a region requiring the fullest possible co-operation of two communities hitherto divided by traditional antagonisms.

On the extreme southern fringe of Silesia the German and Polish populations are confronted with a northward extension of the Czech nation into the upper Oder basin. The Czechs are particularly well represented in and around the town of Teschen, an industrial outpost of Silesia, whose association with the Province is confirmed by the flow of the Oder head-stream on which it stands.

It is obvious that the problem of drawing the western frontier of Poland in strict accordance with national sympathies is one of almost insuperable difficulty; yet the eastern frontier over against Russia is an even greater challenge to statesmanship. The large claims made by Poland in respect of territories occupied mainly by Little and White Russians have already been indicated. If the State were to be confined on its eastern side to lands where the population is overwhelmingly Polish, its frontier would follow a fairly direct north-south course to the west of the Pripet Marshes, along a line from Bialystok to Brest Litovsk, and thence up the valley of the River Bug.

It may be asked why Polish territorial claims have extended far to the east of a line drawn according to the facts of nationality. The answer is to be sought in events of the thirteenth and fourteenth centuries, during a large part of which the treeless plains of Southern Russia and Galicia lay under the tide of Tatar conquest. From Cracow[10] the Polish kings of the fourteenth century steadily won back the Polish and Ukrainian steppes from the Asiatic hordes. They

[10] Cracow, on the upper Vistula and close to the Moravian Gate (leading to the Danube and to Vienna), overlooks the breach in the Central European Highlands through which Danubian civilization has been accustomed to communicate with the East Baltic lands. Lying on the open loess belt, Cracow commands also the main line of advance, south of the Polish forests, from the Ukraine to the heart of Germany. It was the first great centre of Polish national life, and the capital from the eleventh to the fourteenth century.

restored Slavonic civilization as far east as Kiev and the line of the River Dnieper. Europe, and Slavonic Europe in particular, is indebted to Polish civilization for this work of restoration. The reconquered lands of Galicia and Western Ukraine (as far east as the middle course of the Dnieper) were farmed out to Polish noblemen, who thereby became the land-owning class within territory occupied mainly by Little Russians. It was a phase of territorial acquisition reminiscent of the extension of the authority of the Teutonic Knights and their descendants—the Balts—over the East Baltic lands.

One minority within the heart of Poland remains to be considered. Ever since the sixteenth century the number of Jews has been extraordinarily high, even for Eastern Europe. Before the phase of mass migration of Europeans to North America during the second half of the nineteenth century—to which they contributed an important contingent—the Jews of the Polish lands were about one-half of Jewry throughout the world. In more modern time the proportion has been about one-fifth, but the concentration is still higher than in any other country. Until the tragic events of the Second World War there were more than three millions living as town-dwellers, mainly in the eastern and southern districts which had previously been within the frontiers of Russia and Austria, respectively.[11]

Formidable as have been the difficulties resulting from the inclusion of large minority groups within the State, the national problems confronting Poland remain urgent enough, now that its frontiers have been drawn so as to exclude all alien communities. Polish national sentiment, hardened for centuries in the fire of foreign oppression, is passionate and vehement, and dependent to a high degree on the vision of an heroic past. But the main mass of the population is an impoverished and illiterate peasantry to whom the glories of medieval triumphs mean less than they do to an aristocracy of inherited privilege, owning nearly one half the acreage of Poland. National unity is indeed unattainable where the social cleavage is so deep. Moreover, the peasantry was, until 1944, left without an opportunity of sharing effectively in government; and it is doubtful if its social and political aspirations and needs were appreciated by the "Government" which, during the recent war, was in exile.

[11] The Jews of the Tsarist Empire were concentrated within Russian Poland: on the other hand, from Prussian Poland there was, during the nineteenth century, a general dispersal of Jews throughout Germany.

The influence of religion has been particularly potent in the evolution of Polish nationalism. In a long contest with German Protestantism and Eastern Orthodoxy, the Roman Catholic Church has maintained complete authority within Poland, and has been identified with the national struggle for survival against the imperialisms of both Kaiser and Czar; but, if organized religion has proved to be a powerful force working for national unification, it has done little to eliminate the deep socio-economic cleavage within the nation. The widespread supremacy of Roman Catholicism suggests continuous contacts with western civilization, and these contacts have been assisted by geography. Cracow, the centre from which Christianity spread throughout Poland, was at an early time brought into intimate association with Vienna—the Roman Catholic stronghold of Middle Europe—by the easy passageway of the Moravian "corridor."

In addition, though to a lesser degree, uniformity both of ethnic type and of language has assisted the development of national consciousness. Ease of intercourse across the great plain has helped the process of fusion, and has eliminated any marked tendency towards either segregation of ethnic type or regional variation of language. Like most Slavs, the Poles are of short to average stature, pronouncedly broad- or round-headed, and, although there are minor ethnic differences between those of the northern and of the southern districts, they are not easily recognizable. The Polish language is closer to Russian than to any of the Slavonic tongues, yet neither similarity of speech nor consciousness of a common (Slavonic) origin had brought about, before 1939, a *rapprochement* between the two peoples: indeed, in reviewing their relations during the last two decades, an impression is left of almost continuous antagonism. Such hostility, however, was to endure only so long as the true interests of the Polish people were deprived of proper representation in the national parliament.

Most westerly of all the Slavs, the Czechs, by their occupation of the Bohemian plateau-basin, project far into the zone of the Germanic peoples. In earlier years of Teutonic aggression their geographical position was interpreted, in certain quarters, as a threat to German unity; but, in general, there is widespread sympathy for this small Slav community of rather more than seven millions. Isolated from its kinsmen, save on one side, it has stood courageously

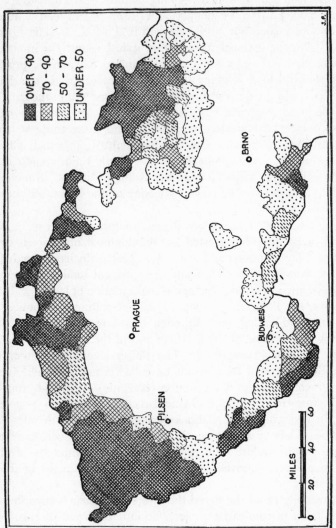

FIG. 12.—WESTERN CZECHO-SLOVAKIA (YEAR 1931): PROPORTION OF GERMANS
IN TOTAL POPULATION (IN PERCENTAGES)

as an outpost of democratic Europe. But, difficult as the political and strategic position of the Czechs has proved to be, as a community they have gained considerably, in an economic sense, from their contacts with the advanced industrial technique of the Germans.

In the early years of the thirteenth century the Czechs were in occupation of the Bohemian plateau-basin in its entirety, right up to the highland rim of the Bohmer Wald, Erz Gebirge and Sudeten Mountains which defines Bohemia on three sides. Eastwards from the valley of the Elbe-Ultava (Moldau)—the nucleus of Bohemia— there is a general increase of elevation towards Moravia, but the rim of the plateau here is not so easily distinguished; and, in response to this indefiniteness of relief, the Czechs at an early time extended into Bohemia from Moravia.

From the thirteenth century onwards, German penetration of Bohemia and Moravia proceeded steadily. It was a colonization to which the Czechs were not unfriendly: indeed, many German artisans were encouraged, by the Slav rulers of Bohemia, to make their settlement and establish their trades. A ring of towns, largely German, grew up within the highland rim of Bohemia, and has remained to this day. Before 1938, the Teutonic element in Bohemia was about thirty per cent of the total population, and was so distributed as to prevent the Czechs, as a majority, from reaching the highland rim anywhere, except on the Moravian side. Within the valleys of the Elbe and, especially, the Ultava, the numerical supremacy of the Czechs was undoubted. They are situated for the greater part within the lower part of the plateau-basin, where altitude does not exceed 1,500 feet. German penetration, though mainly confined to the hilly ramparts of Bohemia, was very deep in places and especially so in the north-western corner—the basin of the Eger River. Here the considerable resources of coal and iron-ore were mined by colonists from Saxony and Thuringia as early as the thirteenth century. Continuous with the Eger zone of Germanism was, before 1945, a strip of the same nationality, some ten to twelve miles in width, which followed the Erz Gebirge eastwards into the Sudeten district where it overlooked the corner of Upper Silesia. It was rare for the German areas to be without large Czech minorities, which might be as high as forty-nine per cent of the total; whereas in the Czech areas of Central Bohemia the German elements were usually insignificant, save in one or two towns.

Moravia was also affected by German penetration, from both the Austrian and Silesian sides, during the thirteenth century and later. It is estimated that prior to the founding of the Republic of Czecho-Slovakia the population of this Province (formerly Margravate) was two and a half millions, of whom about three-fourths of a million were Germans. The latter were distributed, in the main, close to the Silesian and Austrian borders, but were also an important element in certain of the towns, including Brno (Brünn).

By the sixth century the distinctive language of the Czechs had evolved, but Czech nationality was of slower growth. During the later medieval period the Kingdom of Bohemia expressed the national ideal, but Czech political independence vanished in the military disaster of 1620 (Battle of the White Mountains), after which time and until 1918 Austrian political and economic control was complete. Nevertheless, Czech nationalism retained its vitality throughout the period of Austrian hegemony in Bohemia. It expressed itself particularly in cultural, including literary, activities which, to the credit of the Hapsburg dynasty it must be said, were tolerated, at least intermittently. Antagonism towards Austria was not continuous nor was it deep-seated, and before the First World War the majority of Czech patriots would have been satisfied with the concession of local autonomy, within the framework of the Austro-Hungarian monarchy.

There can be no doubt that long settlement within a well-defined region of geographical individuality has aided the cause of Czech national unity as much as any other factor. Religion, in this case, has not been a unifying force, for, although a majority are Roman Catholics, a Protestant tradition is strong in parts of both Bohemia and Moravia, and has been so since the time of John Huss.

Close political association of the Czechs and Slovaks which has brought the new State of Czecho-Slovakia into existence is based on similarities of language and religion, whilst kinship of race is regarded as a further indisputable argument for union. Yet there are important divergencies of tradition between the two communities which Czech statesmen may not have sufficiently considered, and for which the explanation is, in part, derived from geography. Their affinities of race, language, and religion are not in dispute—a majority of the Slovaks being Roman Catholic and a minority Protestant as in the case of the Czechs—but in their economic interests and political outlook, necessarily influenced by their different environments, they are contrasted.

Slovakia is a wooded, mountainous land—the culmination of the lofty Carpathians—and the Slovaks are hillsmen of old and conservative traditions, who were forced to take refuge in their present home at the time of Magyar conquest of the Danubian Plain. At the

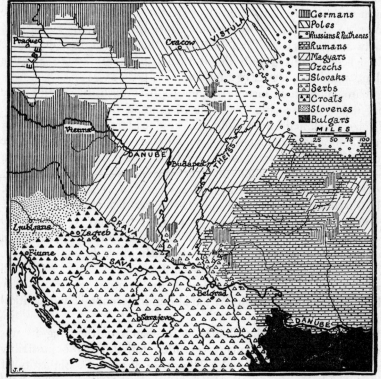

FIG. 13.—THE NATIONALITIES OF THE DANUBIAN BASIN (1920)

foundation of the State of Czecho-Slovakia two considerable lowlands were attached to Slovakia, but their population is Magyar in the main, as was known at the time.

The economic difficulties usually associated with a mountainous terrain are exemplified by Slovakia. There is isolation from the main currents of Central European life, and a low standard of farming and industrial practice which compares unfavourably with that of the

Czechs. Moreover, despite the presence of considerable mineral wealth, there was, in the long period of Magyar control, no large-scale mining or manufacturing, which would have encouraged a concentration of population.

We picture the Slovaks as a small scattered community of little more than two millions, the equivalent of the population of Wales, though the Slovaks occupy a much more extensive territory, and are even more thinly distributed than are the Welsh people. From the Western Beskids they overlook the Moravian "corridor," and extend eastwards across the Tatra Plateau to the Eastern Beskids. There they become mixed with the Ruthenes, who, in Eastern Slovakia alone, number a quarter of a million.

Throughout their history the Slovaks have been drawn into close but unhappy association with the Magyars of the Hungarian Plain. Their detachment from Bohemia, headquarters of the Czechs, is, geographically, well-nigh complete, so that, but for the oppressive *régime* formerly imposed on them by the Magyars, there would have been no compelling inducement for the Slovaks to look westwards to the Czechs for sympathy and co-operation. The final trend of the Slovakian valleys is southwards to the great Danubian Plain, where contact over a wide front is made with the Magyars. Under normal conditions Slovakian timber and mineral ores and Hungarian cereal wealth would be complementary to each other in mutual trade. Unfortunately, in the years between the World Wars, racial and cultural animosities which reflected the contrast of two widely different environments proved too strong for economic and political *rapprochement*.

The treatment of the Slovaks at the hands of the Magyars was heavily oppressive over many centuries, forbidding the possibility of Slovakian autonomy under Hungarian hegemony. Similarity of religious observance, in the dominant Roman Catholicism of both Hungary and Slovakia, has, unfortunately, been powerless to obliterate an ancient antagonism. On the Magyar side, hostility is expressed by an assumption of superiority, based on a tradition of military conquest, and by resentment against the treaty makers of Trianon (1920) because of their inclusion of close on a million Magyars and their lands within Czecho-Slovakia.[12]

---

[12] The official Czecho-Slovak estimate of the number of Magyars within the State was about 700,000 in 1931. Of these 580,000 were in Slovakia. The Magyars, however, claimed that the figures were much higher.

The authority of the Roman Church is strong in the life of the Slovaks, and the *rôle* of the clergy in politics is highly influential. Such clerical influence, indeed, was responsible for much of the Slovak agitation for secession from the Czech-controlled Republic in the years before the Second World War.

THE MAGYARS

In our treatment of the peoples of Central Europe a special place is reserved for the Magyars, not only because they are of Asiatic origin—with Ugro-Finnic and Turki affinities of race and language—but also because they have retained throughout the last millennium an attitude of national exclusiveness which is remarkable even in Europe.

Cradled on the steppes of West-Central Asia, they migrated westwards, and in the ninth century established themselves, during the last episode of the Great Migrations, on the Danubian Plain, at the very heart of Europe. There they found an environment of dry grassland closely resembling their earlier home, and conditions were well suited to the continuance of a semi-nomadic society, characterized by a pastoral economy. They absorbed Asiatic elements, such as the Avars, who had previously occupied the Great Plain, and expelled those Slavonic peoples who had succeeded in retaining a foothold in Hungary during the centuries of invasion from 'the east.'

Thus they have been able, for over a thousand years, to prevent direct contacts between the Western Slavs and the Jugo- (i.e., Southern) Slavs who occupy part of the Balkan Peninsula. Moreover, with the general acquiescence of Teutonic authority, the Magyars proved to be a most formidable hindrance to Pan-Slavic political ideals. Yet, in the process of time, the Jugo-Slavs were able to encroach from their Balkan stronghold on to the Great Plain, thus to set at nought the ambition of the Magyars to absorb into their nation-state all peoples and lands within the mountain borders of the former kingdom of Hungary.

After their entry into the Great Plain the semi-nomadic mode of life of the Magyars underwent little change for a long period. Indeed, it was not until the early decades of the nineteenth century that the basis of their economy was converted from pastoralism to tillage. The cultivation of cereals, especially wheat, then displaced the rearing of sheep and horses from first place in the national economy. Some poorer stretches of natural grassland remain in pasture, and the seasonal movement of flocks and herds, so deeply rooted in Magyar tradition, is not yet entirely discontinued.

A feature of particular geographical interest in the general distribution of the Magyar people is the detached group, known as Szeklers (i.e., frontier guardsmen) who occupy part of the upper basins of the Rivers Maros and Oltu in the far interior of the plateau-basin of Transylvania. The Szeklers are surrounded by Rumans, save on their western side, where they are in touch with a German community, known as Saxons.[13] The presence of Magyars and Germans as far to the east as Transylvania is explained by the pressing need for the defence of the Hungarian Plain against the onslaught of the Tatars in the thirteenth century. Transylvania, though not invulnerable, was capable of strong defence, and, under the control of Hungarian kings, became the eastern bulwark of the Magyar home. Both Szeklers and Saxons remain unabsorbed by Rumanian nationalism, and constitute a threat to the political integrity of Rumania, as long as that State lays claim to all Transylvania. Re-union with the main body of the Magyars is the supreme ambition of the Szeklers, advocated with a vigour natural to a community whose traditions are those of frontiersmen.

We now attempt to define the geographical limits of the Magyars. It will be recalled from our earlier reference to the Slovaks that the latter keep to the Carpathians and leave the neighbouring plain to their old oppressors. From the right bank of the Danube, below Bratislava, the Austro-Hungarian frontier runs southwards and divides Magyars from Austrians. It leaves most of Lake Neusiedler on the Austrian side, and avoids the foothills of the Alps in Burgenland, after which the River Raab is crossed. The Croatian Yugo-Slavs at this point become neighbours of the Magyars, and the nationality frontier trends eastwards, almost exactly coinciding with the line of the River Drava. On this flank the Magyars are, as mentioned earlier, far from the highland edge of the Hungarian Plain.

Eastwards from the confluence of Danube and Drava, as far as the River Tisa (Theiss), the Yugo-Slavs remain neighbours of the Magyars. The intermingling of the two peoples, however, becomes

---

[13] The name "Saxon" has been applied indiscriminately to settlers of German origin and speech in South-Eastern Europe.

intricate, especially near the lower course of the River Tisa, where the Rumans also are a bordering people. Close to the junction of the westward-flowing Maros and the Tisa—in the region of the Banat—Rumans, Magyars, and Yugo-Slavs are all well represented, but in such geographical confusion that it is impossible to draw a frontier without injustice.

Finally, from the neighbourhood of the town of Arad (on the Maros), going north-eastwards, the Magyars extend close to the foothills of the Transylvanian Highland all the way to the head-waters of the Tisa, where contact is made with the Ruthenes.

Encirclement by so many nationalities is an uneasy position for the Magyars. Most of their neighbours are Slavs, but with none have relations been of the friendliest; and the Slovaks and Croats have particularly bitter memories of long and calculated oppression. A complete linguistic hiatus between the Magyars and all the surrounding peoples is, and has always been, a hindrance to international co-operation: the more so as, from the Magyar standpoint, language is the essential basis of nationality.

It is not too much to say that Hungary lives in the fear of ultimate Slavonic domination. The dread of that possibility alone made tolerable to the Magyars their long association, as junior partners, with imperial Austria; but the fear of Pan-Germanism is only a degree less real, in their estimation. When federation with Austria occurred, near the close of the seventeenth century, and the right of succession to the throne of Hungary passed to the Hapsburg dynasty, the menace of Germanization came very close. It was repelled only by the intensity of Magyar national feeling.

In contrast to neighbouring Slav countries, where democratization of land-ownership has extended, Hungary's territorial system had changed little before 1944. Nearly half the land remained in large estates of over 2,000 acres, and the proportion held by peasant proprietors had not been greatly enlarged, despite the declared intention of Government to broaden the basis of land tenure and to reduce the excessive number of landless labourers. Social and economic reforms are needed as much as in Poland, but—as also in that country—they are likely to be postponed if ever the "old order" should be restored.

As consciousness of race and language plays so large a part in Hungarian nationalism, brief reference to it follows. Philologists have disputed whether or not the Magyar (non-Aryan) tongue is derived more from ancient Finnic than from Turki. It appears to have borrowed freely from both during the migrations of the Magyars, prior to their entry into Europe. During eleven centuries of residence in Central Europe the original semi-Mongoloid ethnic characteristics have been to a large extent eliminated through intermarriage with their Slavonic and South German neighbours; and the majority of the present Magyar generation bear physical traits which associate them closely with the "Alpine" type.

THE RUMANS

By the sanction of custom, the northern limit of the Balkan Peninsula is made to coincide with the line of the lower Danube, as far upstream as its junction with the River Sava, whose west-to-east course provides the north-western frontier. Such a division of South-Eastern Europe is obviously arbitrary. It is satisfactory only for very general purposes, and has no validity as a cultural boundary. This is clearly apparent as soon as the similarity of the Rumans to their southern neighbours, the Yugo-Slavs and Bulgars, is appreciated.

The claim of the Rumans to be of non-Slav origin is based solely on a linguistic inheritance from Latin of the Imperial era. In the first century A.D. Rome carried her conquests into the lower Danube valley—the Wallachia of to-day—where her legionaries and officials intermarried with the inhabitants and latinized them superficially. After the Roman withdrawal, in the third century, Slavs and Asiatic peoples entered the region and destroyed the work of Rome; but the ancestors of the modern Rumans took refuge in the Transylvanian Highland, where they cherished their Latin speech. In more peaceful days the lower Danube Plain was re-colonized from Transylvania by Romanized peasants. Thus the Rumanian nation came into being by the geographical union of the Transylvanian highlanders and the Wallachian plainsmen[14]—both tenaciously holding to the speech of Imperial Rome. Arguing from history and language, the Rumans contend that they are of origin different from that of the Slavonic peoples by whom they are almost surrounded.

But adherence to an ancient language does little to determine the way of life of the modern Rumanian peasantry, and their history is

[14] An echo of the former migrations between Wallachia and Transylvania is still recorded in the practice of transhumance; for each summer flocks and herds are driven from the Danubian steppes to the mountains: in winter they return.

more than a brief Roman episode. There can be little doubt that a Slavonic element was strong in their composition at an early time, and that it has become increasingly important. In ethnic type, institutions and cultural affinities there is, saving language, little to distinguish the Rumans from their Slavonic neighbours. Despite the close attachment to the Latin tongue, Rumanian religion is not of Roman origin. It is Byzantine, and a great majority of the people are members of the Orthodox Church. The "divide" of religion in South-Eastern Europe, between Roman Catholicism and Eastern Orthodoxy (in its various national forms), runs for part of the way along the north-western frontier of Rumania, over against Hungary and Slovakia. It is one of the main cultural boundaries of Europe and has done much to hinder friendly international relations. Estranged as Rumans and Magyars are for other reasons—including the difficult problem raised by the position of the Szeklers—their contacts would be greatly eased by religious tolerance.

The geographical nucleus of the modern Ruman nation lies in the combined Provinces of Wallachia and Moldavia. There the nation grew to full strength at a time when the Balkan Peninsula as a whole lay under Ottoman conquest;[15] and there the Rumans represent an overwhelming majority of the population. Rumanian claims cover, in addition, not only the entire plateau-basin of Transylvania. They involve also a number of outlying provinces, including the Bukovina, Bessarabia, the Dobrudja, and the Banat, in all of which Rumans from a fair proportion though not a majority of the population.[16]

The Bukovina centres on the upper basin of the Prut where Cernauti (Czernowitz) is the regional capital. It is an attractive land of rich soils to which population has gravitated from several sides, with consequences of high density and social complexity. An accurate estimate of the composition of the population is well-nigh impossible without an impartial census, but it seems clear that the Rumans, far from being a majority, are less numerous than the Ruthenes, who number about 320,000 out of a total of approximately 850,000. Other important groups are, or were until 1944, Germans—mostly artisans

[15] The wide course of the lower Danube and its fringe of marsh proved a strong natural defence which the Turks were unable to force.

[16] In 1939 the total population of Rumania was 19,900,000, of whom about 14,000,000 were Rumans; and, of the latter, nearly all belonged to the Orthodox Church.

and traders—and Jews who, here as elsewhere, keep almost exclusively to the towns.

Bessarabia, divided from Moldavia by the line of the River Prut, is the largest of several provinces recently claimed by Rumania, without a title based on nationality. This fertile land of wheat and maize production is as complex in national composition as the Bukovina. The most that can be said with any degree of certainty is that Rumans and Russians are approximately equal, and that each is more than 35 per cent of the total population of about 2,800,000. Northern Bessarabia is predominantly Ruman, whilst towards the south, where Ukrainians outnumber any other group, there is a considerable proportion of Tatars, whose ancestors were a conquering people in the twelfth and thirteenth centuries. Jews are estimated to exceed 200,000—which is higher than the Tatar figure—and are widely distributed in towns throughout the Province.

Southern Bessarabia comes up to the edge of the extensive delta of the Danube whose marshy and sandy tracts offer no opportunity for close settlement.[17] Farther south between the northern swing of the lower Danube and the Black Sea the Dobrudja of dry steppes is a land in dispute between Ruman and Bulgar. Only in its northern district is there a Ruman majority: elsewhere the Bulgars predominate, despite widespread expropriation of their lands for the benefit of Ruman colonists, which occurred early this century.

When tracing previously the limits of Magyar nationality, the highly fertile wheat and maize region of the Banat, east of the lower Tisa and south of the lower Maros, was referred to as a complex of nationalities. Only the eastern part[18] covering the south-western foothills of Transylvania is occupied mainly by Rumans: elsewhere either Magyars or Yugo-Slavs (Serbs) predominate.

THE BULGARS

Related by race as they were at one time to the Magyars, the Bulgars provide an instance of a nation whose Asiatic origins are now forgotten as a result of long-continued contacts with the surrounding Slavs. When first known, the Bulgars were a Finnic people,

---

[17] The contrast in population density between the deltas of the Rhine and Danube, the two arterial rivers of Central Europe, is extreme. The figures are: over 500 per square mile for the Rhine delta; under 25 p.s.m. for the Danube delta.

[18] In particular, the counties of Temes and Kraszo-Szoreny.

occupying territory between the Volga and the Ural Mountains. They crossed the lower Danube during the seventh century, and settled the land between the Balkan Mountains and the great river. Colonists from the main body went farther south, across the Balkan Mountains into Eastern Rumelia, which is the basin of the upper and middle Maritza. The physical characteristics of the Bulgars changed as they fused with the Slavs, in whose midst they settled; and to-day, though they vary between themselves in their ethnic traits, as a whole they are distinguished with difficulty from their Slavonic neighbours. They were never a numerous people, and to-day are hardly more than six millions, thinly spread over a country much larger, and more fertile, than Scotland.

Bulgarian Christianity is of the Orthodox Church, a fact which should contribute to a better understanding with both Ruman and Serb, who also were converted by Byzantine missionary enterprise. The Bulgar language is Slavonic, for the original Finnic speech was abandoned after the settlement of the lower Danubian basin. But affinities of race, religion, and language have done little to harmonize the relations between the Bulgars and their Slavonic neighbours. Between Serb and Bulgar the feud has been particularly long and deadly: moreover, it has been aggravated by the selfish policies certain Great Powers have followed in furthering their own Balkan interests.

From the standpoint of national development the Bulgars have suffered more than any Balkan people by long subjection to the Ottoman Turks. The latter overran Bulgaria in the fifteenth century, and from then until the last quarter of the nineteenth century the Bulgars were unable to obtain autonomous rights from their conquerors. After 1885, however, the hold of the Sultan steadily weakened, and in 1908, taking advantage of the revolution of that year in Turkey, the people declared their complete independence. But in the present century the career of the Bulgar nation has so far been disastrous. They have participated in four major wars in a little more than thirty years, and the national resources of man-power and economic wealth have been repeatedly exhausted. Their military enterprise began in an endeavour to evict the Turk from the Balkans, and was continued for the furtherance of territorial claims—sometimes justified—against Rumania, Serbia, and Greece.

Within the two regions most intimately associated with the history of the Bulgars, namely, the southern half of the lower Danubian basin and the basin of the upper and middle Maritza (Eastern Rumelia), there is but one considerable alien minority. During the period of Ottoman conquest much of the best land of Bulgaria was appropriated for Turkish settlement, and to-day the descendants of the colony number about half a million, practically all of whom are Ottoman Moslems. They live on excellent terms with their Bulgar neighbours and have no *irredentist* tendencies. Moreover, they are not in one compact group but are widespread, especially in the eastern half of the country.

There are numerous Bulgarian minorities living in alien lands, and two or three of them, in addition to the Dobrudja Bulgars already mentioned, demand attention. On the western flank of the Maritza Basin, Bulgars extend up to and, in places, beyond the hydrographic "divide" which separates the Maritza and the Morava. Here the nationality frontier between Serb and Bulgar is rather blurred and difficult to determine. The swing to the south made by the Maritza, after turning the flank of the Rhodope *massif*, gives that river an Aegean instead of a Black Sea outlet; whilst the river-valley provides a natural corridor to the coast. It is not surprising, therefore, that the Bulgars covet this routeway to a sea much more accessible than is the Black Sea to ocean commerce; but they have no just claim, on grounds of nationality, to the lower Maritza, for the people of the vicinity are mainly Greeks and Turks. Farther to the west, however, on the maritime frontage of Western Thrace, there are numerous Bulgar "pockets" amongst the Greeks, especially behind the port of Dedeagatch: and beyond Thrace, in Eastern Macedonia, Bulgar colonists of the Rhodope *massif* have moved south towards the Aegean. A large and compact group goes up to the left bank of the River Struma above Lake Takhino, and is there within 20 miles of the sea. Again, however, as in Western Thrace, an eastward extension of Greek population shuts out the Bulgars from direct access to the Aegean. We may expect to find, in a later chapter, that the political partition of Macedonia and Thrace is a matter of the utmost concern to the Bulgar nation.

THE SOUTHERN SLAVS

It will be convenient to consider next the three groups of the Yugo-Slavs, namely, the Serbs, Croats, and Slovenes who, in our time, have federated under Serbian leadership. Right at the outset it must be said that, even though community of race and similarities of language favour the political union of these three peoples, geography is markedly hostile. The Serbs gather round and within the Morava valley, the great central corridor of the Balkans. The Croats and Slovenes are detached from the Serbs by the difficult terrain of the Western Balkans including the barren Dinaric ranges; and, respectively, their orientation is towards the Adriatic coast and the Danubian Plain. How these divergencies affect the political "cement" of Yugo-Slavia will subsequently be discussed.

Two consequences of the contrasted space relations of the Serbs and the Croats are notable. One is that the former were directly affected, and the latter only indirectly, by the long period of Turkish hegemony in the Balkans. The other, that the Croats, quite early in their Balkan settlement, came under the Christianizing influence of Italy, and so accepted Roman Catholicism, whilst the Serbs, from the sixth century onwards, accepted Byzantine civilization and were converted to the Orthodox Church.

The sturdy Serbian peasantry was permitted by the Turks to maintain its agricultural life without much disturbance, but its militant patriotism was aroused to demand and attain political independence. Liberation from Turkish hegemony came in 1878. Thereafter Serbian ambitions were focused on the attainment of a Greater Serbia for all those Slavs who spoke the Serb language, either in its standard or in its slightly different Croatian form.[19] Greater Serbia, according to this ambition, would have brought in the following districts and their peoples; first, Serbia proper, including the Morava basin and the upper Vardar valley; Montenegro (immediately to the north of Albania), whose well-nigh impregnable highland was the refuge of Serbian patriots after their crushing defeat at the hands of the Turks late in the fourteenth century; the Croatian lands, in the interior of the mountain-ribbed plateau of the Western Balkans, as well as along the Dalmatian coast and on the Slavonian lowland, between the Drava and Sava Rivers.

The question of the union of Croats and Serbs is in some respects closely similar to that of the relations of Czechs and Slovaks. Although the Croatian vernacular is but slightly different from the

[19] In the fourteenth century a Serbian kingdom covered the greater part of the Balkan Peninsula, and Skoplje (Uskub) was then its capital. This was before the Ottoman conquest.

Serbian there are points of marked contrast in the two traditions,
and to treat the two peoples as if they were one is to ignore geography,
as well as history. A linguistic difficulty arises out of their difference
of creed. As the bulk of the Serbs belong to the Orthodox Church,
until 1917 largely organized from Russia, they use the Russian

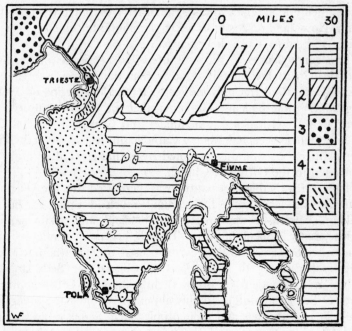

FIG. 14.—NATIONALITIES OF THE ISTRIAN PENINSULA AND ITS NEIGHBOURHOOD

1. Areas where Croats are over 90 per cent of the population
2. Areas where Slovenes are over 90 per cent of the population
3. Areas where Italians are over 90 per cent of the population
4. Areas where Italians are between 50 and 90 per cent of the population
5. Areas where Italians are between 15 and 50 per cent of the population

alphabet, whilst the Roman Catholic Croats have adopted Latin characters. In itself the difference of religion is a serious hindrance to
co-operation, and along with it goes a difference of cultural outlook
for which geography is largely responsible.

A large proportion of the Croats live on the peninsulas and islands
of the Dalmatian coast, and are detached by the barren limestone of

the Dinaric Alps, not only from the Serbs, whose main base is the Morava valley, but also from the Croats of the interior, whose main centre is Zagreb—second city of Yugoslavia. The Croats of the littoral have long been the neighbours of Italian trading colonists, who, from the time of the Roman Empire onwards, have occupied every useful harbour along the Dalmatian coast. Inevitably, many Croats have taken to a maritime life, evidence of which was their large share in the manning of the Austro-Hungarian navy, before and during the First World War.

Competition for territory between Croat and Italian is particularly severe at the northern end of the Dalmatian coast. The Istrian Peninsula is well divided between the two, with Italians dominating the west coast from Trieste to Pola, and the Croats a majority elsewhere. Before Trieste was annexed by Italy, nearly thirty years ago, its inhabitants were mainly Italians, but, in the crowded suburbs, Slavs (both Slovenes and Croats) were in a majority. Excluding Trieste, the Istrian Peninsula had a clear majority of Slavs (mainly Croats) over Italians. Farther south the Italian-speaking colonists are detached in small widely-separated groups. They occupy ports which, in the Middle Ages, either under the protection of Venice or independent of it, flourished as entrepôts. Such were the city-states of Zara, Spalato (Split), Ragusa (Dubrovnik), and Cattara (Kotor). To-day the citizens of these ports of former greatness are bilingual, but in Zara alone there were 12,000 who preferred Italian speech, long before its annexation by Italy. The persistence of Italian influence on the Dalmatian coast is, quite obviously, related to the abundance of excellent harbours, and to the absence of similar advantages along the featureless littoral of Eastern Italy.

Despite their westerly situation within the Balkans, the Croats who occupied the inner side of Dalmatia were considerably influenced by Turkish civilization, from the fourteenth century onwards. The influence was mainly religious, and through it many Croats turned to Islam, although those farthest from the headquarters of Turkish power were never conquered. On a bigger scale, many Serbs of Southern Serbia accepted Islam. For this reason, a considerable proportion of the Southern Slavs became known as "Turks," to the utter confusion of attempts to enumerate the true Turkish population of the Balkans.

The third group of the Yugo-Slavs—the Slovenes—is the smallest in number, but also the most compact, geographically.[20] In culture and language the difference between them and the Serbs is greater than that between the Croats and the Serbs. As a consequence of their geographical situation, close under the Alpine wall, the Slovenes have been brought into close contact with Austria. At one end of

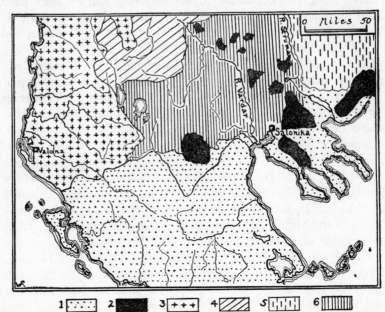

FIG. 15.—SOUTH-WESTERN BALKANS: THE DISTRIBUTION OF NATIONALITIES (1920)

1. Greeks
2. Turks
3. Albanians
4. Serbs
5. Bulgars
6. Macedonian Slavs, the greater number having Bulgar affinities

their territory they come down to the Adriatic along the inner coast of the Gulf of Trieste, whilst eastwards they go beyond the upper waters of the Drava to the Magyar frontier. The town of Lyublyana (Laibach), on the upper Sava, is the principal focus of Slovene life, and, in 1919, a national university was there established.

Through the land of the Slovenes, an old and important highway runs between Vienna and the head of the Adriatic at Trieste, utilizing

[20] In 1939 the population of Yugo-Slavia was about 15,700,000. Apart from alien minorities, there were 6½ million Serbs, 2¾ million Croats, and 1¼ million Slovenes.

the Semmering Pass so as to avoid a considerable detour around the eastern edge of the Austrian Alps. This road, which passes through Lyublyana, is responsible for much of the interchange of culture between Italy and Austrian Germany which has so deeply affected the life of the Slovenes. From Italy came the influence of the Roman Church which is paramount in Northern Yugo-Slavia, whilst to Austria—and Vienna, in particular—the Slovenes owe the comparatively high standard of life which distinguishes them from the more backward, but possibly more virile, Serbs.

THE ALBANIANS

To the south of the Drin river-valley, which opens a way—however indirect—from the littoral to the Morava-Vardar "corridor," the Serbian population gradually gives place to the Albanian.[21]

Although distinctive from the ethnic standpoint, the Albanians are not to be thought of as representing a coherent national entity. A sense of common nationality is not yet fully awake, for the majority are organized in clans, each with local authority. Clan rivalry and religious antagonism have kept the country in a chronic condition of internecine strife, whilst the dissected nature of the terrain tends to promote disunity. Although the authority of the Turks over Albania was never considerable, their religion penetrated widely. To-day the majority of the landowners are Moslems. Those Christians who adhered to their faith were dispossessed of lands and became the serf class. To aggravate the religious difficulties within Albania, Christianity is organized under two different Churches—the Orthodox and the Roman. It may indeed be said that nowhere in the Balkans is the clash of creeds more acute.

Life on the rugged and rather arid Albanian highlands is, of necessity, mainly restricted to pastoralism. The people as a whole are goatherds and shepherds, who move seasonally with their animals between the lower and the higher slopes. They are rarely in nucleated groups, and, to the number of about a million and a quarter, are dispersed over a countryside about twice as extensive as Wales. As mountaineers of long tradition, they prefer the lofty interior to the coastal lowland, and have thereby permitted Italian interests to become established, particularly at the ports of Durazzo and Valona.

[21] The Albanians call themselves Skipetars, or "rockmen," so emphasizing their highland environment.

Independence and turbulence of outlook have characterized Albanian history. Aided by the formidable natural defences of their country, the clansmen have strongly resisted, not only the Turkish invaders, but also the much more numerous and tenacious Slavs, who first settled on the frontiers of Albania about the seventh century. Long contact with the Slavs has undoubtedly affected both their language and their ethnic composition. Ethnologists, however, are agreed that they retain certain features—including remarkable tall-ness[22]—of the pre-Slavonic people of the Western Balkans. Their language, though heterogeneous in its abundance of Slavonic, Turkish, and Greek words, is based on a pre-Slavonic vernacular, similar in some respects to the Latin of Rumania.

THE GREEKS

Going southwards along the coast, the Albanians give place to Greeks some 20 miles beyond Valona, and inland their southern limit is close to the 40th parallel. The Greeks are distributed in two regions of widely different geographical conditions, and although, in all, they number only seven millions, they are more widely scattered than any people of the Balkans. First, there is the broad highland mass of Epirus and Thessaly, dominated by the lofty Pindus chain and fringed by two dissected coastal plains; second is the maze of peninsulas and islands which give a special character to the Aegean environment and from which the word "archipelago" is derived.

The first of the two regions includes Greeks, some of whom live more than 50 miles from either sea. In the second, all are necessarily maritime and belong to that ethnic and cultural type which is widespread throughout the Eastern Mediterranean. Epirotes and Thessalians have felt the full force of the impact with the Yugo-Slavs. They are much modified from the dolichocephalic and brunet stock, called "Mediterranean," which is thought to be the autochthonous element, and is still dominant, throughout the Aegean archipelago and the mainland shore. The northerners on the slopes of the Pindus are not only Slavicized in ethnic features, but are similar to the hillsmen of neighbouring Albania and Serbia in their pastoral mode of life. For their part, the coastlanders of the Peloponnese (Morea)

[22] The people of Albania and the Yugo-Slavs immediately to the north of them are amongst the tallest of the entire world. The writer remembers a visit to the market of Trebinje near Dubrovnik, where, out of 100 men gathered together by chance, more than half were six feet or over.

and of the islands, from Crete in the south to Thasos in the north, are traders, sailors, and market-gardeners. Nevertheless, these distinctions of race and occupation, amongst the people of Greek language and Orthodox creed,[23] count for little when measured against the solidarity of Greek nationalism; for the shepherd of Epirus and the trader of the Piraeus merge in one loyalty of nationhood.

Such particularism of outlook as exists is largely determined by the distribution of population density in the various provinces. There are one or two high concentrations around ports of the south and east, and easily first of these is in the small Department of Attica (including both Athens and the Piraeus), where the average density exceeds 400 to the square mile. By contrast, Epirus and Thessaly are thinly settled, as indicated by a density of about fifty per square mile. As compensation, the influence of the Epirotes and Thessalians in the national life is strong because of their virility and hardiness, qualities which are stimulated by the winter rigours of their mountain environment. Before leaving the subject of the distribution of population, it should be emphasized that, as a whole, Greece is far from being a crowded land. In this respect it is in marked contrast to the peninsula of Central and Southern Italy where, though geographical conditions are opposed to high density, settlement is twice as congested as in Greece.

Urged by his genius for maritime commerce, the "Mediterranean" Greek, of both ancient and modern times, has moved out as a colonist to and beyond the outer limits of the Aegean. He has organized the trade of the southern coasts of the Black Sea and has planted his settlements in every Levantine port. So it came about that the Greek was accepted as an invaluable element in the life of the coastal districts of the Turkish Empire, where his trading and horticultural skill was welcomed rather than merely tolerated. But this expansion has produced serious problems, involving Greek political rights in a number of lands where numerically they are not the most important element. Such difficulties were particularly true of the first thirty years of the twentieth century, when Greek irredentism greatly increased.

In modern times the most urgent question concerned with Greek minorities in alien lands has been the fate of the Hellenic colony in

[23] According to the official census the number of Greeks who are not adherents of the Greek Orthodox Church is negligible.

Turkey. Until 1923 there were in the western coastlands of Anatolia, and more particularly in the city and district of Smyrna, approximately one million Greeks. Smyrna itself, with nearly 400,000 inhabitants, was in the early years of the century the largest city of the

FIG. 16.—THE DISTRIBUTION OF NATIONALITIES IN THE SOUTH-EASTERN ANGLE
OF THE BALKANS (YEAR 1919)

1. Greeks   2. Turks   3. Bulgars

N.B.—The distribution shewn preceded the exchange of population between
Greece and Turkey

Greek world. This rapidly growing and compact alien colony represented a challenge to the reborn nationalism of republican Turkey. It was forced to accept repatriation, and between 1922 and 1925 virtually the entire body migrated to Greek territory and was resettled, mainly in Western Thrace.

Greece lays claim to the entire littoral of Macedonia and Thrace

—at least as far east as the lower Maritza—on grounds of nationality and of historical association. Although the maritime frontage is unquestionably Greek in allegiance, in the nearby hinterland "Macedonian Slavs" and Bulgars are overwhelming majorities in their respective areas. We have already defined Macedonia, in terms of physical geography, as the combined basins of the Struma and Vardar rivers, and it is there that the "Macedonian Slavs" are concentrated. They are mostly bilingual, and usually speak either Bulgar or Serb, though a minority are of Hellenic speech. There is little doubt that those who prefer Bulgar as their vernacular are a clear majority, but, whatever may be the linguistic preference of the "Macedonian Slavs," it seems that their national sentiment is sufficiently aroused to resist incorporation within any of the South Balkan States. At the same time, if circumstances demand that their territory should be allotted to one of the Powers, justice, not to speak of their own preference, would seem to point to Bulgaria as that Power.

THE TURKS OF THE SOUTHERN BALKANS

Until the Balkan Wars of 1912-13, Macedonia was part of the Ottoman Empire and had been so for more than four centuries. The Balkan boundary-changes of the early years of this century produced a steady shrinkage in the territories controlled by the Turks; and, as a rule, when their military authority disappeared, they preferred to migrate as refugees rather than remain under Christian domination. Thus, when Ottoman rule was eliminated in Macedonia, about 100,000 Turkish residents moved either eastwards into Thrace or overseas to Anatolia. This process of retreat towards the south-eastern angle of the Balkans was greatly accelerated in the opening year of the First Great War, when both Greece and Serbia were hostile to Turkey. The number of Turkish refugees from these countries combined was at least a quarter of a million in that single year; whilst a counter-movement developed, as a consequence of the expulsion of an approximately equal number of Greeks from Turkey.

As the expulsion of minorities under war-time conditions was already a normal Balkan occurrence before the First Great War, it is not surprising that, in the subsequent peace negotiations, attempts were made to reach agreements for exchanges of population, not only in the interests of particular countries, but of international welfare. Yet, although certain agreements were ratified, the carrying out of a "voluntary exchange" by an international commission proved virtually impossible. Expulsion was more general, and involved, as we have mentioned, the evacuation of more than one million Greeks from Anatolia—in addition to about 200,000 from Eastern Thrace—between the years 1922 and 1925. At the same time, some 356,000 Turks left Greece, though by the terms of the Agreement of 1923 neither the Moslems of Western Thrace nor the Greek colony (exceeding 110,000) of Istanbul were required to abandon their homes.

No longer were there any considerable minorities of Turks left in any part of the Balkans, save only the groups of Moslems within the eastern half of Bulgaria. Turkey, shorn of its empire, is a re-strengthened, because homogeneous, nation-state which, though based mainly on Asia Minor, extends also across the Bosphorus and over Eastern Thrace to the line of the lower Maritza.[24] It is probable, however, that if Turkish authority over Istanbul had been contrary to the interests of those States which determine the balance of power in Europe, it would have disappeared from the continent long ago.

Strategically, the control of the Straits is of first-class importance to all those States whose interests converge in the Mediterranean Basin. Here is one of the greatest junctions of communications, where the Mediterranean route from the Black Sea is crossed by the land-bridge linking Europe and Asia. Istanbul was, under its old name of Constantinople, both a mart, with an almost unrivalled range of trade, and the European meeting-place of Occident and Orient. It remains under the sovereignty of a second-class Power, for the sufficient reason that the Great Powers of Europe permit no one of their number to augment its own strategic advantage by annexing the Straits. The cosmopolitan character of the city's population reflects its wide range of trading interests. Turks are a majority, but, in addition to the large Greek colony already mentioned, there are big groups of both Armenians and Bulgars.

As regards race, the original Turki-Tatar traits of the Ottoman Turks in Europe have been largely eliminated after several centuries

[24] According to the Turkish census of 1935, the population was 16,158,000, which included no considerable alien minority other than the Greek colony of Istanbul.

of intercourse with Slavonic and other Balkan peoples. Nevertheless, the Turks are clearly distinguished from their neighbours in respect of culture. The combination of Moslem faith and Asiatic speech has hitherto set them apart from their European neighbours, and has proved a particularly strong bond of nationality. Moreover, because of their lack of interest and skill in husbandry the line of division between them and the Slavs is well emphasized. Traditions of the camp and caravan die hard, yet, in our own time, a social and economic revolution within republican Turkey, led and guided by its first President, has done much to develop a progressive outlook.

THE GERMANIC PEOPLES

We have left to the last a survey of the distribution of the German-speaking communities. The military problem which Germany has repeatedly forced upon mankind during the past seventy or eighty years is the most compelling of its kind which modern Europe has known. On that account it is difficult for a European to be dispassionate and objective when investigating German claims to sovereignty over a large part of Central Europe. Yet the attempt to be just and impartial should be made in the interests of European society as a whole.

The great numerical strength of the Germans—in aggregate more than eighty millions—must be considered in relation to the virility and dynamism by which, as a community, they are characterized. These are characteristics which, from time to time, express themselves in aggressive or contemptuous action towards neighbouring peoples: yet the best German thought has a long tradition in liberal philosophy and the arts, as well as in applied science. Unfortunately, during the last quarter of a century it is the latter whose exploitation has appealed to the minds of the majority of Germans. To the geographer the most significant of all facts concerning the Germans is their occupation and, seemingly inevitable, control of the central and nuclear position within the continent of Europe. The German homeland is there; and how to nullify the geographical advantage possessed by Germany is likely to remain—so long as the spirit of nationalism endures in Europe—the most urgent of all questions for those military and economic strategists whose countries are hostile to, or fearful of, Germany.

At the outset we shall consider how the present distribution of the German-speaking peoples has come about.

When first known to history, in the first century B.C., the German tribes, with their distinctive Indo-European language, were situated on the southern and south-western margins of the Baltic Sea. From this homeland they migrated slowly, over a period of several centuries, both westwards and southwards, urged onwards by the pressure of Slavonic peoples behind them. In the fifth century A.D. tribes, including the Franks and Alemanni (cf. modern French "Allemands"), who had been in touch with Roman civilization—though outside the Empire—invaded the Rhineland and Northern Gaul. For the next few centuries there was a steady advance southwards up the Rhine and Elbe valleys and into the intermediate areas. On their eastern side, over against the Slavonic world, the German peoples were, until about A.D. 1200, limited by the line of the lower and middle Elbe and its tributary, the Saale. The latter takes an approximately south-to-north course before joining the main river above Magdeburg. Then, in the early years of the thirteenth century, came German eastward expansion in its various forms of conquest, conversion of the Slavs, and the colonization of towns.

The Altmark ("Old March") was the first zone to be occupied by the eastward-pressing Germans. This was as early as the tenth century, and the name still appears on the map, out in the plain within the concave bulge of the River Elbe, below Magdeburg. The Altmark was organized at first for the defence of the naturally vulnerable flank against the Slavs, but stage by stage the military frontier was pushed eastwards and what had been a march-land became an integral part of the German homeland.

All territory between the lower middle Elbe and Oder rivers was, in the thirteenth century, brought under Teutonic influence. It became the Mittelmark, out of which Brandenburg, the nucleus of the later Prussia, was created. The terrain was not attractive, for, owing to glacial action and the uncertainty of river-drainage, much of the surface was, and still is, occupied by marsh and lake or by sandy heath, little suited to farming enterprise. Through the heart of the Mittelmark (later Brandenburg) there flows a complex system of sluggish waters, all converging on the east-to-west line of the Havel and Spree rivers which, between them, traverse the greater part of the distance between the Oder and the Elbe. Yet the situation

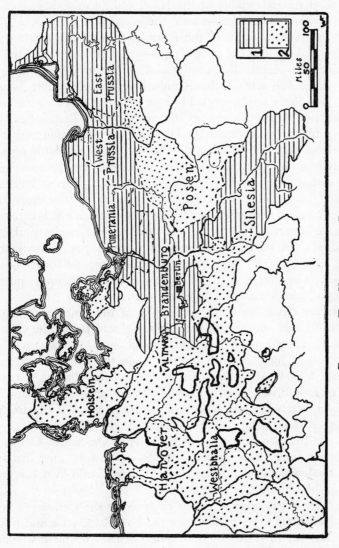

FIG. 17.—THE KINGDOM OF PRUSSIA

1. The extent of Prussia prior to 1815   2. Acquisitions in the period of 1815-1866

of Brandenburg was not without certain geographical advantages. By virtue of the navigability of the Havel and Spree and their connexions—natural or artificial—with the arteries of the Elbe and Oder,[25] transport by water to the Baltic and North Sea coasts was available. Berlin—founded about 1250—was well served by these communications across the centre of the North German Plain, though the actual site of the Brandenburg capital, amidst lakes, marshes, and sterile sands, seemed to have little else to recommend it.

In the late fourteenth century the authority of Brandenburg—already sufficiently important to be raised to the dignity of an Electorate of the Holy Roman Empire—extended eastwards across the Oder into the Neumark, which, in due course, was incorporated. Farther east still, lay the Poznan district of the Kingdom of Poland. And so it came about that two marcher-zones, on the medieval fringes of German authority, were welded into a State which became the "centre of gravity" of the northern zone of the German-speaking peoples. But the advance eastwards of German power inevitably brought into the State large numbers of Slavonic and other non-Teutonic communities, with whom the German colonists intermarried, so losing their claim to ethnic purity.

Our earlier discussion of the geography of the East Baltic communities included reference to the colonizing activities of the Order of Teutonic Knights. The first conquests of the Order occurred in the first half of the thirteenth century, when the territory between the lower Vistula and the Niemen—the original Prussia,[26] later known as East Prussia—was annexed. German settlement followed immediately afterwards, the land being parcelled out to a colonizing peasantry. Although the rise of Poland in the fifteenth century resulted in the destruction of the Teutonic Order the German colonists remained, save in the north-to-south strip, immediately west of the lower Vistula, which after the First World War became known as "the Polish Corridor."

The reader is reminded of earlier reference to the German settlements of medieval times within both the East Baltic zone and East Central Europe. In regard to the Baltic Germans no more will be added; nor is it necessary to make further reference to the Germani-

[25] The canal linking the Spree to the Oder across about twenty miles of country was, of course, a fairly late development.

[26] Its soft-wood forests gave it its name—"the land of spruce."

zation of the borderlands of Bohemia, other than to recall that in the thirteenth and fourteenth centuries German colonization in both Bohemia and Southern Poland was encouraged by Slavonic princes. German craftsmen helped in the foundation of towns, and themselves became the nucleus of a burgher class which persisted down to modern times. A series of such towns grew up along the fertile, low plateau-zone extending eastwards from Upper Silesia into Galicia and beyond. Lemberg (Lwow) was one of the most prominent of these settlements which remained German "islands" within the Slavonic countryside.

Farther to the south, in the Kingdom of Hungary, which included Slovakia and Transylvania amongst other lands, invitations to German colonists brought in skilled artisans. They undertook to exploit the mineral ores of the Hungarian mountain borders and to play their part in the defence of the Kingdom. The Saxons of Transylvania represent, as we have seen, a compact German group descended from these medieval settlers.

By the close of the Middle Ages, German expansion to the east had been checked. There was no further advance until the nineteenth century, and the correspondence is close between the geographical distribution of German speech at the close of the Napoleonic Wars and that of the late fifteenth century. The next impulse to colonization came in the second half of the nineteenth century, as a consequence of the industrial revolution in Germany and of the demand for the exploitation of all available mineral resources. So is explained the expansion of German population at the expense of Polish within the mineral-bearing lands of Upper Silesia, in all of whose industrial towns the German population greatly increased between 1870 and 1900.

During the eighteenth century there was very considerable increase in population density within Prussia, a kingdom which had grown from its nucleus of Brandenburg to dominate almost the entire North German Plain as far west as the lower Rhineland. Very energetically the Kings of Prussia undertook the reclamation and settlement of the infertile lands which made up a high proportion of their territory. And not only German colonists were encouraged: Dutch, Huguenot, and even Czech settlers were introduced, with the result that, ethnically, the population of the North German Plain became more composite than before. The process of intensive development of the poorer soils, together with the annexation of land, greatly increased the population of Prussia during the latter half of the eighteenth century. At the beginning of Frederick the Great's reign, in 1740, the inhabitants of the Kingdom numbered some two and a half millions on an area of approximately 50,000 square miles; at the end of the reign in 1786 the population was nearly six millions on an area half as large again.

The eastern and south-eastern limits of the German-speaking peoples have now been defined with fair approximation,[27] as also on the south-western flank of the German zone, in Alsace and Lorraine (v. Chapter II, section on France); but there remain for mention the frontiers on the north-west and south.

In the latter direction the geographical complexity of the Alps is reflected in a complicated distribution of languages. By the close of the twelfth century, German colonists from the north had penetrated the entire Alpine zone of present-day Austria; and, in the opening years of the thirteenth century, the Germanization of the highlands, south of the Tyrol, began. Utilizing the Brenner and other passes, the Teutonic settlers made their way southwards—at the expense of Italian influence—into the high valleys of the Adige and its tributary, the Isarco. Still farther down the main valley they settled beyond the junction of the two rivers, near Bolzano.

In the course of centuries, German speech within this district of Alto Adige became predominant, but farther south, in the Trentino, still well within the Alps, the inhabitants of Italian language were able to hold their own. This, in brief, was the linguistic geography of the Italo-Austrian border-country when, in the late nineteenth century, Italy—for the first time politically united—pressed Austria to cede the Trentino and at least the southern part of Alto Adige. She claimed that this concession to Italian nationalism would be consistent with the geographical distribution of German and Italian speakers.

Under the threat of war from Italy in 1915, Austria felt obliged to offer her neighbour the greater part of the Trentino. The concession was not regarded by Italy as adequate, and Austria was

[27] The isolated groups of Germans long resident in both southern and eastern districts of European Russia have not been included, for their geographical detachment from the German zone of Europe may be regarded as complete. In 1941, following the German attack on the Soviet Union, the Germans of the middle Volga were, in the interests of Russian security, removed to Siberia.

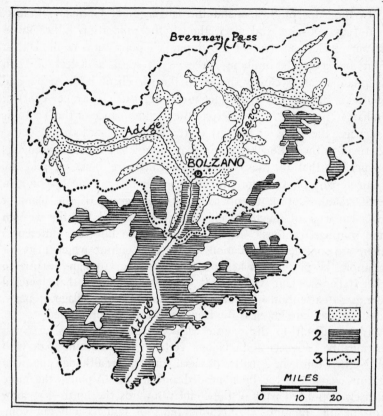

FIG. 18.—SOUTHERN TYROL. DISTRIBUTION OF AUSTRIAN AND ITALIAN
MAJORITIES (1919)

1. Areas where Austrians formed a majority
2. Areas where Italians formed a majority
3. Boundary between Alto Adige and Trentino
(This map is re-drawn from *The New World*, by Isaiah Bowman, published by
Messrs. Harrap & Co., Ltd., London, to whom kind acknowledgment is made)

coerced into a more substantial offer. This would have placed the
international frontier within three miles of Bolzano—a more equitable
division of the Tyrolese Alps than that of 1914 or of 1919. After
the First World War, by insisting on a frontier as far north as the
Brenner Pass, the Italian Government brought into the State a
quarter of a million Austrian Germans, whose *irredentism* became as
vocal as that of the previous Italian minority within Austria.

In the Alps of Switzerland the languages of Germany, France, and Italy converge and meet, though the proportion is heavily in favour of German. Out of the Republic's population of more than four and a quarter millions, 72 per cent speak a dialect of High German which is closely similar to the speech of both Alsace and southern Baden. The remainder use either French (21 per cent) or Italian (6 per cent).[28] Yet, despite the predominance of the Teutonic language, the Swiss of no part of the country regard themselves as German in the national sense; so that social and political movements —such as that of the Nazi Party—which are born in, and are characteristic of, Germany, usually awaken little or no response in Switzerland. Out of twenty-five cantons, German is the main or only language of nineteen, and these comprise all but the western and southern cantons.[29] Moreover, apart from linguistic differences there are considerable variations in material culture which may, for example, be perceived when moving from the German-speaking to the Italian-speaking cantons. It cannot be denied that material standards—attention to sanitation, the condition of village property, and the like—are lower as the frontier of Italy is approached.

It is difficult to distinguish with certainty the basis of Swiss nationality. Language and religion[30] certainly have nothing to do with it. Neither can it be a matter of racial affinity, for, although the main ethnic element is the broad-headed and stocky "Alpine," the more densely populated parts of the country towards the north-west show considerable mixture with Nordic traits of tallness and fair complexion, together with a tendency towards dolichocephaly. The geographical difficulties attending communication between most of the cantons would seem to be adverse to the development of a common national sentiment and purpose. Yet there can be no doubt that it was similarity of geographical conditions which, in the first place, led to a realization, on the part of the cantons, of their common interests in both peace and war.

Geography can and does, as we have seen elsewhere, exert a very

[28] Romansch is spoken by about 1 per cent, or 45,000 persons. In 1937 it was made the fourth national language.

[29] Italian is spoken by a majority in one canton, namely Ticino, which is south of the Lepontine Alps.

[30] About 57 per cent of the population are Protestant—mainly Calvinist—and approximately 41 per cent Roman Catholic.

powerful influence upon the process of nation-building. Yet an English author who has written extensively on the evolution of nationality in Europe is prepared to deny that Switzerland is a nation-state on the grounds that the Swiss nation is "a purely political-territorial" conception;[31] as if, in the case of most nation-states generally, long occupation of a given territory were not an essential consideration in the growth of national sentiment and

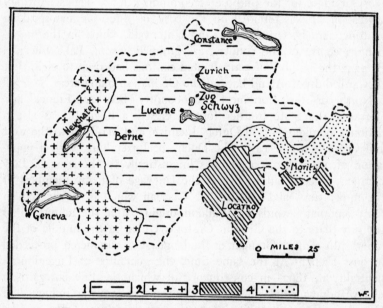

FIG. 19.—SWITZERLAND: DISTRIBUTION OF LANGUAGES

1. German   2. French   3. Italian   4. Romansch

cohesion. To claim that the German Swiss are not distinguished from their neighbours in Germany by anything but a difference of political forms[32] is a strong argument in favour of the Nazi concept of a Greater Germany. The doctrine, enunciated, for example, by one of its major advocates, Ewald Banse, is that, because the Swiss are in all respects, save geography, a part of the Reich, they should be incorporated. By the same argument, the right of Australia to inde-

[31] v. C. A. Macartney: *National States and National Minorities*, London, 1934, p. 154.
[32] *Idem.*

pendent nationhood might be denied. The present writer prefers to believe that there is in the Swiss nation a spirit, born of place as well as of time, which has a greater power to distinguish the Swiss from the Germans than the similarity of language and of material culture has to unite them.

Swiss nationalism has had nearly seven centuries in which to evolve. The first alliance or confederation of cantons occurred in the year 1290, for the purpose of common defence against Austrian aggression. It was founded on the basis of three German-speaking cantons, namely, Uri, Schwyz, and Unterwald, which, in the mountainous centre of the country, are grouped around Lake Lucerne. By 1353 the number of confederated cantons had risen to eight, but they still did not extend beyond the German-speaking area.

North of the Lorraine border-country between France and Germany the State frontier follows closely a linguistic, as also a national, boundary—with Dutch, Flemish, and Walloon to the west and German to the east. The Duchy of Luxemburg, with a population of about 300,000, belongs linguistically to the zone of Low German dialects; but French is the language of many members of the upper class, and even in the German which is widely spoken there are many words of Walloon origin. After the admission of the tiny State to the German Customs Union in the middle of the nineteenth century German, as the language of commerce, proceeded to oust French. At the same time, the guarantee of Luxemburg's neutrality in 1867—in consequence of which the Prussian garrison was withdrawn—did nothing to weaken the growing influence of Germany. Situated as it is on the south-eastern flanks of the Ardennes Plateau and within the drainage system of the Moselle, the current of its industrial and commercial life tends to flow Rhinewards. Yet, whether or not it would be generally agreed that the term "nation" should be applied to the citizens of Luxemburg, there is no doubt that a large proportion, if not a majority, of the inhabitants wish to be politically independent.

The frontiers which divide Germany from the Netherlands and Denmark, respectively, run closely in accordance with the facts of nationality and language. In the case of the Dano-German line, a boundary adjustment, twenty-five years old, in favour of Denmark, has resulted in an equitable solution. The frontier with the Netherlands remained fixed—down to the time of the Second World War—

for a very much longer period. Despite the similarity of the lowland landscape on the German and Dutch sides of the international line, the two nations are quite clearly marked off from each other. As the

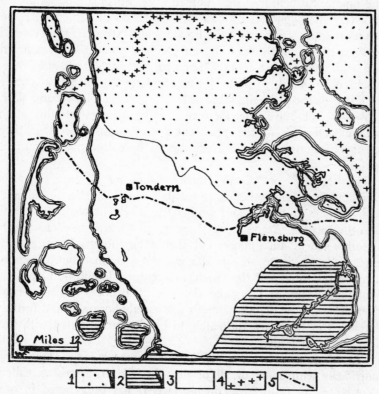

FIG. 20.—THE DANO-GERMAN NATIONALITY BOUNDARY IN SCHLESWIG (1919)

1. Areas where Danes were more than 75 per cent of the population
2. Areas where Germans were more than 75 per cent of the population
3. Areas of mixed Danish and German population where a minority of either was not less than 25 per cent of the population
4. International frontier of 1914
5. International frontier of 1919

frontier isolates no considerable minority on either side, there was not, until the invasion of 1940, any important territorial question at issue between Germany and the Netherlands.

The Dano-German frontier question is complicated by the

extension of German language and sentiment northwards into the Danish Peninsula. Holstein has been German for much the greater part of its history, but Schleswig was not so until the second half of the nineteenth century. After war, in 1864, Prussian annexation led to a very thorough and ruthless Germanization of Schleswig. From the northernmost district of the Province about 60,000 Danes—equal to more than one-third of its non-German population—emigrated before the end of last century. Even so, the district remained overwhelmingly Danish in both language and sentiment, as was clearly indicated by the plebiscite taken at the close of the First World War.

We cannot leave the German-speaking peoples at this stage without reference to the persistent propagandist claim that they are united as much by racial affinities as by culture, language, and sentiment.

The "Nordic" or "Aryan" theory claims for all true Germans membership of a hypothetical race of tall, blond long-heads endowed with courage, initiative, and wisdom to an extent characteristic of no other people. Accordingly, there is one "master-race" to which all other stocks are inferior and should be subservient. Ironically enough, the originator of this idea was not a German but a Frenchman. In the middle of the nineteenth century, Joseph de Gobineau wrote his *Essai sur l'inégalité des races humaines*. It had a considerable vogue in France before it was eagerly borrowed and further developed in Germany, ultimately to be closely associated with the name of Adolf Hitler.

That there exists in North-Western Europe a large number of individuals with some or all of the physical characteristics called "Nordic" is an easily ascertainable fact. It has been noted in our reference to the Scandinavians and some other peoples of the Atlantic fringe of Europe. What anthropologists strenuously deny, on the basis of abundant evidence, is that, as a whole, the people of Germany belong to this type. As for the Prussians, whose claim to "Aryan" ancestry is the most arrogant of all, they are among the least "Nordic" of all Germans. Tall stature, fair hair and eyes, together with dolichocephaly are quite commonly found in the north-western angle of the country as, for example, in Hanover and the western parts of Schleswig and Holstein; but as distance increases from this "Nordic" corner—both eastwards and towards the south—there is a general displacement of the "Nordic" stocks by such "Alpine" peoples of

stocky build and marked brachycephaly as the majority of Württem-
bergers and Bavarians and the most typical of Brandenburgers.
Just as the Prussians east of the Elbe—up to which river, it will be
recalled, the Slavs extended in early medieval times—merge imperceptibly with the Polish (Slavonic) type, so does the broad-headed
Austrian German fuse with the very similar stock of Slavonic
Bohemia. During the First World War, Professor F. G. Parsons
measured the heads of soldiers from all parts of the German Empire
and thus summed up his anthropological observations: "The more
one thinks of it, the more one is convinced that since the sixth
century the broad-headed 'Alpine' (Slav) race has been slowly and
steadily supplanting the long-headed 'Nordic' type, not only in
Prussia but in every part of Germany."

Such facts as these are well known in German scientific circles,
but because the preponderance of broad-heads in the German population does not tally with accepted racial theories there is no alternative for the racialists other than to discredit and discard the cephalic
index as a test of race. They then proceed to publish a new absurdity, namely, that the shape of the head is a matter of accident.[33]

German claims to racial exclusiveness and purity are easily disposed
of, and yet the people as a whole could hardly be more united in
their national outlook if they were as homogeneous in race and
culture as they have been taught to regard themselves. Germany has
yet to learn that a nation's human resources are the richer for being
varied, and that the people of each region has its particular contribution to make to the sum-total of national genius. This is a doctrine which has long been understood and accepted in the
neighbouring country of France. Whether or not variations in mental
activity and genius within the German-speaking zone of Europe may
be closely related to differences of ethnic origin, it is well authenti-
cated that there is regional variation in philosophical outlook and
artistic achievement. For example, it is supposed, with impressive
evidence in support, that the upland dwellers of South-Central and
Southern Germany—including Austria—are more artistic, notably in
musical composition, than are the lowlanders of Prussia.

[33] For scientific statements concerning "race" in Germany, the reader is recommended to consult W. Z. Ripley, The Races of Europe, 1899, and Coon, The
Races of Europe, 1939 (which is intended to be a modernization of Ripley's
classic).

The German State, as we know it to-day, dates only from 1871. In that year the Empire was proclaimed. German nationalism, however, evolved early, and its beginnings may be traced to the growth of Prussia from its nucleus of Brandenburg. It was a sense of kinship and of common tradition which, aided by community of language, made political unification a practicable experiment. The petty States which relinquished their individual sovereignties were of varying degrees of territorial size and of importance, and on the map of the region between Rhine and Oder they made a complicated patch-work.[34] Despite the political detachment of Austria from the Reich, which persisted down to 1938, and the long-continued rivalry of the Hohenzollern and Hapsburg dynasties, the people of Austria and of the other South German States recognized a mutual attraction based on cultural sympathy, itself largely a response to similarity of environment. It was on this sympathy that Hitler could depend when planning the absorption of Austria.

Germany is not, as France may claim to be, the natural cradle-land of a nation. Between the northern plain and the southern plateaux there is a sharp distinction, and no determinist could possibly argue, from a study of the orographical map, that the union of Prussia and Bavaria was inevitable. But German nationality, which so long preceded the establishment of a State incorporating the majority of Germans, has not been as closely associated with "natural frontiers" as has French nationality.

There is a fundamental difference between the French and German types of patriotism which has been well expressed by Vidal de la Blache. In his view, the land of France to a Frenchman represents a personality to which he is devotedly attached: on the other hand, Germany to a German is an ethnic idea—a conception of the unity of the German-speaking peoples of Europe.

Because Berlin was the capital of the Prussian political nucleus, from which Germany grew, it became, almost inevitably, the headquarters of the empire which Prussia dominated. It is well placed as the metropolis of the North German Plain, but is little representative of the interests of Bavaria or of the south in general. If the domination of the Reich by Prussia is to cease, it would seem not only desirable but also essential that the capital should be moved

[34] As late as 1819 the loosely organized Confederation consisted of 39 German States, each with its separate customs organization.

elsewhere. Leipzig, in the extreme north of Saxony, where northern lowland and southern highland merge, is a much older city whose central geographical situation and illustrious traditions fit it well for metropolitan rank. Its historic record has less to do with military organization for ruthless conquest (always associated with Berlin) than with jurisprudence, the arts of literature and music, and commerce. Germany might help to restore its prestige among the nations by permitting Leipzig, rather than Berlin, to express the national genius.

SELECTED BIBLIOGRAPHY

AITOFF, D.: "Peuples et langues de la Russie," *Ann. de Géogr.* vol. 15, 1909, pp. 92–5.

AMMANN, H.: *Die Italiener in der Schweiz*, Basel, 1917.

Atlas Graphique et Statistique de la Suisse, Berne, 1914.

Atlas de Finlande (atlas and 2 vols. of text), Helsingfors, 1911.

BARKER, J. ELLIS: *The Foundations of Germany*, London, 1916.

BATTISTI, C.: "Il Trentino," Novara, 2nd ed., 1917.

BEAUVOIS, E.: *La nationalité du Slesvig*, Paris, 1864.

BENEŠ, E.: *Bohemia's Case for Independence*, London, 1916.

BEYNON, E. D.: "Migrations of the Hungarian Peasants," *Geographical Review*, 1937.

BOYD, L. A.: "The Marshes of Pinsk," *Geographical Review*, New York, 1936.

BRAILSFORD, H. N.: *Macedonia: its Races and their Future*, London, 1906.

BRAUN, G.: *Die nordischen Staaten: Norwegen, Schweden, Finnland: Eine soziologische Länderkunde*, Breslau, 1924.

BRAUN, G.: *Die nordischen Deutschland*, Berlin, 1916.

BRUCE-BOSWELL, A.: "The Teutonic Order," *Cambridge Medieval History*, Chapter IX, vol. VII (pp. 257ff.).

BRUNHES, J., and VALLAUX, C.: "German Colonization in Eastern Europe," *Geogr. Rev.*, vol. 6, 1918, pp. 465–80.

BRUNIALTI, A.: *Trento e Trieste dal Brennero elle Rive dell' Adriatico*, Turin, 1916.

COOLIDGE, W. A. B.: *The Alps in Nature and History*, New York, 1908.

COON, C. S.: *The Races of Europe*, New York, 1939.

CORNISH, V.: *Borderlands of Language in Europe and their Relation to the Historic Frontier of Christendom*, London, 1936.

CVIJIC, J.: *La Péninsule Balkanique*, Paris, 1918.

DAINELLI, G.: *La Dalmazia: Cenni geografici e statistici*, Novara, 1918.

DAWSON, W. H.: *The Evolution of Modern Germany*, new ed., 1919.

DE LA GARENNIE, D.: "La Ruthénie tchecoslovaque," *Ann. de Géogr.*, vol. 33, 1924, pp. 443–56.

DEMANGEON, A.: "La Bulgarie," *Ann. de Géogr.*, vol. 29, 1920, pp. 401–16.

DE MARTONNE, E.: "Essai de carte ethnographique des pays roumains," *Ann. de Géogr.*, vol. 29, 1920, pp. 81–98.

DE MARTONNE, E.: "L'Europe Centrale," *Géographie Universelle*, p. 623, vol. IV, Part II, Paris, 1931.

DE MARTONNE, E.: *La Valachie: Essai de monographie géographique*, Paris, 1902.

Dictionnaire Géographique de la Suisse, 6 vols. and atlas, Neuchatel, 1902–1910.

DOMINIAN, L.: *The Frontiers of Language and Nationality of Europe*, New York, 1917.

EAST, G.: *An Historical Geography of Europe*, London, 1935.

ECKHART, F.: *A Short History of the Hungarian People*, London, 1931.

FLEURE, H. J.: *The Peoples of Europe*, London, 1922.

FREEMAN, E. A.: *The Historical Geography of Europe*, 2 vols, 3rd ed., by Bury, 1903.

GILLETT, A. M.: "A Sketch of the Historical Geography of the Black Earth Region of Central Russia," *Scott. Geog. Mag.*, Jan. 1922.

GOOCH, G. P.: *Nationalism*, London, 1920.

HOUTTE, H. VAN: "Frontières naturelles et principe des nationalités," in Académie royale de Belgique, Brussels, *Bulletins*, 5e ser., vol. 21, Nos. 3–5 (1935), pp. 81–97.

JESSEN, F. DE: *La Question du Slesvig*, 1906.

JORGENSON, —.: *La Question dano-allemande*, Copenhagen, 1900.

KANT, E.: "L'Estonie: principaux aspects géographiques," *Annales de Géographie*, vol. XLI, 1932.

KLYUCHEVSKY, —.: *A History of Russia*, trans. Hogarth, 5 vols., 1911–31.

KNATCHBULL-HUGESSEN, C. M.: *The Political Evolution of the Hungarian Nation*, 2 vols., London, 1908.

KNOWLES, L. C. A.: *The Economic Development of Europe in the Nineteenth Century*, 1932.

KRETSCHMER, K.: *Historische Geographie von Mitteleuropa*, 1904.

MACARTNEY, C. A.: *National States and National Minorities*, Oxford, 1934.

MARRIOTT, J. A. R., and ROBERTSON, C. G.: *The Evolution of Prussia: the Making of an Empire*, Oxford, 1915.

MARRIOTT, J. A. R., and ROBERTSON, C. G.: *The Expansion of Prussia*, 1915.

MARTONNE, E. DE: "Europe Centrale," Tome IV, *Géographie Universelle*, Paris, 1930.

MILOJEVIC, B. Z.: "The Kingdom of the Serbs, Croats, and Slovenes," *Geogr. Rev.*, vol. 15, 1925, pp. 70–83.

NEWBIGIN, M. I.: *Geographical Aspects of Balkan Problems*, London, 1915; also 2nd ed., 1919.

NEWBIGIN, M. I.: *Southern Europe*, 1932.

NOWACK, E.: "A Contribution to the Geography of Albania," *Geogr. Rev.*, vol. 11, 1921, pp. 503–40.

OGILVIE, A. G.: "A Contribution to the Geography of Macedonia," *Geogr. Journ.*, vol. 55, 1920, pp. 1–34.

PARTSCH, J.: *Central Europe*, New York, 1903.

PEISKER, T.: "The Expansion of the Slavs," *Cambridge Medieval History*, vol. II, Chapter XIV.

PITTARD, E.: La Roumanie, Paris, 1917.

PULLERITS, A. (editor): Estonia: Population, Cultural and Economic Life, Tallinn, 1937.

RIPLEY, W. Z.: The Races of Europe, New York, 1900.

ROMER, E.: Atlas géographique et statistique de la Pologne, 2nd ed., Warsaw, 1921.

RORH, F. J.: "Home Colonization in Germany," Internatl. Rev. of Agric. Economics, vol. 3, 1925, pp. 28–72.

RUYSSEN, T.: Les Minorités Nationales d'Europe, Paris, n.d.

SALTS, —.: Lettlands Wirtschaft und Wirtschaftspolitik, Riga, 1930.

SETON-WATSON, R. W.: Racial Problems in Hungary, London, 1908.

SETON-WATSON, R. W.: The Rise of Nationality in the Balkans, London, 1917.

SETON-WATSON, R. W.: The Southern Slav Question, London, 1911.

TAMARO, A.: La Vénétie Julienne et la Dalmatie: Histoire de la nation italienne sur ses frontières orientales, 3 vols., Rome, 1918.

TELEKI, P.: The Evolution of Hungary and its Place in European History, New York, 1923.

TOYNBEE, A. J.: Nationality and the War, London, 1915.

USHER, A. P.: "The History of Population and Settlement in Eurasia" (with maps), Geogr. Rev., January 1930.

VINCENT, C.: Nationality in Hungary, London, 1919.

WALLIS, B. C.: "Central Hungary: Magyars and Germans," Geogr. Rev., vol. 6, 1918, pp. 421–35.

WALLIS, B. C.: "The Peoples of Hungary," Geogr. Rev., vol. 4, 1917, pp. 465–81.

WALLIS, B. C.: "The Slavs of Northern Hungary," Geogr. Rev., vol. 6, 1918, pp. 268–81.

WEILENMANN, H.: Die vielsprachige Schweiz; Eine Losung des Nationalitäten-problems, Basel and Leipzig, 1925.

WRIGHT, J. K.: The Geographical Basis of European History, New York, 1928.

4.

The Partition of Europe
After the First World War

THE POLITICO-GEOGRAPHIC SETTING IN 1914

    Reduced to the simplest terms of political ge-
ography, the Europe of the early twentieth century was a medley of
States, comprising five great Empires,[1] two other imperial Powers of
lesser magnitude (Italy and Turkey), and twelve small Powers. Of
the latter only one, namely Spain, reached twenty millions in population, the other eleven being under eight millions in each case. The
five great Empires, together with the two of secondary magnitude,
were grouped in one or other of the grand alliances which, mutually
hostile, had been called into being, ironically enough, in order to
preserve the political stability of Europe: whilst the twelve small
Powers, most of which were outside the two great alliances, had no
more than an insignificant influence on the high policies by which
the affairs of the European peoples were directed.

    The Triple Alliance of Germany, Austria-Hungary, and Italy—to
which both Bulgaria and Turkey were, as it later proved, attached,
but from which Italy deserted within the first year of the First
World War—was a most formidable *bloc* of territories and peoples,
occupying practically the entire middle zone of Europe. Its opponents of the Triple Entente were widely separated—Great Britain
and France being not less than 800 miles from Russia—and, in the
event of war, they could not assist each other directly, by land or
sea. But the military strength of the Central Empires, weakened by

---

[1] Germany, France, Russia, Austria-Hungary, and Great Britain; the last-named
the mother of an empire, virtually all of which lay outside Europe.

the defection of Italy, was, to an extent—much greater than in the case of their opponents—dependent on the loyalty of alien subject peoples. The majority of the latter were Slavs, none of whom were enthusiastic in the cause of German, Austrian, or Magyar domination. Russia in Europe had relatively few citizens who were not Slavs.[2] Its own nationals, on whose loyalty it could unquestionably depend, were an overwhelming proportion of the total population. On the other hand, Austrians and Magyars together were but a minority of the population of the Dual Monarchy.

France and Great Britain were homogeneous nation-states of unparalleled experience, without any important minority problem save that of Northern Ireland. Their imperial territories lay overseas—in the case of Britain at vast distances from the mother-country—so that their military resources could not be fully concentrated on the European front at the outset of the war.

The military prestige of France stood high, if not still supreme, in 1914; this almost a century after Buonaparte's downfall. Military strength is based ultimately on organized man-power, but the authority of France in Europe was found to depend largely on the record of past achievements: it was without the backing of a numerically adequate population. By 1914 her national strength had reached a peak of about forty millions, and the momentum of natural increase seemed to have ceased.[3] Germany, on the other hand, had already attained sixty-five millions, apart from the large Teutonic elements in the Dual Monarchy, and was showing a highly satisfactory rate of natural increase.[4] These advantages, possessed by Germany, offset, to a considerable extent, the disadvantages—shared with its main ally, Austria—of having large and potentially hostile minority groups within its frontiers.

In respect of industrial wealth and its organized exploitation, Germany alone in 1914 was more than the equal of Russia and France combined; and, as in the case of the marshalling of her armies,

[2] The non-Slavonic population of Western European Russia in 1914, namely, Finns, Esths, Letts, and Lithuanians, together with Tatars in the south, barely reached 10 out of over 100 millions.

[3] In 1913 the birth- and death-rates were approximately equal. By 1919 the population was 200,000 less than in 1913, not counting the deaths directly attributable to the war or to the influenza scourge of 1918.

[4] The population of Germany rose from 45,234,000 in 1880 to 64,903,000 in 1910.

Great Britain's resources could not be brought to bear at once upon the enemy. France was particularly deficient in coal, both in output[5] and quality, and there was no comparison between her fields and those of Germany. Moreover, having lost the greater part of Lorraine to Germany, France was deprived of a corresponding proportion of the iron-ores of the richest field in Europe.

Of all the Powers involved in the international crisis of 1914, Germany alone had supreme confidence in the ability of her army and her industrial machine to undertake war on a continental scale. That confidence was not misplaced, as events proved. Had the war been limited to the European continent, both in its distribution of belligerents and the extent of its operations, the result might well have been reversed. As it was, Germany, not for the last time, lacked a proper appreciation of the possible repercussions of the war in other continents and oceans; and, continental Power that she was, she completely under-estimated the importance of control of the sea.

An excess of confidence in her military strength was, however, not the only mood of Germany in 1914. In seeming contradiction, fear was also present—the fear which had actuated German statesmen since the days when Prussia strove, both to unite the North German Plain and to close that "draughty corridor open at both ends" to attack from either France or Russia. Though known to be less capable of launching aggressive war, France and Russia were powerful foes, even when measured by German standards of military capacity, and to their armies geography opposed no natural barrier. The North European Plain is wide open to the east, and the only natural obstacle to the westward advance of armies is the belt of marshes and lakes, in the Masurian district of East Prussia, which could be, however, easily outflanked on its southern side. East Prussia, by its easterly projection, was the province most exposed to attack, and when war came the Russian army could not be prevented from investing Königsberg for a time.[6] Over to the west, where the great plain narrows, the two small Powers of the Low Countries lay across the easiest way of advance between France and Germany, but their neu-

[5] In 1913 the production was 40 million metric tons, whilst the German total was over 190 millions.
[6] Until near the close of 1944, Germany had fought two great European wars, each of over four years' duration, without experiencing the invasion of her frontiers at any point, save in the case mentioned.

trality was no more of a shield than their weak military establishments.

Although in the past eighty years Germany, on three successive occasions, has been the aggressor, the possibility of an invasion—made easy by geography—from North-Eastern France was by no means overlooked by her soldiers, as the building of the "West Wall" in 1939 was clear evidence. From the First World War the Germans inherited the claustrophobic fear of a campaign on two widely separated fronts which might draw together across German soil. An attempt to eliminate at least one of the fronts by the methods of *Blitzkrieg* was inevitable, from the German standpoint.

GERMAN PLANS FOR THE CONQUEST OF EURO-ASIA

In 1914 the military conquest of Europe was regarded by Germany as the necessary prelude to the fulfilment of grandiose economico-political plans for the domination of the heart of the Old World. The project was the outcome of a geographical idea which had been maturing for some years. The First World War led to its only temporary abandonment, and it was received with a new-found enthusiasm, especially in the period from 1933 onwards to the Second World War.

Even the immediate aims of Germany in 1914 were not limited to the mere defeat of the two land-Powers which she regarded as penning her in on her eastern and western frontiers, respectively. It was intended that France and Russia should be eliminated for all time as Great Powers. The destruction of Russia was regarded, from the long-term point of view, as the more important, mainly because its vast but half-empty lands, stretching beyond Europe deep into Asia, seemed to offer unlimited scope for Teutonic colonization and industrial development. It was the policy of *Drang nach Osten*—inherited from the Middle Ages—on an enormous, a megalomaniac scale. Yet it was not undertaken solely for the lust of conquest. German imperialists, gathering together geographical ideas from many sources, not confined to Germany, were concerned primarily with the search for security in a world of competing national sovereignties.

In 1904 Mr. (later Sir) Halford Mackinder's lecture, entitled "The Geographical Pivot of History," read before the Royal Geographical Society, was published.[7] Except within a very restricted geographical

[7] *The Geographical Journal*, Vol. 23, London, 1904.

circle it aroused little comment at the time in Britain; but in Germany its ideas were quickly absorbed into the imperial design.

Mackinder regarded the vast plains of European Russia and Siberia, together with the great plateaux farther east in the very heart of the continental mass—all then as now within one empire—as the pivotal region of the world. This was the empire of Russia, the development of whose resources had been hardly begun. Those resources of soil, forest, and minerals would be developed by a rapidly rising man-power already far exceeding a hundred millions. Moreover, Russia alone of the Powers possessed vast continental space which sea-power could not seriously affect and which, in its self-sufficiency, was independent of maritime enterprise. Such incomparable economic and strategic assets as these pointed inevitably, in Mackinder's view, to a dominating position in world affairs. "In the world at large," he wrote, "she (Russia) occupies the central strategical position held by Germany in Europe." Later in the same paper the fear of an alliance between Germany and Russia is disclosed, and to meet such a contingency the author recommended an opposing alliance of all the maritime Powers, though such a proposal was virtually a contradiction of one part of his thesis, which was to discount the permanence—and consequently the strength—of any such combination against the pivotal Power.

Germany's reading of the thesis and its subsequent development by Mackinder was, in effect, to substitute German control of the great Euro-Asiatic continental mass for that of Russia.

At the end of the First World War, Mackinder developed his idea, with the results of that great conflict in mind.[8] He then viewed the origin of the war as due to "a German effort to subdue the Slavs who were in revolt against Berlin." It was his claim that, had Germany stood on the defensive on her comparatively short frontier towards France and thrown her full weight against Russia, the war would likely have ended with Germany in command of the "Heartland" (comprising Eastern Europe together with Western and Central Asia).[9] Warning France and Great Britain that their victory in the war might be more apparent than real, Mackinder continued: "When our statesmen are in conversation with the defeated enemy

[8] v. H. J. Mackinder: *Democratic Ideals and Reality—a Study in the Politics of Reconstruction*, London, 1919.

[9] *Op. cit.*, p. 193.

some airy cherub should whisper to them from time to time this saying:

> 'Who rules East Europe commands the Heartland:
> Who rules the Heartland commands the World-Island:
> Who rules the World-Island commands the World.' "[10]

The speedy recovery of Germany after 1919 Mackinder foresaw as inevitable and, in order to meet it—in the interests of European peace—he proposed that the zone separating Germany and Russia should be partitioned between "self-contained nations," as, indeed, was carried out.[11] An identical project for building a "middle tier" between Germany and Russia is still very widely encouraged in circles where fear of Germany and Russia—and, indeed, of both—is ever present. It is an idea to which we shall necessarily return on a later page. Meanwhile, let it suffice to say that the project of a "middle tier" is doomed, so long as the population of that zone, expressed in terms of military strength, is far too small to withstand the assault of either the Russian or the German armies or, more obviously still, of the two in combination.[12] Indeed, if there is any design which would have as its inevitable, however unintentional, result, the bringing together of Russia and Germany, it is this.

Mackinder's conception of the geographical basis of world-power received much more sympathetic attention in Germany than in Britain, for two reasons: first, geographical ideas occupied a much more prominent place in German than in British education; second, the doctrine of land-power was much more attractive to a continental than to a maritime nation.

Out of the ferment of geographical thought in Germany which was stimulated, though not created by Mackinder, there developed soon after the First World War the study of *Geopolitik*—the investigation of the dependence of political policies on the character of the earth, not objectively, but in its application to the furtherance of

---

[10] *Op. cit.*, p. 194.

[11] "The condition of stability in the territorial rearrangement of East Europe is that the division should be into three and not into two State-systems. It is a vital necessity that there should be a tier of independent States between Germany and Russia."

[12] We may estimate the population of the Soviet Union (whose development Mackinder did not foresee) as 200 millions; that of the Germany of 1939, over 80 millions; that of "the middle tier" (comprising Poland, Czecho-Slovakia, Hungary, Rumania, and the Powers of the Balkan Peninsula), about 65 millions.

Germany's imperialistic ambitions. It was a time when the ideology of the sovereign nation-state was supreme in the minds of the victorious nations. Such an ideology, with its identification of nationhood with statehood, was prepared to extend sovereignty to even the smallest of European nations, with populations not more than one or two millions.

By contrast, *Geopolitik* was concerned only with "space-conquering forces" and with empires of continental dimensions. Its exponents claimed for it a complete break with a tradition which cherished a narrow, provincial nationalism. The doom of the small nation and an inevitable trend towards the building of super-states of vast dimensions were confidently predicted. Certainly the statesmen present at Versailles and subsequent conferences completely neglected to consider the possibility of a Great Power arising on the ruins of an older—and less competent—one, within the land-mass of Euro-Asia. If their training and habit of mind had permitted them to envisage such a possibility the partition of Europe which they sanctioned would certainly have been fundamentally different. As it was, they preferred to draw a *cordon sanitaire* around Euro-Asia and to ignore that the geographical heart of the world came within their terms of reference.

It is of incidental interest to our discussion of German politico-geographical thought during the period between the World Wars that a German professor, one Karl Haushofer, who accepted Mackinder's pivotal theory, became the leader of the geopolitical school of thought[13] and succeeded in impressing his views on Hitler. Particularly after the incorporation of Austria within the Reich did Haushofer influence the policy of Germany. Up to that time there were a number of cross-currents which confused the geopolitical outlook of the Nazi leaders: for example, there was Hitler's original plan for an understanding with England which was carried further by Rosenberg in his crusade against Bolshevism—all of which was a contradiction of the view of certain influential members of the German General Staff, who preferred an alliance with Russia. Indeed, in his public utterances, as late as the early part of 1938, Hitler did not go beyond a demand for the inclusion within a Greater Germany

[13] The founder of *Geopolitik* was a Swede named Rudolf Kjellen. His ideas are set out in a number of works including *Grundriss zu einem System der Geopolitik*, Leipzig, 1920.

of all German-speaking communities who were outside the frontiers of the Reich.

After the occupation of Czecho-Slovakia, the geopolitical doctrine demanded, for such a dynamic and technically efficient community as the Germans, the right to go beyond the frontiers of their home-land—alleged to be overcrowded—into territories occupied less densely by non-German people, too backward or indolent to develop them. Such, in short, is the basis of the demand for living-space (*Lebensraum*) which, obviously enough, has no regard for the terri-torial freedom of other peoples. It takes for granted the priority of German rights to land, by virtue of the superiority of the master-race (*Herrenvolk*) over all non-Germanic peoples. Moreover, it is the ex-cuse for an expansion into Euro-Asia which would make the Teutons the lords of the Old World.

As it is well known that the contention of Germany's geographical insufficiency merely conceals a lust for world-power, the scientific examination of the supposed need for *Lebensraum* would hardly seem to be necessary. We may, however, compare the density of popula-tion within the Reich with that of a number of other European countries.

For the whole of the Reich—including Austria—the figure is ap-proximately 345 per square mile, which may be placed against 700 per square mile for Belgium or England and Wales. There is only one province of Germany, namely Saxony, which, with a comparable area, equals the density of Belgium; no other approaches it even re-motely. And it cannot be objected that, in respect of either soil fertility or mineral wealth, the land of Germany is unusually de-ficient. In England and Wales the proportion of unusable land is at least as high as it is in the Reich.

Moreover, the eastern lands which Germany covets are not without their own considerable densities. The Ukrainian soils and mineral fields were, in the First World War, as in the Second, the main objec-tive of all Teutonic campaigning in Eastern Europe. In this part of Russia the rich, black *chernozem*, together with some of the light-coloured *loess*, may well be described as the granary of Europe. It supports a density of population of about 200 per square mile, which, for an almost entirely rural area, is a fair density, judged even by Western European standards. There is a very urgent problem of living-space both in Europe and in Asia, but it is not one in which the German people are specially involved.

When its claim to expansion in Europe was challenged, Germany was prepared to raise the issue of the proprietorship of the tropical and sub-tropical zones of the world. Only by annexations, similar to those of Germany in Africa during the late years of the nineteenth century, is it possible—so runs the argument—for a highly industrialized Power to assure itself of the sources of raw materials and of the markets for manufactured goods which are required by an ever-expanding industrial system. To be permitted to trade under restrictions, however small, within the tropical empire of some other Power is not enough. It has to be admitted that there is cogency in such an argument so long as the Powers regard their dependencies as their exclusive possessions.

The argument for German "living-space" was put more persuasively and soberly than usual, as well as without that extreme offence to other nations which has been so characteristic of modern Teutonic literature, by Friedrich Naumann in his book *Mitteleuropa*, published early in the First World War.[14] As a philosopher, Naumann was specially concerned with the economico-geographical factor in the development of empire, and of the German Empire in particular. His contention was that the world of the near future would be divided between a few Super-States of vast populations and resources, numbering some five or six in all, which would grow by annexing and absorbing smaller entities. The time would come, though then distant, when the Super-States would federate to form the United States of the World; but in the immediate future there would be fierce competition, and probably war, between them.

Naumann illustrated what he considered to be inevitable, from the evidence provided by commerce and industry, wherein combines and trusts, by their ever-increasing power of ruthless competition, make it difficult or impossible for small firms to survive. It was, he argued, in the interests of neighbouring countries to throw in their lot with Germany, which had already built up the greatest industrial machine on the continent of Europe and, in addition, a considerable tropical empire. These marginal countries would thereby share in the prosperity and protection which Germany alone could extend to them.

Naumann's conception of a Central European Super-State, ranking

[14] The work was translated into English and appeared as *Central Europe* in 1916.

with the U.S.A., Russian Euro-Asia, the British Empire, and a Sino-Japanese empire of the Far East, would have granted Germany the hegemony of Austria-Hungary—already closely attached, both politically and economically—and of the Balkan Peninsula; and, indeed of all Europe outside the empire of Russia and the British-controlled Atlantic fringe. Within this Central European Super-State there was to be little provision for national autonomy which, from Naumann's point of view, was a mere irrelevance. To him the maintenance or the creation of a system of small and weak States on a nationality basis was a vain attempt "to put the clock back," to deny an inevitable process of evolution.

THE PRINCIPLES UNDERLYING THE PEACE SETTLEMENT AND THEIR APPLICATION

The Allied statesmen who met at Versailles and later conferences were confronted with the problem of deciding the future political status of a wide variety of communities made free by the disintegration of four empires—Germany, Austria-Hungary, Turkey, and Russia. The latter was, from the standpoint of the Western Powers, in a different category from the other three, in that until 1917 Russia had been an ally; so that there could be no justification for their taking an active part in the dissolution of the Tsarist Empire.

Whatever the mood of the statesmen who were responsible for the new partition of Europe, the temper of the victorious nations was one of idealism. The slogans of the time—"A world safe for democracy," "A war to end wars," "The rights of small nations," "Self-determination," and the rest—were the texts of a political religion which had been shaped in the heat and stress of war and which could be relied on to influence mankind just as long as the horrors of war remained vivid in human memory. By their own professions, and in some cases by their own convictions, the statesmen were committed to a settlement which placed one consideration paramount over all others. It was the right of every national community, no matter how small, to decide, as a sovereign body, its own political and economic system, without conditions imposed from without. The new frontiers were to be, therefore, as far as possible, strictly in accordance with the distribution of nationalities. This was a decision that presented frontier-drawing commissions with problems defying solution, especially within that east-central zone of Europe whose national complexities have already been discussed at some length.

This regard for national susceptibilities may be criticized from the standpoint of the wider interests of Europe, but, in its seeming regard for the small Power, it was certainly commendable. Moreover, it was closely in line with the political traditions of the two nations—Great Britain and France—which, because of their prestige and military power, were able to dominate the European peace conferences. Their ideal of national self-determination was derived from centuries-old experience. As the benefits which it had brought to the French and British peoples were obvious, what was more natural than that similar benefits should be extended to those less fortunate peoples of Europe who, temporarily and at a most critical juncture, were in their care?

Whether or not the new European system would work satisfactorily from the economic standpoint does not seem to have been more than a secondary consideration. In this respect much was left to chance, as if the bitter and ancient animosities which the Great War had re-kindled would soon subside. Economic difficulties, it was thought, would be resolved in time by continual adjustments between neighbouring Powers, though international history gave little warrant for such a likelihood. Furthermore, the possibility of another world-wide conflagration was so remote in 1919 that no positive measures—as distinct from the ineffective formulae of the League of Nations for dealing with aggressors—were devised for the protection of the newly-created, or revived, States. From the outset of their careers, they—one and all—were embarrassed by military insecurity.

Reviewing in retrospect the frontier changes as a whole, the number of instances of departure from principles of international justice was too great to be justified. In general, they were the result of prejudice, natural to statesmen who were nationally—not internationally—minded. The nations which fought for the Allied cause, or reluctantly served as Slavonic conscripts of Austria and Germany, were treated generously in the allocation of territory. On the other hand, the frontiers of every State, whose nationals had been hostile, were drawn narrowly and, in some cases, harshly. Wherever a frontier-rectification was made, which could not be justified by an impartial interpretation of the principle of nationality, a former ally gained at the expense of a former enemy. Sometimes it was a matter of granting a belt of commercially valuable territory, such as a frontage on the navigable Danube, or a railway zone, to some former ally or well-disposed nation: at other times, territory was ceded—though never to an ex-enemy—in order to grant a strategic advantage, such as the control of the crest-line of a mountain chain. Yet again, claims to territory, beyond limits defined by nationality, were granted on historic grounds, the appeal to history frequently depending on an interpretation of events as remote as several centuries earlier.

THE FRONTIERS OF GERMANY, 1919-35

The central position of Germany in Europe, and the importance, both political and economic, of several of the borderlands which she lost in 1919, suggest that detailed study of the partition of Europe should begin there.

The losses of European territory incurred by Germany, though very considerable, were not crippling, and were restricted in most cases to areas whose inhabitants of German speech were a minority of the total population. In aggregate, the loss was about 27,000 square miles, supporting a population of about 6½ millions, according to the census of 1910.[15] (This estimate does not include the Saar Basin, to which further reference will be made later.) On the other hand, Germany would have expanded by the addition of Austria—32,000 square miles with 6,500,000 people—if the Allied Powers had permitted the union demanded by the Austrian National Assembly in March 1919 and on several later occasions. The setting aside of the principle of national self-determination in this case was due to a persistent fear of Germany—on the part of France, in particular—and to a determination that Germany should not be strengthened by an increase of territory and population.

[15] The areas (with populations) ceded by Germany were:

	Population	Area (sq. miles)
Western Poland (part of Silesia, Posen, and the Polish Corridor)	3,854,971	17,816
Alsace and part of Lorraine	1,874,014	5,607
Northern Schleswig	166,348	1,542
Memel	141,238	1,026
Danzig	330,630	739
Eupen and Malmédy	60,003	400
Part of Upper Silesia (to Czecho-Slovakia)	48,446	122
Total	6,475,650	27,252

Although the territory ceded to France was not as extensive as that annexed by the re-born Poland it was of greater value to German industry. Moreover, it was possible for Germany to contend, not only that both Alsace and the eastern part of Lorraine were, for the greater part, German-speaking, but also that the political allegiance of the people had not been accurately tested. The French claim to the two Provinces was based on history; they were part of France until Prussia tore them away in 1871. But the appeal to history was double-edged, and the German argument was that the Provinces were German soil until annexed by the French in a series of conquests during the seventeenth and eighteenth centuries. The decision of 1919 was that of *force majeure*, for the Gallic mood would not permit the discussion of any alternative to complete restitution.

As indicated earlier, there is no sound geographical argument for joining Alsace and Lorraine together irrevocably: yet statesmen too frequently regard them as if they were a single entity which, by its very nature, cannot be divided. Unfortunately, in 1919, the people of these disputed lands had no opportunity to express, uninfluenced, their political preference. Rather too easily was it assumed that the Lorrainers of German speech, as well as the Alsatians, were resolved to be part of France. No plebiscite was held after the War, and, even if it had been organized, its impartiality would not have been above suspicion. In Alsace, during the last seventy years or more, there has been a movement favouring complete separation from both France and Germany, in order to eliminate the main cause of strife between these two Powers. Other impartial observers of the problem, as it was prior to the rise of the Nazi Party, have favoured a solution which would allow Alsace, at least, to join the South Germans in a federated State, able to hold its own against Prussia.[16]

After 1918, a strenuous, but abortive, attempt was made by France to eradicate German language and culture in both Alsace and the German-speaking parts of Lorraine, which, in reverse, was precisely the kind of policy in which Germany indulged during the period from 1871 down to the First World War. Many of German sympathies either chose, or were persuaded, to leave the two Provinces, just as there had been an exodus of French-speaking inhabitants during

[16] v. A. J. Toynbee: *Nationality and the War*, London, 1915, p. 46. v. also Appendix C.

the time of German annexation.[17] The attempt to gallicize Alsace and German-speaking Lorraine produced much local resentment, which the French were obliged to take into account in a compromise which accepted bilingualism.

When, in 1923, the French temporarily extended their occupation of the Rhineland to include the coal-mining district of the Ruhr, fears were entertained that they intended to remain permanently on the left bank of the Rhine, downstream from Alsace as far as the Dutch frontier. Had not Marshal Foch publicly stated that the Rhine was the best frontier to ensure the future protection of France! A movement to detach from Germany the Palatinate (Pfalz) and other lands farther downstream on the Rhine was supported by a small minority of local opinion, but was actively assisted by the French Government. Great Britain recognized, however, that there was no mandate for such a project from the German inhabitants of the areas concerned, and France came to recognize the impossibility of the plan.

The economic advantages which France gained by the re-incorporation of Alsace and German-speaking Lorraine were to some extent off-set by the political disadvantage of bringing into France a population of nearly two millions, many—though probably not a majority—of whom were of doubtful loyalty. Moreover, the annexation brought in no important source of fuel, and it was coal which France required much more than iron. Before 1914 France consumed twenty-two million tons of coal more than she produced, and the acquisition of ex-German Lorraine with its vast metallurgical industry greatly increased the dependence on imported fuel. Of iron-ore France had a fair sufficiency before 1914, after which Eastern Lorraine added a reserve that Germany had formerly exploited at the rate of twenty-one million tons of ore per annum. Indeed, France entered the period of post-war reconstruction with larger reserves of iron-ore than were possessed by any European Power, though for their utilization her dependence on Ruhr coal was as complete as ever it had been.

As compensation for the war-time destruction of the Lens-Valenciennes collieries, France claimed, and was awarded, the coal-seams,

[17] During the period 1871-1910 about 400,000 inhabitants of Alsace-Lorraine emigrated to France. Some 500,000 immigrants (mostly German) came in during the same period.

together with the mining plant, of the Saar Basin, a plateau-hollow
of about 750 square miles, just over the frontier of Lorraine. The
population was known to be almost entirely German in language
and sentiment, so that the annexation of the region, which France
at first demanded, could not be justified. The League of Nations was
granted the administration of the Saar territory for fifteen years, after
which a plebiscite was to be taken to discover the political allegiance
of the inhabitants, though it was well known to every responsible
statesman that no decision other than reunion with Germany would
be reached by the population. It was further stipulated that if, or
when, the Saar returned to Germany, the coal-mines were to be
bought back from France.

The plebiscite taken in 1935 was a foregone conclusion, but was
skilfully exploited by Adolf Hitler in the interests of the Nazi Party.
It would have been wiser for France and Britain to have allowed the
return of the Saar to Germany without the publicity of a popular
vote. As it was, the new Teutonic militarists were able to turn the
plebiscite to excellent account for purposes of propaganda. The Saar
coal, mined to an annual amount of over fifteen million tons, was of
great use in the industrial life of France, but, owing to its poor
coking quality, could not replace the Westphalian product in the
furnaces of Lorraine.[18]

Only ten miles west of the Saar Basin lies the frontier of the
Grand Duchy of Luxemburg, whose southern district comes within
the Lorraine iron-field. With its geography and economic life orien-
tated towards Germany—it is Ruhr coal which converts Luxemburg
ore into steel!—almost inevitably, before 1914, the Duchy belonged
to the German Customs Union. In 1919, however, the economic tie
with Germany was severed, and Belgium then hoped to attach the
Duchy, economically, to itself. A plebiscite resulted in a vote for
economic union with France, one consequence of which was that
Belgium feared the Duchy might be absorbed within France. In the
event, France declined to act on the result of the plebiscite, but
approved of the removal of the customs frontier between Belgium
and Luxemburg. This was effected in 1922. Perhaps the most disap-
pointing feature of the negotiations for the future of Luxemburg was
the emergence of Belgian fear of France, so clearly demonstrated.

[18] For a full discussion of the frontier changes which affected the Saar and other
borderlands of Germany, the reader is advised to consult the six volumes of *A
History of the Peace Conference of Paris*, edited by H. W. V. Temperley, 1920.

And this despite a comradeship in arms of over four years against their common foe and oppressor!

After the recent war it will be difficult to alter the status of the Grand Duchy so long as political union with France or Belgium or Germany is repugnant to the great majority of its citizens. On the other hand, without some guarantee of independence and neutrality, more effective than any in the past, the Luxemburgers cannot hope for security.

The Belgian Government went to the Peace Conference determined to alter the frontier with Germany where it crosses the northern district of the Ardennes Plateau. Here, in the vicinity of the two small towns of Eupen and Malmédy, the Germans in 1914 held the advantage of terrain, where it sloped down from the frontier towards the Meuse in the interior of Belgium. It was a geographical advantage of which Germany made the fullest military use in her preparations for war. The Belgian claim did not, however, depend solely on a strategical argument: in addition, it invoked both history and the universally accepted principle of self-determination. Within the districts of Eupen and Malmédy there were about 60,000 inhabitants,[19] most of them closely similar to the Walloon population of Southern Belgium. In 1815 the two districts had been awarded to Prussia, and at that time the local language was unquestionably French. After a century of germanization the proportion of French speakers had greatly declined. By 1918 it was not more than eighteen per cent, of which the greater part were the townspeople of Malmédy. Whether or not these facts justified Belgium in annexing the two districts, the Allied and Associated Powers had no hesitation in awarding her claim.[20] And the events of more recent years do not suggest that the reward will be set aside in the general re-shaping of the German frontiers.[21]

In compensation for the loss of Eupen and Malmédy, Germany

[19] In 1910 the figures were: Malmédy, 34,768; Eupen, 26,156.

[20] No plebiscite was taken, though the pretence of one was made. By the terms of the Peace Treaty a register in which the inhabitants might, if they wished, record their preference for German administration of Eupen-Malmédy, was kept open for six months. The news that such voting would be public and under Belgian supervision had the desired effect. Only a tiny fraction of the German speakers signed the register.

[21] To the district of Eupen was added, in 1919, the small town of Moresnet, situated in the near neighbourhood of Aachen. Important for its zinc deposits, Moresnet had previously been neutral to both Belgium and Germany for over a century.

made a claim—based on the principle of national self-determination —to a district of German speech farther south on the Ardennes Plateau.[22] It lies within the Belgian frontier, with the town of Arlon as its nucleus, but between it and Germany there is the entire width of the Duchy of Luxemburg. Its cession to Germany, therefore, would have offered practical difficulties, apart from which, in the mood of 1919, any proposal to transfer a part of Belgian territory would have been regarded as unworthy of consideration.

No other territorial change affected the western half of Germany, except the cession of a small area of Schleswig to Denmark. Alone of the new boundaries of post-war Europe, the Dano-German line seems to have been accepted with almost complete international approval; or such was the case before the domination of Germany by the Nazi creed. In consideration of the embittered history of Schleswig—taken from the King of Denmark by an aggressive Prussia—the Danes showed in 1919 a degree of moderation which was an excellent, if disregarded, model for other nations then in a position to stake out territorial claims. Denmark declined to claim the return of all Schleswig. She asked for, and received, no more than a minimum territorial concession. A frontier in strict accordance with the facts of nationality was her need, and she had no wish so to expand across Schleswig as to incorporate large numbers of German nationals. No doubt, however, in addition to the fairness and moderation which characterized the Danish attitude, there was the dread of arousing an *irredentist* movement backed by a Germany fast recovering from the War.

In 1920 the plebiscite which Prussia had promised (in 1866), but never granted, was held in Northern Schleswig. It was appreciated that the central and southern parts of the Province were almost entirely German in both speech and sympathy; and, therefore, they were left outside the area of the plebiscite. Northern Schleswig was divided into a northern and a southern zone for the purposes of voting. The result was as expected—the northern choosing union with Denmark and the southern electing to remain within the Reich. The alignment of the frontier which followed could not have been more equitable; yet, in the event, it was inevitable, so intermixed

[22] There are about 35,000 German-speaking inhabitants in the district of Belgian Luxemburg.

were the two nationalities, that a few thousand Germans and Danes should be left on the wrong side of the border.[23]

Flensburg, the largest town near the Dano-German frontier, was, at the time of the plebiscite, both port and market for the entire eastern district of Northern Schleswig, and as it lies just within the area of German speech it was left to Germany. There may have been no alternative to this decision, but it had the consequence of dislocating the trade both of Flensburg and of the district, north of the border, which Flensburg formerly served. Germany's gain was to some extent countered by the loss of the small town of Tondern, an outlier of German speech, set within the zone of Danish loyalty and close to the North Sea coast. On balance, there was no serious cause for complaint on either side. The settlement proved generally successful, and is not likely to be set aside in the peace which follows the Second World War.

No strategic considerations, it is to be noted, were involved in a decision which was based almost entirely on ethnographical arguments. Denmark realized that a frontier across the plain of Schleswig, no matter how advantageously drawn, could never grant her security. Her own man-power (based on a population of only three and a half millions) and resources, diminutive in contrast to the great strength of her southern neighbour, together with a realization of the exposure of the Danish mainland and islands to attack, led her to regard military defence as largely illusory. For this and other reasons she was prepared to go farther along the road to military disarmament than any other European Power.[24]

In regard to the 1919 frontiers of Eastern Germany we remember that the capitulation of Germany in 1918 cancelled the Treaty of Brest Litovsk, which a defeated and virtually disintegrated Russia had signed only a few months before. The policies of the Western Powers and of Germany were alike in at least one respect, namely, in their intention to establish between Central Europe and Great Russia[25] a "middle tier" of states extending from the Arctic to the Black Sea. The Western Powers were conscious of their inability—

[23] The frontier left about 50,000 individuals—including both Germans and Danes—outside their respective countries.

[24] The budget for the armed forces in 1939-40 was equivalent to £4 millions, which represented only £1 per head of population.

[25] All European Russia, less White Russia and the Ukraine.

for geographical reasons—to guarantee the political structure of East-Central Europe. On the other hand, Germany at Brest Litovsk had decided to make of the "middle tier" a permanent Teutonic protectorate.

In 1919, Polish and Lithuanian independence brought to the fore, as an international issue, the political relationship of the German communities of the East Baltic littoral with their non-Teutonic neighbours of the interior. These Germans, of East Prussia and Memel-land in particular, are detached from the body of Germany by a narrow wedge of Polish population which reaches the Baltic to the west of the Vistula delta.

Memel-land, which lies beyond East Prussia across the lower reaches of the Niemen River, presented Europe with a considerable problem in political geography. The policy which determined its political status was defended as an attempt to respect the principle of national self-determination. The territory was not to be allowed to remain in Germany, yet the port of Memel with its decisive German majority could not be ceded to Lithuania. It was the kind of dilemma to which those who partitioned Europe inevitably came, and from which there seems to be no escape except by the way of federation. Lithuania, proud and self-conscious in her revived statehood, could not be expected to tolerate a partition which deprived her of sovereignty over her natural outlet to the Baltic; and it could not have been a surprise to the Western Powers when, in 1923, she defied both them and the League, and annexed the Memel territory.[26] And so with the consent of the Powers, but as a result of her own defiance of them, the German-controlled outlet of the Niemen River passed to Lithuania, a large part of which is the natural hinterland of the Lower Niemen. Farther north, the old German city of Riga and its Dvina hinterland had come, in a more legitimate way, under Latvian sovereignty.

Within the "Polish Corridor" the considerable German population—in 1919 it was estimated to be 418,000—diminished greatly in more recent years, as a result of pressure which induced many to move across the frontier into Germany. Yet it is well known that during the long period of its incorporation within Prussia the process

[26] The annexation was confirmed in 1924, by the Memel Convention, the principal signatories of which were Great Britain and France.

of germanization had been continuous. Although there can be no certainty, owing to mutually contradictory estimates from German and Polish sources, it seems that in 1919 the Polish inhabitants were a bare majority of the total population. Unfortunately for the peace of Europe, the sanction of the "Polish Corridor" meant that East Prussia was completely detached from Germany. This major operation in political surgery was justified in order to satisfy Polish national and commercial aspirations, and particularly the desire for a maritime outlet. Yet, apart from sentiment, it is difficult to maintain that a strip of the Baltic shore is vital to Poland's existence, any more than the need for a maritime frontage is essential to the life of Switzerland or Czecho-Slovakia, or some other landlocked State. Given such freedom of trade as Switzerland normally enjoys, Poland could develop both continental and overseas contacts, by suitable arrangements with neighbouring States, and without exclusive rights over the nearest part of the Baltic coast. This, however, is a matter of high controversy, and opinion on it will differ as long as international trade is organized on a competitive basis.

A matter on which there is little room for controversy to-day concerns the separation of East Prussia from the remainder of Prussia. It was probably the most serious of all the errors that the statesmen of 1919 committed. As we have seen, the significance of East Prussia in the story of German political development is not to be dismissed lightly, and more important than the land in this instance is the community—if it is possible for one to be considered separately from the other. The detachment of the East Prussians from the main body of their compatriots was likely to have two consequences: first, they would not cease to agitate for reunion with their kinsmen, just as any other people with a similar historical and geographical background would do; secondly, Germany as the parent nation would nurse a desperate grievance which would embitter her relations with Poland, and could only lead to renewed war.

As it appears to the present writer, there can be only one decision which, if it will not secure peace, will make peace a reasonable possibility. If Poland is to retain what is now known as the "Corridor" (i.e., Pomorze), the entire East Prussian population should be moved to the main body of Germany; and with the East Prussians the Germans of Danzig—and for that matter the German citizens of

Memel—should also go. There have been a number of recent precedents for such a wholesale transfer of population, and the results have, in time, been generally beneficial. One of them, the exchange of Greek and Turkish populations between 1923 and 1925, was on a scale equivalent to the proposed evacuation of East Prussia; whilst a precedent in the Eastern Baltic region was the agreement of 1939 between Germany and Russia for the transfer to Germany of the "Balt" population of Estonia, Latvia, and Lithuania. Hardship to the individual and enormous, though temporary, economic difficulties would undoubtedly be involved, but they would be as nothing compared with the suffering incidental to a European conflict which this kind of *irredentist* question is likely again to bring about. (In 1945 the problem of East Prussia reached a new, if temporary, solution. It was partitioned between Poland and Russia, and Germans were expelled on a scale not yet fully known.)

In regard to East Prussia, the political action of the victorious Powers of the First World War was to decide by plebiscite the future allegiance of the population in the southern district of the Province, particularly that part south of the town of Allenstein. As indicated on an earlier page, the population there included over 400,000 inhabitants of Slavonic speech. Yet they showed no desire to be admitted to Poland, and voted for Germany. The frontiers of East Prussia could not, therefore, be greatly altered, without violation of the principle of self-determination.

The creation of the political unit known as the Free City of Danzig (comprising an area of over 700 square miles and a population approximately 400,000) was another instance of the tendency of the victorious Powers to favour excessive partition. As in the similar case of the Memel Territory, there was general dissatisfaction, loudly expressed not only by Germany, which lost a former Hansa stronghold of predominantly Teutonic population, but by the Danzigers and by Poland also. Re-occupation of Danzig by Germany was the first act of the Second World War.[27]

Prevented from annexing Danzig—the natural outlet of the Vistula Basin, as its commercial history records—Poland selected a site at Gdynia, on the west side of the Bay of Danzig, and proceeded, at great cost to itself, to build a rival port. The growth of Gdynia

[27] On September 1, 1939, Danzig was by decree reincorporated in the Reich. On September 8, 1939, Great Britain expressed its intention to regard the Free City as territory in the unlawful occupation of Germany.

has been to some extent at the expense of Danzig,[28] though the latter has also shared, if to a lesser degree, in the commerce of Poland.

The intention of the victorious Powers was to grant Poland adequate trading facilities in Danzig, as was shown by the inclusion of the Free City within the Polish customs frontier and the strong Polish representation on the Harbour Board. Difficulties were inevitable, however, because of the administrative separation of Danzig from its commercial hinterland. Poland's irritation at the limitations imposed on her sovereignty throughout the lower Vistula region was, however, matched by German complaints of attempts to "polonize" the Free City and of restrictions placed on the commercial inter-relations of East Prussia, Danzig, and Germany.

Two further frontier rectifications involved Germany in considerable losses of territory. One case was the Posen (Poznan) Province, the other, Upper Silesia.

The loss of Posen Province and the "Polish Corridor" virtually reduced Prussia on its eastern side to the limits of the year 1810. Posen covered an area of about 11,000 square miles and, although much was of indifferent agricultural quality, it had been farmed better by the Germans than the Warsaw district and Galicia had been by Russia and Austria, respectively; whilst in industry the towns—including Posen itself—were more advanced, despite the local scarcity of mineral wealth, than those of the Austrian and Russian parts of Poland.

Yet Germany had no possible justification for the retention of Posen, and the annexation of much the greater part of it by Poland was generally approved. Within the urban areas of the western fringe of the Province, where it meets the Silesian and Brandenburg borders, there was, however, in 1919, a small majority of Germans; which suggests that, if ever it should be considered a matter of justice to compensate Germany for the loss of the "Polish Corridor" and the Free City of Danzig, it should be done by adding to Brandenburg and Silesia a narrow strip of Posen territory, not exceeding fifteen miles in east-to-west extent. By this means a considerable proportion of the Germans remaining in Poland would be reunited to Germany, and this might well be an advantage as much to Poland as to Germany.

[28] In 1938 the volume of cargoes handled at each of the two ports was as follows: Gdynia, 9,173,000 tons; Danzig, 7,127,000 tons.

The proportion of Germans in the population of Upper Silesia and their importance in its urban and industrial life were much too considerable to allow Poland to annex the region as a whole, though her claims were wide and based partly on Silesia's place in the Kingdom of Poland six centuries ago. The plebiscite of 1921, on the basis of which the Germano-Polish frontier was drawn, reflected correctly the predominance of Germans in Upper Silesia, as far up the valley of the Oder as a line drawn between the towns of Beuthen and Ratibor. That is, over about two-thirds of Upper Silesia. What, therefore, more fair than that two-thirds of the territory should remain in Germany,[29] whilst the south-eastern fraction should be ceded by Germany? The frontier was drawn accordingly, yet this decision, which was based solely on national self-determination, was one of the most unworkable of all the territorial transfers of the time. Indeed, it would have produced a major economic disaster, from which Poland more than Germany would have suffered, if a local modification of sovereignty had not been effected by an agreement between Poland and Germany.

The statesmen responsible for the Upper Silesian frontier were prepared to regard the following as of secondary importance:

(i) that much the greater part of the Silesian coal-field—greatest in Central Europe. if the Ruhr resources are excepted—together with the greater part of the rich ores of iron and zinc, were left on the Polish side of the frontier,[30]

(ii) that the urban and industrial organization of practically the entire area was due to German settlement, and that all towns ceded to Poland, including Katowice, the largest, contained considerable German populations,

(iii) that the partition of Upper Silesia, although corresponding to the numerical strengths of the two nationalities, was not a geographical division in accordance with the distribution of the German and Polish communities.

[29] Out of about 1,170,000 votes cast, some 700,000 were for Germany and 470,000 for Poland—numbers whose proportions are equivalent to the allocation of territory to Germany and Poland respectively.

[30] Of the 67 coal-pits in the region, Poland received 53, with an even higher proportion of coal output than these figures indicate.

This last criticism is the most serious of all, from the standpoint of political geography, and suggests that the principle of national self-determination was so interpreted as to justify a previously made territorial decision. It is not overlooked that about one-half the total Polish population of Upper Silesia was left on the German side of the frontier. The inference is warranted that, irrespective of the wishes of the inhabitants or the economic welfare of the region as a whole, Poland was to receive the lion's share of the mineral fields. The frontier which seemed to most superficial observers of the time to be fair to Germany, in that about two-thirds of the province went to her, was drawn in the economic interests of Poland.

The partition proved to be unworkable, and embittered the already difficult relations between Poland and Germany. The two countries declared a war of tariffs, and closed their markets to each other's products. A modus vivendi for the region had to be sought in its desperate need, for the frontier cut across not only industrial connexions, but also transport, gas, electricity, and water services. By the opening of the Second World War the problem had not been solved, and it remained to test the capacity of American and European statesmanship at conferences of the United Nations. But this much was done: Poland and Germany signed a Convention by which the life of the region might have been reintegrated, had all its 600 articles been adhered to by both sides. If the political strife between the two countries, centring mainly on the Free City and the "Polish Corridor," could have been averted, there might have been a chance for the fulfilment of the Convention.

THE AUSTRIAN REPUBLIC

By the Treaty of St. Germain (1919) Austria was reduced to almost exactly one-quarter of its former area.[31] It thus became a true nation-state of some seven millions, occupying a sparsely populated mountain-land which closely resembles, in geographical character, its western neighbour, Switzerland, though about twice the latter's area and population. The cession of the imperial territories of Bohemia, Galicia, Bosnia, and Herzegovina was actually less damaging to the young republic than the necessity to support the former imperial capital, Vienna, one of the six largest European cities of the time. The fame of Vienna was not derived from its metropolitan leader-

[31] From 116,000 to 34,000 square miles.

ship of a district comprising only the Austrian Alps and a tiny frag-
ment of the Danubian Plain. It was the recognition of its status as
capital—administrative, cultural, and commercial—of over fifty millions, living within the extensive and varied territories of the Danubian Basin and its borderlands. Deprived of its imperial authority
and of its commercial contacts with Central Europe, Vienna
languished and seemed likely to die. It appears that the agonies of
the starving city were not foreseen by the statesmen of St. Germain. At the outbreak of the First World War the population was
over two millions: it had been increasing rapidly for many years.
By December 1919, Vienna had lost 160,000 of its citizens, and the
majority of those who remained were close to starvation. The
excessive burden on the young State which Vienna represented was
one of the reasons for the petition of Vorarlberg, the westernmost
Province, to secede from Austria and unite with Switzerland.[32]

When the federation of Danubian lands is achieved—as it must
be one day, if there is to be peace in Europe—Vienna will return to
its rôle of capital of Central Europe, for which geography intends it.
Meanwhile, its size in relation to the resources of Austria is too
great. It possesses between one-quarter and one-third of the population of the State—a position of unbalance which is equalled in no
other European country. The first need of Austria, whose area is
mainly mountainous and yet 50 per cent of whose population is
urban, is an assured food supply. As only 24 per cent of the land
is under any form of cultivation there is a very large dependence
on imports, and no improvement in agricultural standards can make
much difference to this dependence. Taking into account the
exhaustion of Austria in 1919 and its need for supplies, it is surely
a reflection on the sagacity, not to say humanity, of the Allied statesmen that the young Republic was required by the Treaty of St.
Germain to deliver farm-stock to Italy, Rumania, and Yugoslavia.

By 1922 Austria was in desperate straits; revolution and collapse
seemed imminent. Then were the Western Powers through their
instrument—the League—forced to act by extending a loan of £25
millions, for they feared not only revolution in the heart of Europe,

---

[32] Switzerland declined to accept Vorarlberg on two main grounds. The first
was financial, as the mountainous province would have been a liability. The
second was less official but equally important, namely, that the Protestant majority
in Switzerland did not desire an increase of Roman Catholic voting strength.

but also the incorporation of Austria by a sympathetic Germany. Union with the latter was repeatedly forbidden by France and Great Britain—in 1919, 1921, and 1922—without reference to a plebiscite which the Austrian National Assembly demanded. Yet in 1937 and 1938, when Austria feared she would be unable to withstand the armed aggression of Germany, and looked to the Powers to enable her to remain independent, she applied in vain.

That under normal conditions Austria will wish to unite with Germany there is little room for doubt; and there seems no reason —save the general distrust of Germany—why it should be denied. Austrians are Germans as much as are the Bavarians or any other southern group of German-speaking peoples, and differ only in the fact that, until 1938, they had never been united politically with Prussia. Until the Republic was founded in 1919, Imperial Austria claimed to be the inheritor of the Holy Roman Empire. That imperial tradition was finally abandoned at the close of the First World War.

It is possible that, because of her recent tragic experience under Nazism, Austria, more fearful of political Germany than ever before, may choose to emphasize such racial and cultural differences as distinguish her citizens from those of Prussia. As long as the horrors of the Nazi period are remembered, the Austrians may be attracted by the example of their neighbours, the Swiss, who, though predominantly of Germanic language and culture, have rejected with the utmost decision any suggestion that their nationhood should be merged with that of Germany.[33]

Where contact is made with Switzerland, Germany, and Czecho-Slovakia, the drawing of the Austrian frontiers provides no serious international problem; but where Austria has frontiers against Italy, Yugoslavia, and Hungary, the fixing of limits, strictly in accordance with nationality, is more difficult. Most critical of such problems is associated with the Italo-Austrian frontier, in the Central Alps.

It will be recalled that in 1915, before Italy was at war with Austria-Hungary, the latter offered to cede that part of the Southern Tyrol where Italians were a decisive majority of the population. By going to war on the side which, she calculated, would be victorious,

[33] According to the announcement of policy made by the representatives of the Soviet Union, Great Britain and the United States at Moscow in November 1943, the return of Austria to independent status was then decided.

Italy obtained, under the terms of St. Germain, the entire drainage area of the River Adige, including both the Trentino and the Alto Adige. Her frontier thereby followed closely the crest of the Central Alps and covered the vitally important Brenner Pass, easiest passageway between the Upper Danube and the great Plain of Lombardy. Obviously enough, the frontier was determined by considerations of strategy. Arguments of the Italian General Staff, to ensure that Italy should not again be exposed to its hereditary enemy, commanding the Alpine crest-line, carried the day.

By incorporating the entire basin of the Adige River, Italy brought within her frontiers nearly a quarter of a million Austrian Germans, whose resistance to the transfer was strenuous. Allowing for exaggeration of their complaints, there can be little doubt that as a "minority" their treatment by Italy did not conform to the standards sanctioned by the League of Nations. Italy, whose foreign policy has so long been concerned with *irredentist* claims on her neighbours, was increasingly embarrassed by the presence of this alien and hostile minority. But for the Italian alliance with Nazi Germany, cemented after the absorption of Austria within the Reich, the question of the Austrians of the Alto-Adige would certainly have become acute in Italo-German relations.

On her eastern and south-eastern borders, where Austria meets Hungary and Yugoslavia, respectively, in the zone of transition from the lofty Alps to the Danubian Plain, an attempt was made by the statesmen of St. Germain to align the new frontiers strictly in accordance with the limits of nationality. The elongated territory known as Burgenland, extending from the Danube opposite Bratislava as far as the line of the River Raab, was formerly a part of the Kingdom of Hungary. It is essentially a borderland, covering part of the foothill country of the Eastern Alps, and coming out into the Danubian Plain to the east of the Leitha Mountains which, with the Little Carpathians, serve to detach the Vienna Basin from the Hungarian Plain. Throughout Burgenland the wishes of a majority determine its allegiance to Austria, rather than to Hungary, to which it formerly belonged. Its transfer to Austria was the sole instance of an ex-enemy Power gaining territory as a result of the First World War. It will be noted, however, that the loss was suffered by Hungary, an ex-enemy nation. On geographical grounds the cession of Burgenland to

Austria was commendable, in that it added an area, however small, of cultivable land to the agriculturally impoverished Republic.[34]

In the same latitude as the southern border of Burgenland, but farther west and inset well within the Eastern Alps, is the long depression followed by the River Drave. From its principal town it is known as the Klagenfurt Basin. It was believed possible that a majority of the population within the southern part of the Basin and on the frontier of Yugoslavia might prefer union with the latter, and a plebiscite was held. As the southerners voted for inclusion in Austria it was not considered necessary to hold a plebiscite in the district north of the Drave, around Klagenfurt itself, where, it was estimated, the Germans (Austrian) would probably have a majority. Had the southerners voted for Yugoslavia and the northerners for Austria, a small region—unified in its economic life—would no doubt have been partitioned, with disastrous consequences for its welfare.[35]

CZECHO-SLOVAKIA: A COMPOSITE STATE

President Masaryk and his colleagues, founders of the Republic of Czecho-Slovakia in 1918, assumed that the similarities of language, tradition, and national sentiment were so close as to justify the incorporation of the Czechs and Slovaks within a unitary state. If the political position of the Slovaks had been one of equality with the Czechs the Republic's career in the years between the wars would certainly have been less troubled than it was by internal difficulties. The Slovaks protested, with considerable justice, that a status of inferiority, which was contrary to the constitution of the Republic, resulted in their political and economic needs receiving inadequate attention. The legislative and executive control was largely in the hands of the Czechs, and, although Masaryk's statesmanship was the most enlightened in Central Europe, autonomy for the Slovaks was not conceded. In justification, the Czech argument stressed both the more backward national development of the Slovaks and their small numbers—barely two millions as against six million Czechs.

The selection of Praha as the state capital, though a natural one to the Czechs, for whom it had been for centuries the geographical

[34] The area of Burgenland is about 1,500 square miles, which, with a population of 300,000, shows a density higher than that of any province of the Republic, except Lower Austria.

[35] Klagenfurt and its district has a very considerable industry, of varied character, but with metal and electrical production predominating.

focus of the nation, was calculated to emphasize the concentration of political power within the hands of the Czechs. It is a city which, in the nineteenth century, lost most of its one-time cultural links with the Slovak people[36] who, in their political and economic subordination to Hungary, had acquired closer associations with Buda-Pest. Moreover, the geographical orientation of Slovakia, southwards towards the Hungarian Danube and away from the enclosed plateau-basin of Bohemia, conflicted with any tendency towards association with the Czechs and with their cultural focus on the Ultava.

It would have been a wise decision to have selected as Czecho-Slovak capital some city—preferably Brno (Brünn)—of Moravia, which, though Czech in nationality, is much more accessible than Praha to the Slovak community. Brno (265,000 inhabitants in 1939) is the second town of the State both in size and dignity, and occupies a focal position as a particularly important route-centre, not only of Moravia and Czecho-Slovakia but of Central Europe as a whole. It is well fitted by geography to be the connecting link between the —at present divided—interests of the Czechs and Slovaks.

After the dissolution of Czecho-Slovakia in March 1939, the assumption was widespread in Britain, where the refugee Czech Government was, for some years, established, that Czecho-Slovakia would be revived, with its former frontiers—as confirmed by the Treaty of St. Germain—in their virtual entirety. Further, it was taken for granted that the Czechs and Slovaks formed one, not two, nations and that there was no necessity fundamentally to revise the constitution of the Republic. These assumptions must be carefully investigated, and on two fundamental points the will of the Slovak people should be expressed without fear of external pressure. A plebiscite taken in Slovakia should alone decide whether or not the inhabitants wish to be joined with Bohemia and Moravia in a single State; secondly, if the vote is for union with the Czechs, there should be a guarantee of wide powers of autonomy to the Slovaks, similar to those promised, though never granted, by Masaryk in 1918. It seems clear that the Slovaks can be persuaded to co-operate with the Czechs on a basis of equal partnership, but on that basis only: this the Czechs now recognize.

[36] Before the nineteenth century there had been a period during which the influence of the Czech literary language spread from the University of Praha into Slovakia.

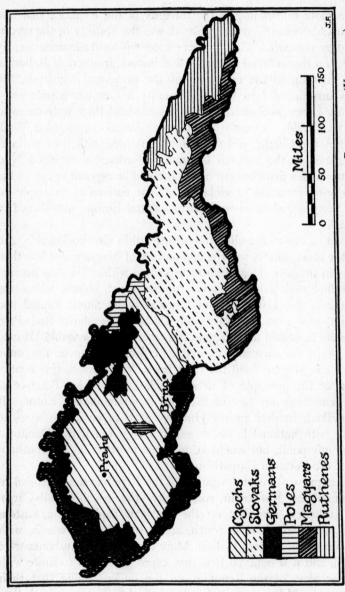

Czechs

Slovaks

Germans

Poles

Magyars

Ruthenes

•Praha

Brno.

Miles

0   50   100   150

J.F.

Fig. 21.—Czecho-Slovakia: Distribution of the Main Elements in the Population (Year 1930)

Even more threatening to the integrity of the Republic than the differences between Czech and Slovak was the hostility of the several large alien minorities who were enclosed within its boundaries. By insisting on the so-called "natural" and historic frontiers of Bohemia, which went up to the crest-lines of the peripheral highlands, the Czechs introduced into their community a German population—popularly known as Sudeten Germans—of about three millions, who were considerably in excess of the entire Slovak community. Well-treated by the Czechs, and reasonably contented with their political lot, the case of the Sudeten Germans, nevertheless, provided Nazi Germany with a first-class grievance. It could be exposed as one of the most glaring instances of violation of that nationality principle on which the political reconstruction of Central Europe was alleged to be based.

Second in size to the alien minorities within Czecho-Slovakia, and of all the most hostile, was the community of Magyars, not less than 600,000 in number. They were incorporated within Slovakia because of Czecho-Slovak insistence on a frontier which should follow the left bank of the Danube, from Bratislava—the Slovak capital and river-port—down to a point some thirty miles above Buda-Pest. The desire to obtain an adequate frontage on the navigable Danube was perhaps commercially excusable, especially as over the same distance the Magyars held the right bank. Nevertheless, this contravention of the principle of national self-determination deserves as severe censure as any case of the kind in contemporary Europe. If the Slovakian frontier against Hungary were to be drawn so as to coincide with national limits, it would hardly touch the Danubian Plain at any point, but would keep to the foothills on the southern flank of the Western Carpathians.

The narrow eastern prolongation of the Republic was intended to incorporate the Ruthenian community—the so-called Sub-Carpathian Ruthenes—who live on the southern flank of the Eastern Beskids, where they are in touch, across the Carpathian axis, with their kinsmen of Eastern Galicia. More than 400,000 Ruthenes were involved, and it is believed that they expressed a wish to unite with the other Slavs of the Republic, on the understanding that their autonomy would be recognized in the federal State, which both they and the Slovaks believed they were joining. Never were the dominant Czechs actively oppressive towards the Ruthene majority. Yet autonomy was withheld, the excuse being that wide differences in cultural standard and tradition between Czech and Ruthene made difficult the award of self-government. It is true that, without administrative experience as they were, the Ruthenes would have needed much guidance in the earliest stages of their autonomy, but there seems to be no good reason why the Czechs should not have fulfilled a solemn promise to their more backward compatriots. The recent union of the Sub-Carpathian Ruthenes with the Ukraine frees the Republic of a serious embarrassment.

One other alien minority, important but smaller than the others, was a source of political weakness to the Republic. It was an outlier —not more than 75,000—of the Polish people, extending across from Upper Silesia and Western Galicia into Moravia. The frontier here was not particularly unjust to the Poles, for Czechs as well as Poles were left on the wrong side of the border. Indeed, it would not have become a critical issue between the two nations, but for the valuable coal and iron deposits in the district of Teschen. Though on a smaller scale the intermixing of Czechs and Poles in the rich mineral-field of Teschen recalls German and Polish inter-penetration of the Upper Silesian field, of which indeed the Teschen district is a southerly extension. The partition of the Teschen coal and iron zone adhered fairly closely to the linguistic frontier, and left to Czecho-Slovakia the western half of the territory, including the best seams of coking coal. On the other hand, Poland was awarded, in addition to the eastern half, the industrial town of Teschen, where much of the industry of the district was organized. Poland might well have been more sympathetic than she was to the need of her neighbour for coking coal, of which commodity she herself had come to possess, in Upper Silesia, one of the most considerable reserves in Europe.

The partition of a district as closely knit, in the industrial sense, as Teschen showed a complete disregard of the economic life of the community, for it detached the principal town from its effective hinterland. Moreover, at the time (1939) of Hitler's destruction of Czecho-Slovakia, little was heard of the contemporary annexation by Poland of the western part of the Teschen district, which she had never ceased to covet. It was an act as reprehensible and as callous as that for which Germany was justly condemned.

Burdened with three large and one small alien minority—all very active—and taking into account the increasingly unfriendly relations of the Czechs and Slovaks, the young Republic from the outset was sorely tried in its efforts to prevent disruption. Moreover, its military position, especially after the incorporation of Austria within Germany, was extremely difficult. Bohemia, its centre of gravity, might be attacked from three sides as well as cut off, via the narrow "waist" of Moravia, from Slovakia. Once Germany was rearmed, the military salvation of the Republic depended on the intervention of her ally, France, and of those of her friends not expressly bound by treaty to defend her. The re-birth of the Republic in 1945 was signalized by a close military alliance with Soviet Russia, the Power which alone, because of the facts of geography, can guarantee Czecho-Slovakia against the possibility of a renewed German menace.

Yet another internal problem which will confront the Republic in the future, as it has in the past, is the difficulty of bringing the outlying regions fully into contact with the headquarters of government by a modernized system of communications. The configuration of Czecho-Slovakia, dominated by a succession of highlands, is hostile to the development of a national system of highways. In former imperial days the majority of routes which traversed the land of the Czechs and Slovaks diverged from each other, and were merely links in long-distance lines which served Central Europe as a whole. Thus, for example, the main highways of Bohemia led from Southern Germany to Vienna, whilst those of Slovakia converged southwards upon the middle Danube, and on Buda-Pest in particular.

We have touched on the difficulties of a country which, nevertheless, is endowed with a varied and very adequate basis of food-supply and industrial production. Czecho-Slovakia, unlike Austria, can feed its population. At the same time it has developed a well-balanced industry, based on considerable fuel and ore resources, not to speak of Slovakian timber reserves richer than those of Austria. On the basis of the technical skill of the Czech artisan and farmer, generally wise statesmanship and the varied natural endowment of the land, Czecho-Slovakia became in the years between the World Wars by far the most prosperous of the "succession states" that arose from the Peace Treaties. Yet its prosperity would have been greater still had it been free to trade—without tariff hindrances—with the territories which enclosed it. Nor must it be overlooked that the prosperity of Czecho-Slovakia was to some degree at the expense of its two defeated neighbours, Austria and Hungary, both of which were heavily penalized by loss of territory in the Peace Treaties.

To Czecho-Slovakia is the credit for appreciation of the impossibility of maintaining international health on the basis of the existing system of national sovereignties. Regional associations or alliances of Powers for common economic and political ends, such as the Czecho-Slovak Government proposed on several occasions before 1939, may be open to serious objections, mainly because of the likely development of inter-regional competition and strife; but at least they would represent some advance on the chaos into which Central Europe fell in the twenty years between the World Wars.

HUNGARY OF THE TREATY OF TRIANON

On all sides save the western—against Austria—the new Hungary was left considerably less in area and population than would have been the case if national self-determination had been a strictly observed principle of frontier delimitation. The three bordering nations, to whom Magyar-occupied lands were ceded, had all been friendly to the Western Powers during the First World War.

In the course of our reference to the frontiers of Slovakia, the annexation of Magyar territory on the left bank of the Danube, from Bratislava downstream, was indicated. To Yugoslavia, on the southern frontier, was ceded land occupied by not less than a quarter of a million Magyars, who represented a majority in their districts. The frontier was so drawn as to deprive Hungary of any share in the fertile lowland within and to the west of the Banat, to whose complexity of population reference was made on an earlier page. If the views of the majority of local inhabitants had been taken into account, the Hungarian frontier would have been extended southwards, so as to include an additional thirty miles along both banks of the Tisa River, in a downstream direction.

Once again, this time in the drawing of the eastern frontier, there was discrimination against the Magyars. From the point where the Hungarian, Slovakian, and Rumanian boundaries all met, in the upper course of the Tisa, southwards to the convergence of Hungary, Rumania, and Yugoslavia, the frontier kept wholly within the Danubian Plain. In consequence, Rumania was granted a fringe of lowland to the west of the Transylvanian Plateau, though this annexation was not warranted by the geographical limits of her nationality.

If the frontier of Hungary on this side had been carried east to an average depth of twelve miles, at the expense of Rumania, there would have been no injustice to the legitimate claims of the latter. Unfortunately, as often happened in 1919, it was decided to set aside the basic principle, on which partition was justified, in favour of an economic concession to a friendly people.

Immediately to the west of the foothills of Transylvania a railway passes southwards, by way of Oradea, Arad (a big junction on the Maros River), and Timisoara, to the Danube, immediately above the Iron Gate. To it Rumania laid successful claim on the grounds of the need of her westernmost provinces to be brought into direct contact, through its agency, with the capital of Bucharest. There was also the Rumanian intention to tap the westward-flowing commerce of the outermost Transylvanian valleys, whose natural orientation is towards the Plain of Hungary. Neither of the reasons given was adequate, for the railway mentioned is not the only connecting link of its kind between Western Transylvania and Bucharest; whilst the desire to divert the natural flow of trade away from Hungary is suggestive of the worst forms of economic nationalism, especially when it is remembered how enormous, in aggregate, were the territorial annexations of Rumania after the First World War.

Closely circumscribed within its new frontiers, Hungary lost more than one-half of her former dominions, including a considerable proportion of territory wherein Magyars were a clear majority. In addition, she was deprived of the very considerable Szekler element—several hundred thousands strong—which, in the interior of Transylvania, passionately maintained its Magyar associations. It is generally agreed, however, that Hungarian possession of interior Transylvania is not justified by the presence of an "island" of Szeklers.

The Vienna Award of 1940, by which Germany tipped the Transylvanian balance in favour of Hungary, had an even shorter life than the frontier clauses of the Treaty of Trianon. This at least could be said, however, on behalf of the German partition of Transylvania: that it took into account both Magyar and Ruman claims, and made some attempt to adjudicate reasonably between them. This was not because Germany in 1940 was more virtuous than were Great Britain and France in 1920, but because in 1940 both Hungary and Rumania were allies of Germany. As the frontiers made by Germany during the Second World War were repudiated after that conflict, the details of the Vienna Award need not be examined too closely. It was worthy of note, however, that, in order to attach a large proportion of the Szeklers of the upper Maros and upper Oltu valleys to Hungary, a long triangular wedge of Hungarian territory was drawn south-eastwards from the north-eastern frontiers of Trianon Hungary, as far as the great angle of the Transylvanian Alps between Wallachia and Moldavia. Judging from the deep penetration of this Hungarian "wedge" into the very heart of Rumania, and from the echoes of Rumanian protests which reached Britain, it would seem that Germany showed an excess of favour to its Magyar ally.[37]

Returning to the Hungary of Trianon, it is conceded that the economic prospects of the State, despite its extensive territorial losses, were considerably more hopeful than were those of Austria. The latter was left with its nationality frontiers intact, but with an inadequate geographical basis for the support of its population, much of it urban; whilst Hungary, though deprived of a deep fringe of lands, to which she had the title of nationality, retained the fertile centre of the Danubian Plain. The soils of the latter are not uniformly rich, for swamp and sterile sand are present in patches, but, taken as a whole, Hungary is still one of the best-endowed wheat and maize lands of Europe. Farm production, which includes great herds of sheep and cattle, as well as abundant grain, is more than sufficient for the needs of the population. Apart from Budapest there is no city of great size, and the capital itself, with eleven hundred thousand inhabitants, is not the equal of Vienna, nor has it as large a proportion of the national population as the Austrian metropolis possesses.[38] Consequently, when Hungary was shorn of vast domains, its population was not reduced to starvation, nor was the threat to the economic and political stability of the State as considerable as in the case of Austria. On the other hand, the country seemed unlikely to develop industries on more than a modest scale, owing to the scarcity of fuel and metallic ores.

More threatening to the future of Hungary than the loss of wide territories was the nation's adherence to a medieval conception of land-tenure. Considerably over one-third of the country was divided

[37] During the Second World War, Hungary gained at the expense of Yugoslavia also. Part of the Banat was detached from the latter.

[38] The population of Hungary in 1939 was rather more than 9 millions. Apart from Budapest there is no town larger than 150,000 inhabitants.

between large estates of not less than 2,000 acres each. Although a promise was made to endow both the landless labourer and the impoverished peasant with adequate plots, there had been, before 1944, little reform of the kind. The clash of interests on the issue of land-tenure remained a source of grave weakness to the State; but it was not to be disregarded indefinitely even by a government of big land-owners.

The political alliance of Germany and Hungary, which common defeat in the First World War served to strengthen, was significant of their anti-democratic outlook. They fostered a common aim, which was to overthrow the Treaties of Versailles and Trianon, and recover their lost territories. An additional circumstance favoured their co-operation. To Germany the Hungarian surplus of grain and live-stock was invaluable because of its abundance and accessibility; whilst Hungary was completely dependent for metallurgical, textile, and other manufactured products upon her highly industrialized neighbour and ally.

GREATER RUMANIA

When it emerged from the First World War, Rumania demanded annexations which brought it to twice its pre-war dimensions of territory and population. Before 1914 it was a nation-state formed from the union of the two great Sub-Carpathian provinces of Wallachia and Moldavia, their limits clearly defined by the river-lines of the Danube and Prut, and by the great crescent of the Transylvanian Alps. The sparsely populated Dobrudja, framed by the angular bends of the lower Danube, was a small Rumanian appendage with a frontage on the Black Sea.

As we have seen, the limits of Ruman nationality extend well beyond the frontiers of Wallachia and Moldavia into Bessarabia, the Bukovina, Transylvania, and the Banat. In none of these, however, can Rumania claim that her nationals are so large a majority as to justify annexation. Yet, in 1919, seizing the opportunity when all her hostile neighbours—Hungary, Bulgaria, and Russia—were militarily helpless, she occupied, with the permission of the Western Powers, all lands where a Ruman minority was considerable. Transylvania, the southern Dobrudja, Bessarabia, and the Bukovina were incorporated, together with the eastern part of the Banat, where, however, the Ruman majority was assured.

In 1939 the population of the kingdom closely approached twenty millions, but over 20 per cent of this number were foreign nationals, mainly Magyars (8 per cent of the total population of the State), Russians (6 per cent), Germans (4 per cent), and Bulgars (2 per cent). A high proportion of the Magyars and most of the Germans were at the very centre of the new Rumania, where their presence as hostile elements was a permanent threat to the unity of the State.

The hostility of Soviet Russia, aroused by its loss of Bessarabia in 1920, could not always be ignored. Unfortunately, the Bessarabian question was enlarged and rendered even more dangerous to European peace by the joint action of the Entente Powers in sanctioning the annexation. Great Britain's guarantee of Rumania's integrity, made in 1939 before the outbreak of war, was intended primarily as a warning to Germany, but, by the Soviet Union, its significance was interpreted differently. Russia had never left Europe in any doubt as to her intention to regain Bessarabia at the first favourable opportunity. The conquest of Rumania (1944) was that chance.

The territorial questions at issue between Rumania and Hungary have already been outlined, and there remains for mention the frontier problem within the Dobrudja. This Black Sea province remained wholly in Rumanian hands from the close of the Balkan Wars of 1912-13 until the German domination of South-Eastern Europe in the Second World War. The loss of the southern part of the Dobrudja by Bulgaria in 1913 represented a forfeit of over 2,000 square miles, of whose mixed population 270,000 were Bulgars. Were the international frontier to be drawn strictly in accordance with the principle of national self-determination there can be little doubt that it would leave the Southern Dobrudja to Bulgaria. It remains to be seen, however, if an equitable partition of the province between the two Powers would be acceptable to both. Inevitably, the recent war has transformed the Dobrudja problem. The Red Army's advance to the middle Danube made it certain that Soviet Russia would demand and acquire a dominant interest in Balkan affairs.

The sympathy of Russia for the impoverished but sturdy Slav peasants of Bulgaria is certain to be a considerable factor in the political future of the lower Danubian region. In their turn, the main body of the Bulgars have long regarded Russia as their ultimate protector; but so long as Rumania held the greater part of the Dobrudja, Bulgaria was isolated from the help which the Great

Power of Eastern Europe alone could extend to her. It would suit the interests of both Russia and Bulgaria if they were to be contiguous in the neighbourhood of the Danube delta, and, with the restitution of Bessarabia to Russia towards the close of the Second World War, Bulgarian annexation of the northern part of the Dobrudja would make contiguity possible.

An estimate of the economico-geographical resources of the Rumania of 1919 includes a number of varied, but potentially rich, regions, ranging from the fertile grain-growing lowlands of Wallachia and Moldavia to the forests and mineral wealth of the Transylvanian Plateau. For its size, the land is endowed with latent resources equalled by few European countries. Wheat and maize are grown in rich abundance,[39] there is much timber available for export, and the petroleum supplies are more plentiful than any to the west of Russia. Wells are distributed along the foothills of the Transylvanian Alps, where they overlook the Wallachian-Moldavian Plain, and the oil is collected and refined at Ploesti, some 35 miles to the north of Bucharest. Before 1939 the supply of refined oil was diminishing, though still more than six million metric tons per annum. Later, under German occupation, Rumania's output probably rose considerably, for Germany, though in control of the greater part of Europe, had no other important natural source of supply. German energy in exploiting the Rumanian wells could be taken for granted.

As in the case of most, if not all, the countries of the "middle tier," between Germany and Russia, Rumania is without the economic organization, the equipment, the craftsmanship, and the capital which are necessary for the effective development of her latent resources. National independence is largely illusory so long as she is indebted to some Power or group of Powers which, attracted by the industrial possibilities present, makes of her territory a "sphere of influence."

In one very important respect the economic rehabilitation of Rumania was undertaken by the nation itself after the First World War. By the laws of 1918 and 1921, all lands held in large estates, which were capable of cultivation, were expropriated and converted into medium-sized holdings. The largest farm unit was limited to

[39] Rumania's wheat crop is normally close on 3,000,000 metric tons, which is about eight times the yield of Austria, and greater even than that of Hungary; and the maize crop is twice as abundant.

200 acres, but, at the same time, care was taken to ensure that the expropriated estates were not so excessively sub-divided as to render economic farming impossible. The standard of farming practice was raised by the establishment of agricultural co-operatives, and production prospered in the years before the Second World War. On the other hand, the rich mineral resources of Transylvania remained largely undeveloped, and where their exploitation proceeded it was largely as a result of foreign capital and enterprise.

THE KINGDOM OF THE SERBS, CROATS, AND SLOVENES[40]

When the plan for a State, based on the three Southern Slav communities, was formulated, it was assumed—rather too readily— that the national differences between the Serbs, Croats, and Slovenes were not so serious as to endanger the proposed federation. After the revolution of 1918, when the Austro-Hungarian Monarchy disintegrated, the Croats and Slovenes were willing to join the Serbs within a single kingdom, so long as a generous measure of autonomy was conceded. Many Croats resisted the union with Serbia because of their conviction that the new State was merely a Greater Serbia.

On an earlier page the geography of the three Yugoslav nations was discussed and their divergencies of outlook were indicated. From the evidence it was clear that Serbia would be the dominant partner of the federation. It is the only one of the three nations with a considerable experience of statecraft and of military organization, whilst its number of nationals is half as large again as the combined numbers of Croats and Slovenes. The very ease with which the supremacy of Serbia was assured made that nation reluctant to grant such political concessions as alone would have made possible the permanence and stability of the union.

Belgrade, which is unsuitably placed as Serbian capital, because of both marginal position and extreme vulnerability to attack, is even more unsuited to the rôle of federal capital of Yugoslavia. The peoples of Dalmatia and the entire western half of the State, including both Croats and Slovenes, do not regard the city as in any way representative of their particular interests. To them it is still an alien stronghold, little more sympathetic than Vienna had been to them in the days of Austrian domination. The Yugoslav Parliament, sitting at Belgrade, appeared as an instrument of Serbian policy.

[40] Renamed "Kingdom of Yugoslavia," in 1929. A Republic was proclaimed in 1945.

Outside the old Serbia, whose geographical nucleus is the Morava valley, there are three main concentrations of regional loyalty in Yugoslavia. One is Zagreb, the capital of the Croats and the second city of the Kingdom; second is Lyublyana, the cultural centre of the Slovenes; third is the Croat population of the Dalmatian littoral, grouped mainly around Fiume, Kotor, Split, and Dubrovnik. The cultural contacts of these ports have been more intimate with Italy than with Serbia. It would be difficult for a geographer to expect success for a Yugoslav Federation which failed to concede a generous degree of autonomy, both cultural and political, to the separate nuclei of population into which the Western Balkans is divided.

The Yugoslav frontiers with Austria, Hungary, and Rumania, respectively, have already been discussed in the sections devoted to those countries, and such departures from the principle of national self-determination as were allowed by the Peace Treaties have been noted. It might have been expected that the former frontier with Bulgaria would be unchanged, for it followed approximately the limits of the Serb and Bulgar nationalities. By the Treaty of Neuilly of 1919, however, the eastern boundary of Serbia was extended eastwards at the expense of Bulgarian Macedonia. It went well beyond the hydrographic divide between the River Vardar and the upper waters of the Struma. This alteration[41] was effected for strategic reasons favourable to Yugoslavia. In particular, it was intended to give greater protection not only to Nis, the focus of Central Serbia, but also to communications along the Morava-Vardar "Corridor." From the standpoint of Bulgaria the frontier change was highly disadvantageous, for Sofia, the capital, was less than forty miles from Serbian territory. There could be no clearer instance of the abandonment of the principles on which the Peace Treaties were ostensibly based, and their replacement by the self-seeking of particular Powers.

As the Yugoslav—and particularly the Croatian—population extends to the Adriatic coast along almost the entire length of Dalmatia, from Fiume to Albania, it might have been expected that at least on this—the maritime side—of the new State, there would be no frontier problem. But imperial Italy was ambitious to be a

---

[41] The Yugoslav frontier was advanced in four localities, each of which had a population predominantly Bulgar: they are, from north to south, the Timok valley, Tsaribrod, Boseligrad, and the Strumnitza district.

Power of the Balkan Peninsula and to dominate the Adriatic from both sides.

Italian settlement and cultural penetration along the Dalmatian coast were discussed in an earlier chapter, and we have now to relate the post-war (1919) political partition of Dalmatia to the claims of Yugoslav and Italian nationalism. A geographical coincidence should be noted between the extent of Italian colonization and the occurrence of a narrow zone of "Mediterranean" climate and vegetation—suited to the experience of the Italian!—along the Adriatic edge of Dalmatia. Nowhere does Italian settlement extend more than fifteen miles inland. Moreover, in 1919, Italian territorial claims, based on the historic importance of the Dalmatian cities—Ragusa (Dubrovnik), Spalato (Split), and Cattaro (Kotor)—all of Italian foundation, could no longer be based on the national sentiment of the inhabitants. Only here and there, notably the fringe of Istria and the cities of Trieste and—more doubtfully—Fiume, was there in 1919 a localized numerical superiority of Italians over Croats and Slovenes.

Italy had been induced to enter the First World War by Great Britain and France, which, in the secret Treaty of London (1915), had given their consent to Italian annexation of Trieste, the entire Istrian Peninsula, the northern half of the Dalmatian coast (including Zara), and the Trentino. The natural desire of the Yugoslavs to possess satisfactory ports on the Adriatic led them strenuously to contest the Italian claim to Fiume, in particular. Though both Trieste and Fiume have large numbers, if not majorities, of Italians, the surrounding districts are overwhelmingly Yugoslav—either Croat or Slovene—in allegiance. Each depends for its commerce on access to a hinterland comprising the Northern Balkans and the Danubian Plain, and neither is essential to the life of Italy, as Fiume certainly is to Yugoslavia. Italian annexation of both ports[42] was an indefensible act of aggression, part of the blame for which was shared by the Allied Powers which supported Italy. Close by the commercial centre of Fiume is the suburb of Susak, whose population is almost wholly Croat. Susak was left within Yugoslavia, though its harbour was small compensation for the loss of the first-class port facilities nearby.

The peninsula of Istria, which juts seawards between Trieste and Fiume, was also lost by Yugoslavia, though its population is pre-

---

[42] Fiume was proclaimed a "free city," but was finally annexed by Italy in 1924.

dominantly Croatian, save on the outer coastal strip. And this was not all. In recollection of the terms of the secret Treaty of London (1915), Italy laid claim to some of the best harbours of Northern Dalmatia. Zara was granted to her, and this port possessed the only considerable Italian colony to the south of Fiume. In addition, Italy annexed a number of islands close inshore.

In all post-war Europe there was no parallel to this legalized domination by one Power of its neighbour's littoral. Italy could well claim that the Adriatic was now a Roman lake—as, indeed, it was described by Benito Mussolini—and that no longer were the deep, island-studded inlets of Dalmatia a source of danger to the harbour-less coast of Eastern Italy, as they had been when Austrian submarines lurked in them.

There is no Dalmatian harbour, south of Fiume, which is accessible to a hinterland of more than a few square miles. The ancient ports of Ragusa and Spalato had based their wealth, not on contacts with the Balkan interior, but on a large share of the carrying trade of the Eastern Mediterranean. The trend of the compressed folds of the Dinaric Alps forbids the construction of any but the most difficult mountain-road between the coast and the Danubian lowlands of Yugoslavia; and south of Fiume there is no opportunity of developing a national port. For this reason the Belgrade Government was interested in obtaining access to the Albanian ports of Durazzo and Valona, which, however, were to pass under Italian influence.

On their southern side the Serbian provinces extend down the valley of the Vardar to within 45 miles of Salonika. This great port is by far the most suitable gateway for the commerce of the eastern half of Yugoslavia, and the Serbs have not concealed an old ambition to reach the Aegean frontage by way of the Vardar corridor. Greek control of Salonika seems, however, to be assured so long as the national allegiance of its population is selected as the test of sovereignty.

In magnitude and in the variety of its regions the Yugoslavia of 1919 compared favourably with the other Balkan Powers. Its northern plains provide an abundant harvest of grain—maize and wheat especially—whilst the wide expanses of its deeply-riven plateau conceal a most varied, if dispersed, wealth of minerals. The list of mining products is imposing, and includes soft coal, iron, chrome, copper, lead, bauxite, and antimony, all of which were being developed on a steadily increasing scale in the years before the Second World War. Yugoslavia, unprovided with adequate capital, has been unable to make the fullest use of its mineral resources. Moreover, because the latter are widely scattered and in some cases difficult of access, there has been no inducement to foreign interests comparable in scale with the foreign financing of Rumanian petroleum.[43] Of great detriment to Yugoslavia, as to all Balkan countries, is the tendency for foreign control of mining development to produce minerals for export, not for native industry.

A very large proportion of Yugoslavia's industry is dependent upon the products of native agriculture. Flour-milling, sugar-refining and the preparation of tobacco are three of the most typical activities of the kind. Yet tillage and stock-rearing most characteristically represent the economy of this peasant nation. Before 1914, peasant proprietorship was already widespread in Serbia, and after the First World War it was mainly in the former Hungarian lands of the Drava and Sava basins that large estates existed. These were soon divided into peasant plots, but a serious agrarian problem remained for many years. At first, the majority of the peasant holdings were too small for economic working, and Government was concerned both to increase the size of individual plots and to improve the generally depressed standard of agriculture, more particularly in the arid parts of Dalmatia and the backward districts of Southern Serbia. As in the case of Rumania, the growth of farmers' co-operatives was officially encouraged. By its earnest attention to the economic welfare of the peasantry the Yugoslav Government, in the period between the World Wars, did much to counteract the disintegrating influence of the separatism of Croats and Slovenes. Yet the lot of the peasant throughout the greater part of the mountainous interior, where soils are poor or thin and transport is primitive, remains difficult, as, indeed, it does within the Balkan Peninsula, as a whole.

THE EMERGENCE OF ALBANIA

On an earlier page reference was made to the impediments in the way of Albanian national unity. Although statehood has been recognized, internationally, for more than thirty years, there has been little

[43] Foreign capital is, however, an important factor. Down to 1939 a French company was responsible for a large part of the copper produced, whilst British capital helped in the development of the lead ores.

evidence of increasing national cohesion or of nationally organized resistence to foreign aggression. Close proximity has given Italy the opportunity to complete its domination of the Adriatic by closing the narrow entrance from both sides.[44] After the passing of Turkey from the Western Balkans and the disintegration of the Austro-Hungarian Monarchy, there was nothing but the sporadic and unorganized resistance of Albanian mountaineers to prevent the extension of an Italian protectorate over the immature State.

As late as 1912, when the First Balkan War was fought, the geographical limits of Albanian nationality had not been properly determined. At that time the right of Albania to statehood had hardly been fully recognized by the European Powers. Serbia joined Bulgaria and Greece for the purpose of eliminating Turkish influence in the western half of the peninsula, and planned to obtain outlets to the Adriatic coast at Valona and Durazzo, under her own sovereignty. Her ambitions were not, however, realized—largely owing to the influence of Austria-Hungary. The latter had no intention of permitting Serbian expansion—and a German prince, with the consent of the Powers, accepted the crown of Albania in 1914. During the First World War, Albania lay under the military control of Austria, but it was then that the Western Powers promised to cede to Italy at least the southern part of the country, including the port of Valona.

In all these moves, on which the fate of Albania depended, the clansmen of the country played no effective part. Impoverished and disunited, largely as a result of geographical conditions within their difficult terrain, they were quite unable to co-operate for mutual defence. After the First World War the frontiers of the State were drawn to correspond, for the greater part, with the approximate limits of Albanian nationality. Serbia (Yugoslavia), however, protested that, because of a war-time promise to herself made by France and Britain in 1915, and also because of the presence of a majority of Slavs in the population of the lower Drin basin, the latter should not have been left within Albania. With the Drin valley in her possession, Yugoslavia would have controlled the only direct highway, itself mountainous and difficult, between the Morava-Vardar "corridor" at Skoplje (Uskub) and the Adriatic coast.

Italian imperialism proceeded to weigh heavily on Albania,

[44] The Straits of Otranto are but fifty miles across.

especially after the rise of Fascism. From 1924 onwards, all financial and economic control was in Italian hands and was exerted through the Italian "bridgehead" at Valona. The annexation of Albania by Mussolini in 1939 shocked the democratic world, but was merely the logical conclusion of a process of which, in its earliest stages, the Western Powers had themselves approved.

For the years which succeed the Second World War the status of Albania provides a formidable problem. Without economic and political assistance, its future will be precarious, yet dependence on some Power or group of Powers will menace its sovereignty. Such indeed is the dilemma in which all the weak and backward States of Europe find themselves. With a population of little more than one million, scattered over an inhospitable, mountainous land,[45] Albania's basis of statehood is geographically inadequate, and union with a friendly neighbour, willing to grant it autonomy, would seem to be inevitable, sooner or later. It is possible that such autonomous existence may be secured within the framework of Yugoslavia, or of a wider Balkan federation, as proposed (1945) by Yugoslavia.

THE BULGARIAN FRONTIERS

No country of similar size has suffered more from war than Bulgaria. Within thirty-five years, the nation has engaged in four campaigns, with disastrous consequences to man-power and material resources.

The sympathies of Western peoples have been estranged, largely because of the pro-German policy of the reigning house, itself of Teutonic origin; yet the mode of life and the aspirations of the Bulgarian peasantry are little different from those of the Serbs, who have been assured of the friendship of the Western Democracies. Between Serb and Bulgar there is no difficulty which could not be removed by the elimination of the ambitions of their respective dynasties. Unfortunately, their territorial disputes have been exploited by certain of the Great Powers in their own interests, and there has been little opportunity for friendly relations to develop. Another factor which has worked against stability in Bulgarian political life

---

[45] At the last census, taken in 1930, the population was 1,003,000, over an area of 10,630 square miles. The average density of 94 per square mile conceals no important concentration of population. Less than one-tenth of Albania is cultivated.

is the frequency of the frontier changes to which the country has been subjected, since it gained its freedom from the Turk in 1878.

On the other hand, given peace, the Bulgars have a better opportunity than most Balkan peoples to attain a well-balanced economy. They have two advantages which a disastrous foreign policy has not been able entirely to dissipate. First, the national area is a compact geographical entity composed of a number of regions which make a rich and varied contribution to the agricultural wealth of the State. Within the limits of the Balkan Peninsula no region surpasses, in spaciousness and fertility combined, the basin of Eastern Rumelia, situated between the Rhodopian *Massif* and the Balkan Mountains. It is the heart of Bulgaria, with a many-sided agriculture in which wheat, the principal crop, is accompanied by the vine, cotton, and tobacco. The mineral wealth of the country, though considerable, is little developed.

The second advantage of the country is the democratic basis of land tenure. Most of the peasants are small proprietors with holdings varying between two and six acres. As a whole, despite the extent of mountain, Bulgaria, even within its present narrowly drawn frontiers, is an adequate homeland. Rather more than six million inhabitants occupy some 40,000 square miles. They are overwhelmingly rural in their distribution, and only the capital, Sofia, and the much smaller Plovdi (Philippolis) exceed one hundred thousand inhabitants.

Their economic needs satisfied, the Bulgars are likely to be a contented people now that their Government has become more truly representative of the country's interests. Economic subordination to Germany, steadily increasing year by year, was characteristic of the period between the World Wars. It was an enslavement for which the court party was primarily responsible.[46] Liberation from Germany came finally in 1944, when the Red Army advanced across the lower Danube, to be welcomed by the great mass of the Bulgar population.

Bulgaria lost considerably in territory in consequence of the Second Balkan War. By the Treaty of Bucharest, 1913, she forfeited a share of the partition of ex-Turkish Macedonia between the Balkan Powers. Northern Macedonia, including Uskub (Skoplje), then passed to

[46] In 1938 the imports derived from Germany exceeded those from all other countries combined; in exports there was even greater dependence on the German market.

Serbia, and Southern Macedonia, including Salonika, to Greece. This partition showed little respect for the wishes of the Macedonians who, as we discussed in a former chapter, include many, if not a majority, of Bulgarian speech. In addition, also by the Treaty of Bucharest, Bulgaria lost the southern districts of the Dobrudja to Rumania; and here again, the transfer of territory had nothing to do with the wishes of the inhabitants affected.[47]

Embittered by her territorial losses, Bulgaria was easily tempted by Germany's declared plan for the re-partition of the Balkans, and she joined the Central Powers in 1915. Defeat three years later confirmed the former gains made by Rumania, Greece, and Serbia at her expense, whilst Greece made new and very formidable gains to her detriment.

By the Treaty of Neuilly, 1919, Bulgaria lost in Western Thrace her frontage on the Aegean Sea, though some attempt to lessen the blow was made by economic concessions. Bulgaria was to receive a permanent lease of the port of Dedeagatch, the government of which was to be in the hands of an international commission. To all such proposals Bulgaria objected that they were no satisfactory substitute for full rights of sovereignty over Dedeagatch. If we apply the test of nationality to Greece's successful claim to Western Thrace, the distribution of Bulgar and Greek populations certainly does not seem to warrant the complete exclusion of the Slav State from the Aegean coast. From an earlier reference to Yugoslavia it will be recalled that, by the terms of the Treaty of Neuilly, Bulgaria also lost four small, but strategically important, districts on her western frontier. These went to Yugoslavia, but no care was taken to consult the wishes of the people who were thus transferred.

THE PARTITION OF THRACE

In the previous chapter the great difficulty was noted of drawing the political frontiers of Greece in such a way as to take account both of the scattered distribution of Greek nationals throughout the Aegean, and of the legitimate aspirations of the Bulgars and Turks. In 1919 the Allied and Associated Powers were prepared to be generous to the Hellenic cause, not least because the people had

---

[47] After the outbreak of the Second World War, Bulgaria regained the southern districts of the Dobrudja from Rumania, and the frontier was placed back again at the line of 1912. This involved a gain of 2,800 square miles by Bulgaria.

expelled their pro-German king and had entered the war. Victory in the Balkan wars of 1912-13 had brought Greece big territorial gains in Macedonia and the northern parts of Epirus and Thessaly, but her claim to Thrace was still unrealized. The virtual elimination of Turkey from Europe was expected to be one result of the First World War, and, as Bulgaria also was to be punished for her part in that conflict, Greece had high hopes of annexing the entire seaboard of Thrace, to and beyond the Maritza River.

Claims to Thrace rested mainly on the considerable numbers of Greeks in the population, and less solidly, on the historical prominence of Greek culture at Constantinople. The complex character of population within Thrace prevented any accurate statement, save that it was highly unlikely, even if the Greeks were the largest single element, that they were a majority of the population. A decision was reached not so much by the action of the Western Powers as by the political and military revival of Turkey under Mustapha Kemal. Having defeated the French attempt to incorporate Cilicia within the mandated territory of Syria, Turkey drove the Greek population from Western Anatolia. Moreover, Kemal was able to re-annex Eastern Thrace, as far westwards as the north-to-south line of the lower Maritza, from a point above Adrianople down to the Aegean coast.

In view of the large additions made to her coast-line in Macedonia and Western Thrace, during the first two decades of the twentieth century, Greece cannot complain if Eastern Thrace is withheld. There seems to be no good reason for depriving Turkey of Eastern Thrace, and so the Ottoman retains his foothold in Europe. Equity suggests, however, that the Bulgarian claim to an outlet on the Aegean should receive consideration. Preferably, it should be in Western Thrace, for there is no harbour of importance, open to the Aegean, in Eastern Thrace. The Turco-Bulgarian frontier is a reasonable approximation of the limits of the two nationalities, but they are so intermingled that no boundary could divide them without leaving considerable minorities on either side.

By the Treaty of Lausanne, 1923, which finally determined the frontier between Greece and Turkey, most of the Aegean islands lying close in to the Anatolian coast were left in either Greek or Italian hands. Unquestionably, the populations of almost all the islands are Greek, and the award to Greece was thus justified. The strategic importance of the islands to the defence of the Turkish coast, however, would have been viewed differently had Turkey ranked as a friendly Power. The annexation by Italy of the Dodecanese Islands, off the south-western coast of Anatolia, had no justification. Italy first occupied this group of thirteen islands at the close of the Italo-Turkish War in 1912, though she promised to evacuate them within a short time.

THE EAST BALTIC STATES

The four non-German, non-Slavonic nations, distributed along the eastern littoral of the Baltic, gained their political independence almost automatically with the dissolution of the Tsarist Empire in 1917-18. Of the four, only Finland had experienced some measure of autonomy,[48] so that the sudden accession of sovereign statehood by Estonia, Latvia, and Lithuania, without political apprenticeship, involved a considerable degree of risk. The new Republics had at least one advantage: they were well-defined nation-states and the frontiers which they claimed gave, on the whole, no offence to the principle of national self-determination. Yet limited as they were by the same principle, they were all small in population, and only one exceeded three millions. All were acutely conscious of their vulnerability, squeezed as they were between Germany and Russia, by one or other of which they had been conquered in former time. And they were destined to see their territories overrun again and again before the middle of the present century.

Soviet Russia recognized the independence of the four Republics by the Treaty of Dorpat (1920). Later she showed clearly that she intended to restrict their sovereignty at the first suitable opportunity, but there is no evidence that Soviet Russia is less sympathetic to national autonomy in Estonia, Latvia, and Lithuania than in the non-Slavonic republics of her Union.

Opposition to the possibility of renewed Russian expansion came more particularly from Finland, and the relations between these two unevenly matched Powers could hardly have been worse than they were in the interval between the World Wars. Without doubt, it is the Swedish Finn minority, with political influence out of all proportion to its numbers, which has shown the most marked hostility

[48] Finland was united to the Russian Empire, in 1809, as an autonomous Grand Duchy.

to Russia. Its political authority within Finland has been such that it has been difficult for the outer world to appreciate that there is in the country a considerable population—possibly a majority—whose antipathy to Russian influence is less than to Swedish.

The Russo-Finnish frontier of 1920 was generous to the Finns. They were granted the eastern coast of the Varanger Fjord, and were able to incorporate the very useful, ice-free port of Petsamo. Farther south, the frontier closely followed that of the former Grand Duchy, and Finland had little ground for complaint. Nevertheless, she claimed the right to extend eastwards over the entire region of the forested Karelian plateau, her intention being to incorporate about 200,000 Karelian Finns, intermingled with whom were considerable numbers of Great Russians. The Soviet Union not only rejected Finnish claims to Eastern Karelia, but considered much of the population of more westerly parts of Karelia, hitherto within Finland, to be Russian.

In 1939, however, Russia proposed to Finland an exchange of territory by which Finnish claims over Eastern Karelia might be realized. In return, she asked for certain small areas, regarded as vital to the military, naval, and aerial defences of the Soviet Union. Convinced that Germany was preparing to attack her, Russia intended to strengthen her geographical position in the Gulf of Finland, with special reference to the defence of Leningrad. The great northern metropolis of Russia and its suburbs occupies the narrowest part of the Karelian Isthmus, which separates Lake Ladoga from the Gulf of Finland. Much the greater part of the Isthmus was left to Finland after the First World War, and her frontier at one point came within fifteen miles of Leningrad. Russian military reasons for demanding the cession of the Karelian Isthmus, in return for Eastern Karelia, were therefore easily explained.

The seaward approaches to Leningrad are interrupted by a chain of small islands which are closer to the Russian than to the northern coast of the Gulf of Finland, but, in 1939, were not Russian-owned. The best known of these islands is Suursaari, or Hogland. Russian demands on Finland included not only the Isthmus and the Hogland group, but also Hangö, at the south-western tip of Finland, where an open-sea position permits navigation throughout the winter. In 1940, Russia gained the peninsula of Hangö on a lease of thirty years, but was forced to evacuate it when Germany, shortly afterwards, occupied both coasts of the Gulf of Finland. It is certain that, in her final settlement of accounts with Finland, Russia will demand that Hangö, the islands and the Isthmus shall not be left within the grasp of a Power hostile to her own interests.

In the entrance to the Gulf of Bothnia, and closer to the Swedish than to the Finnish coast, lie the Aaland Islands. Their sovereignty was Swedish until 1921, when, by a recommendation of the League of Nations, they were awarded to Finland. Sweden accepted her loss with very good grace, and her attitude was the more magnanimous in that the Aaland population—in all less than 20,000—was almost entirely of Swedish nationality. Finland claimed that, in foreign hands, the islands were a potential menace to her own security, though Sweden might have argued with equal justice along similar lines. By the terms of an international convention, Finland was not permitted to fortify the islands. The Aaland settlement would have been one of the brightest episodes in the brief career of the League of Nations, but for the exclusion of Russia from decisions important to her welfare as a Baltic Power. Shortly after the defeat of Germany, in 1945, the Swedish majority on the islands gave notice that they were no longer prepared to remain under Finnish sovereignty.

In view of its very small population—rather less than four millions in 1942—the vast area of Finland is something of an embarrassment, because of the demands on man-power for both defence and economic development which are involved. Of its 134,000 square miles—considerably larger than the British Isles—only the southern coastal fringe is at all densely populated, and the northern half of the country has an average density under seven to the square mile. It is, however, the scantily populated areas which support Finland's greatest wealth —her vast forests of conifers. These cover two-thirds of the entire area, and no country of the world has, in proportion to its size, an equal reserve of timber. Inevitably, lumber and its products, notably paper, dominate the export trade, so that all other items combined are not of comparable importance.

Farming is closely restricted to the southern coastal districts, where climate and soil make possible the cultivation of the hardier cereals, particularly oats and rye, as well as the rearing of cattle. Finnish agriculture is on a high technical level and shows the influence of Swedish standards. Long before separation from Russia was achieved, the co-operative ideal had spread to Southern Finland, where it received a new impetus. Co-operative societies not only organize production of commodities for export; they provide loans and equipment to the farmers, in addition to facilities for agricultural education. Despite the high standards of farming, however, the harshness of the Finnish climate restricts cultivation to a very small fraction of the total area, and Finland must import much of her food.

The Baltic Republics situated to the south of the Gulf of Finland are not only smaller in area, population, and economic resources than Finland, but are much more vulnerable to pressure, exerted either by Germany or by Russia. They lie across Russia's path to the Baltic, and their ports, especially Riga, owed their commercial distinction more to their relations with the Russian hinterland than to their local functions.

Estonia emerged as a nation-state, covering an area (18,400 square miles) smaller than Ireland, and with a smaller population (1,100,000) than any country of Europe. The demand of the Estonian peasants for independence was spontaneous, and was welcomed by the Europe of 1918. Yet were there many Europeans who feared that the young State would meet with almost insuperable difficulties in attempting to preserve its integrity. Not sufficient attention at the time was paid to the inevitable resurgence of both Germany and Russia, and to its consequences for the weak countries of the Eastern Baltic.

Within a zone of Europe, where the intermingling of nationalities makes difficult the demarcation of political frontiers, Estonia has the considerable advantage of being free from large foreign elements. Russians, to the number of about 91,000, who come just within the eastern frontier, represent the only important alien group. The German Balts, once of outstanding influence, were repatriated in 1939 by arrangement between Germany and the Soviet Union. Important to the welfare of the State is the geographical compactness of its population. The frontier with Russia and with Latvia is almost exactly co-terminous with the limits of Estonian nationality; for part of the way it traverses Lake Peipus from north to south, and comes to within sixty miles of Leningrad. It satisfied both Estonian and Russian aspirations before the Second World War, and is likely to remain for administrative purposes now that the entry of Estonia into the Soviet Union is an accomplished fact.

In the furtherance of her plan of defence, to meet the expected German attack, Russia in 1939 demanded and seized two large Estonian islands—Hiiumaa and Saaremaa[49]—which lie in the entrance to the Gulf of Riga, together with the very useful winter port of Baltiski. As in the case of her temporary control of the Finnish bases, Russia was forced by Germany in 1941 to abandon all Estonian territory. The occupation indicated very clearly, however, the extent of Baltic control which Russia was likely to demand for her own security when Europe returned once more to peace.

Latvia, but little larger in area than Estonia, resembles it also in the size and compactness of its population. The frontiers which define it leave no considerable Lettish community outside, but even after the recent withdrawal of the German Balts two considerable minorities—Russian and Jewish respectively—remain. Whether or not these alien minorities were the cause, Latvia seemed more ready than were the other East Baltic States to co-operate with the Soviet Union in the years before 1939. The commercial interests of the great port of Riga are necessarily bound up with the economic development of that part of Western Russia which forms its effective hinterland. Thus in the sphere of economic geography the tendency for Latvia and neighbouring parts of Russia to be drawn together supplies an argument for that federation of the small Republic within the Soviet Union which the Second World War brought about. A similar argument might be extended to the East Baltic States generally.

Cut off, after 1917, from the Russian hinterland, the ports of Latvia suffered a period of acute depression. Between 1927 and 1932, however, both trade and industry quickly revived, in response to the Commercial Treaty of that period between Latvia and the Soviet Union; but later there was renewed decline, when relations between the two Powers deteriorated.

Early in the Second World War, Russia occupied certain bases in Latvia which she regarded as vital to her western defences. The ports of Liepaja and Ventspils, on the open Baltic, were the main objectives of her occupying force which, however, in 1941, retreated in face of the German advance.

Unlike her sister Republics of the Eastern Baltic, Lithuania, from the outset of her political career, was threatened with disintegration.

[49] Better known as Dago and Osel, respectively.

Two main factors contributed to the difficulties which arose. In the first place, the Lithuanians, in the south-west and south-east of their national area, are considerably mixed with either Germans or Poles. It has already been shown that, by their control of the lower Niemen outlet at Memel, the Germans had long been able to dominate the commerce of the river. Memel Territory, including the port and a coastal strip, in all about 1,100 square miles, was, in 1919, detached from Germany and placed under international supervision. Later, its unlawful seizure by Lithuania was viewed indulgently by the Powers, and by the Convention of the following year the Territory passed under the sovereignty of Lithuania.

An even greater difficulty confronted the youthful State in its relations with Poland. The city of Vilna, in the uppermost part of the Niemen basin, marks approximately the convergence of the White Russian, Polish, and Lithuanian nationalities. Immediately to the east of the city, White Russians predominate, whilst to the west, between it and Kaunas (Kovno)—the Lithuanian capital—Poles are almost as numerous as Lithuanians. Nevertheless, in Lithuanian tradition Vilna is regarded as the national capital, though its position, outside the zone which is exclusively Lithuanian in nationality, can never make it more than an outpost of Lithuanian influence.

At the end of the First World War, the Military Control Commission of the League of Nations awarded the town and district of Vilna to Lithuania, and at the same time confirmed Polish sovereignty over the town of Suwalki, north-west of Grodno and close to the East Prussian frontier, which had been in dispute between Lithuania and Poland. In 1920, the Polish Government agreed to the Vilna settlement, but within a few hours a Polish army seized the city. Poland attempted to deny responsibility for this breach of faith, though no attempt was made to restore the city to Lithuania. Vilna remained in Polish hands until it was assigned to Lithuania in October 1939, on the initiative of Russia.

Had the League of Nations refused to confirm the Polish seizure of Vilna it might have retained international respect. Its acceptance of the decision of the Conference of Ambassadors (1922), to recognize Poland's occupation of the city, was most damaging to its reputation, especially amongst the small Powers. The warning to the little nations was now clear and ominous: the League had neither a will of its own nor impartiality, but was merely the instrument of the Great Powers which dominated it.

One consequence of the annexation of Vilna was that Polish and Lithuanian relations were strained almost to breaking point. The frontier between the two countries remained closed for eighteen years. A further consequence was Lithuania's complete distrust of the international control of the Memel Territory. Almost immediately after the Vilna episode, the Lithuanians, employing the successful methods of the Poles, seized Memel, and, as in the case of Vilna, the act was quickly recognized by the Powers.

Hostility to Poland brought Lithuania to a more sympathetic mood in her relations with Soviet Russia. It was significant that, when the Great Slav Power occupied the East Baltic States (south of Finland) early in the Second World War, Vilna and a long strip of territory which Poland had annexed in 1920 were conceded to Lithuania. In this way Russia removed the Polish wedge between herself and Lithuania. These territorial changes were made as part of the wider agreement between Germany and the Soviet Union, whose main result was the partition of Poland.

There was little doubt, before the end of the Second World War, that Russia intended to re-unite Lithuania to herself. The frontiers of the new Soviet Republic include not only Vilna and its neighbourhood, but Memel also. As part of the Soviet system, however, Lithuania will no longer depend on the Niemen corridor and the port of Memel for its access to markets. The commercial advantages which federation with Russia will undoubtedly bring—not to speak of the greater possibility of security—should go far to reconcile the more extreme elements in Lithuanian nationalism to the loss of sovereignty. Independent of Russia, Lithuania would always live precariously and with a very restricted economy, for its resources are limited to its timber, flax, and hardy cereals. United to Russia it will share in the industrialization of that great country, and its agricultural standards are not likely to remain as depressed as they were in the period between the World Wars.

Little versed in statecraft as the East Baltic States were, during their brief period of sovereign independence, they were nevertheless aware of the advantages which federation would bring. Unfortunately, they were unable to eliminate those tendencies towards individualism which were well illustrated by their mutual competition in trade and industry. Lithuania was particularly apprehensive of the commercial and industrial advantages possessed by Latvia and of its possible economic leadership of any proposed federation. For their part, Latvia and Estonia, with similar resources of field and forest, were competitive rather than complementary to each other, so that federation seemed to offer to neither any marked economic advantage.

An early, if abortive, attempt of the small East Baltic Powers to co-operate was made in 1920, when their delegates, and those of Poland, met at Riga. Agreement was not reached on any important issue, and since that time further meetings, concerned mainly with economic affairs, have failed to produce a common plan. Yet the urgency of the need for mutual arrangements has been fully appreciated. After the violation of her territory at Vilna in 1920, Lithuania declined to attend any Baltic conference to which Poland was invited. The political relations of the East Baltic Powers, other than Poland and Lithuania, were reasonably amicable, but the differences of language, religion, and tradition—not to speak of ethnic dissimilarities—which divide them, permitted separatist tendencies to triumph, down to the time of the Second World War.

Had federation succeeded, the union of Finland, Estonia, Latvia, and Lithuania would have brought together a population of not more than ten millions, which is but the strength of a comparatively small Power, according to modern standards. Moreover, the material resources of such a federation would be on a very modest scale. There is no important source of industrial strength. Coal and petroleum are deficient and, excepting Finland, opportunities for the development of hydro-electric energy are not particularly extensive. Equally serious is the scarcity of important industrial ores, and in this respect the three southern Republics are again less fortunate than Finland. An East Baltic federation would not, therefore, be the equivalent, in population or resources, of a Great Power. Its security and stability would be rendered precarious, not only by internal stresses but also by external pressure, exerted particularly by Russia, Germany, and Poland. It seems likely that, throughout Eastern Europe, the influence of Soviet Russia will be supreme for one or two decades at least, and that any political system which operates within the East Baltic region will require the sanction of Moscow.

THE EASTERN FRONTIERS OF POLAND

In our reference to the frontier changes affecting Germany, Lithuania, Czecho-Slovakia, and Rumania the boundaries of the Poland which emerged from the First World War have been discussed on every side save the eastern, facing Russia. Except for the partition of the central Carpathians between Poland and Slovakia, all other Polish frontiers were notable for the difficult international issues which they raised. By far the longest boundary between Poland and a neighbouring State was the eastern, and, on this side, the question was not one of merely adjusting local territorial claims in the interests of one side or the other. The issue was whether or not Poland was entitled to one-half of the territory which it acquired on the collapse of the Russian Empire. (v. Appendix B.)

We have already noted that, in regard to the expansionist activities of Poland—in the fourteenth century particularly—a clear distinction should be drawn between actual colonization and the extension of Polish influence, based mainly on the ownership of large estates, within Little and White Russia. The eastern frontier of Poland which most closely approximates to the facts of nationality keeps to the west of the Pripet Marshes. It follows a line from Bialystok to Brest-Litovsk, keeps close to the River Bug for a considerable distance, and then trends to the south-west, so as to leave Lwow (Lemberg) in Russia. The frontier proposed by the Western Powers at the Peace Conference of 1919—the so-called "Curzon Line"—closely approximated to the nationality division, but was rejected by Poland. War followed, between Poland and Russia, as a result of which Marshal Pilsudski was able to annex huge tracts of White Russia and Little Russia. Allied statesmen seem never to have been able to impress upon Poland the danger to its own security incurred by the incorporation of large hostile groups. Certain it was that Poland would lose all chance of retaining the Russian lands as soon as the strength of the Soviet Union grew to exceed its own. On the territorial issue alone there was no possibility of neighbourly relations between the two Powers in the interval between the World Wars.

The extent of territory lying between the "Curzon Line" and the actual eastern frontier fixed by Poland (1919) was not less than 60,000 square miles, or some two-fifths of the entire area of Poland, as it was in August 1939. One of Poland's purposes was to include a considerable area of the Pripet Marshes, whose wastes, almost equally divided between Poland and Russia, became a "marcher" zone between the two countries. Thus, needs of military defence were invoked to reinforce territorial claims, whose main justification depended on a reading of events five centuries old, when much of Western Russia was regained from the Tatars by Polish enterprise. To the north and south of the Pripet Marshes, the way is broad and open between Poland and Russia, as, for example, where the wheat lands of Galicia merge imperceptibly with those of the Ukraine. Geography, indeed, makes impossible the defence of the Polish plains against the full weight of a Russian invasion.

Faced with the bitter hostility of Russia, Germany, and Lithuania —incurred by reason of their large territorial losses—the new Poland began her career inauspiciously. Her principal friend was France, but the sympathetic interest of the latter was based rather on fear of Germany than on more positive values. As Teutonic strength increased, the authority of France in East-Central Europe declined, until the likelihood of her armed intervention on behalf of Poland was completely eliminated. The impossibility of Britain and France, together or separately, guaranteeing the integrity of the Polish frontiers in the face of German or Russian aggression should have been apparent, long before the Second World War, to statesmen equipped with the most elementary knowledge of geography. Yet, both France and Britain were involved in that war because of just such an impossible guarantee.

Added to the enmity of powerful neighbours was Poland's embarrassment of having within her borders large minority groups, which were unlikely ever to be incorporated into the nation. One out of every three of Poland's inhabitants was not a Pole. The Russian element, made up of Little Russian (or Ruthene) and White Russian, constituted about 20 per cent of the total population. Apart from the Jews, whose distribution was widespread throughout the towns of Poland, the minorities, Russian and German mainly, were geographically compact. Over considerable areas they were an actual majority of the population, so that the likelihood of their ever being assimilated was remote, indeed. Moreover, the expulsion or maltreatment of minorities was expressly forbidden by Poland's treaty responsibilities, though the terms of that treaty were not scrupulously respected.

A further complication for the new Poland was the failure of its leaders to satisfy the needs of the peasantry for both land and an adequate share in the government of their country. The basis of that leadership was aristocratic, and there was a marked contradiction between Poland's centuries-old fight against oppression and the undemocratic order which prevailed as soon as national independence was once again attained. A very large proportion of the land—as much as 40 per cent—was left to a handful of landowners, many of whom showed little interest in its cultivation. The landed estates of the gentry were particularly prominent in the eastern parts of the country, where the Russian population was situated. In consequence, the conflict between the Poles and the Russian minority possessed an economic as well as a political aspect. (v. Appendix A.)

Unlike the majority of the countries of the "middle tier," between Germany and Russia, the new Poland inherited very considerable industrial resources which were already widely developed before the First World War. The incorporation of the Upper Silesian coal-field —or the greater part of it—together with deposits of iron and zinc, made Poland potentially one of the leading industrial Powers of the continent. She was fourth in Europe in respect of coal production, and the output of zinc exceeded that of any European country. Moreover, the Galician supplies of petroleum were not only adequate for her own needs, but provided also a considerable surplus for export.[50] The Warsaw-Lodz industrial district, with its own supplies of coal, became, before the close of the nineteenth century, one of the leading producers of textiles in Slavonic Europe.

The industrial activity of Upper Silesia, in particular, but of other parts of Poland also, had been due mainly to German and Jewish enterprise. When the new Poland emerged, it was doubtful how far the nation would be able to organize its own industrial future, free from foreign assistance; for Poland had no industrial class of its own. German and Jewish interests continued to influence development, and Poland did not follow the Russian example of training a technically efficient population, so as to make mining and manufacturing industry a vigorous national enterprise. When she eagerly accepted the challenge to combat offered by Germany in 1939 she went into

[50] Mined coal was over 38 million metric tons in 1938. In the same year the output of zinc and iron ores had risen to the record figures of 108,000 tons and 873,000 tons, respectively, whilst petroleum remained constant at about 500,000 tons per annum.

battle confident that her cavalry, reminiscent of heroic days, would be a sufficient answer to the technically-equipped divisions of her enemy.

SELECTED BIBLIOGRAPHY

"Alsace-Lorraine, L" (vol. 1, *Travaux du Comité d'Etudes*), Paris, 1918.

A *Manual of Belgium and the Adjoining Territories* (with separate atlas), Stationery Office, n.d.

ANCEL, —.: "L'Europe Centrale," *Manuel de la Géographie Politique*, vol. 1.

Atlas de Finlande, atlas and 2 vols. of text, Helsingfors, 1911.

BARKER, J. ELLIS: *The Foundations of Germany*, London, 1916.

BEAUVOIS, E.: *La nationalité du Slesvig*, Paris, 1864.

BENEŠ, E.: *Bohemia's Case for Independence*, London, 1916.

BOWMAN, I.: *The New World*, 4th ed., London, 1928.

BRAUN, G.: *Deutschland*, Berlin, 1916.

BRYCE, R. L'E.: "The Klagenfurt Plebiscite," *Geogr. Journ.*, vol. 60, 1922, pp. 112–25.

CLAPHAM, J. H.: *The Economic Development of France and Germany, 1815–1914*, 3rd ed., 1928.

CLARE, C. L.: *The Brenner Pass*, London, 1912.

COLBY, C. C. (ed.): "Geographic Aspects of International Relations" (*Lectures of the Harris Foundation, 1937*), Chicago, 1938.

DAWSON, W. H.: *The Evolution of Modern Germany*, new ed., 1919.

DEMANGEON, A.: "Belgique, Pays-Bas, Luxembourg" (Tome 2, *Géographie Universelle*), Paris, 1927. See also other tomes of *Géographie Universelle*.

DEMANGEON, A.: "La Bulgarie," *Ann. de Géogr.*, vol. 29, 1920.

DEMANGEON, A.: *La Valachie: Essai de monographie géographique*, Paris, 1902.

DOMINIAN, L.: *The Frontiers of Language and Nationality of Europe*, New York, 1917.

DUMAS, P.: "Le Partage de la Haute-Silésie," *Ann. de Géogr.*, vol. 31, 1922, pp. 1–14.

EISENMANN, L.: "La Nouvelle Hongrie," *Ann. de Géogr.*, vol. 29, 1920, pp. 321–33.

FOUQUES-DUPARC, J.: *La Protection des Minorités*, Paris, 1922.

GILFILLAN, S. C.: "European Political Boundaries," *Political Science Quarterly*, vol. 39 (September 1924), pp. 458–84.

HARTSHORNE, R.: "A Survey of the Boundary Problems of Europe," in Colby, ed., *Geographic Aspects of International Relations*, pp. 163–213.

HARTSHORNE, R.: "Geographic and Political Boundaries in Upper Silesia," *Assoc. Amer. Geographers*, vol. 23 (December 1933), pp. 195–228.

HARTSHORNE, R.: "The Polish Corridor," *Journ. of Geog.*, vol. 36 (May 1937), pp. 161–76.

HARTSHORNE, R.: "The Upper Silesian Industrial District," *Geog. Rev.*, vol. 24 (July 1934), pp. 423–38.

HASSINGER, H.: *Die Tschechoslowakei: Ein geographisches, politisches und wirtschaftliches Handbuch*, Vienna, Leipzig, Munich, 1925.

HOLDICH, SIR T. H.: *Boundaries in Europe and the Near East*, London, 1918.

JASZI, O.: *The Dissolution of the Habsburg Monarchy*, Chicago, 1929.

JESSEN, F. DE: *La Question du Slesvig*, 1906.

JORGENSON, —.: *La Question dano-allemande*, Copenhagen, 1900.

La Commission Européenne du Danube et son oeuvre de 1856 à 1931, Paris, 1931 (contains many maps).

LADAS, S. R.: *The Exchange of Minorities: Bulgaria, Greece, and Turkey*, New York, 1932.

LYDE, L. W.: *Some Frontiers of To-morrow: an Aspiration for Europe*, London, 1915.

MACARTNEY, C. A.: *Hungary and Her Successors*, Oxford, 1937.

MACKINDER, H.: *Democratic Ideals and Reality*, London, 1919.

MAIR, L.: *The Protection of Minorities*, London, 1926.

MARRIOTT, J. A. R., and ROBERTSON, C. G.: *The Evolution of Prussia: the Making of an Empire*, Oxford, 1915.

MARRIOTT, J. A. R., and ROBERTSON, C. G.: *The Expansion of Prussia*, 1915.

MARTNA, M.: *L'Esthonie*, Paris, 1920.

MILOJEVIC, B. Z.: "The Kingdom of the Serbs, Croats, and Slovenes," *Geogr. Rev.*, vol. 15, 1925, pp. 70–83.

MOODIE, A. E.: *The Italo-Yugoslav Boundary*, London, 1945.

MORROW, —.: *The Peace Settlement in the German-Polish Borderlands*, Oxford, 1936.

MOSCHELES, J.: "Natural Regions of Czechoslovakia," *Geogr. Rev.*, vol. 14, 1924, pp. 561–75.

NAUMANN, F.: *Central Europe*, trans. by C. M. Meredith, London, 1916.

NEWBIGIN, M. I.: *Geographical Aspects of Balkan Problems*, 2nd ed., 1919.

NOWACK, E.: "A Contribution to the Geography of Albania," *Geogr. Rev.*, vol. 11, 1921, pp. 503–40.

OGILVIE, A. G.: "A Contribution to the Geography of Macedonia," *Geogr. Journ.*, vol. 55, 1920, pp. 1–34.

OGILVIE, A. G.: *Some Aspects of Boundary Settlement at the Peace Conference*, London, 1922.

PALLIS, A. A.: "Racial Migrations in the Balkans during the Years 1912–24," *Geogr. Journ.*, vol. 66, 1925, pp. 315–31.

PASVOLSKY, L.: *Economic Nationalism of the Danubian States*, New York, 1928.

RATZEL, F.: *Der Lebensraum*, 1901.

ROMER, E.: *Atlas géographique et statisque de la Pologne*, 2nd ed., Warsaw, 1921.

RONAI, A.: *Biographie des frontières politiques du centre-est européen: étude politico-géographique consacrée à l'histoire des frontières*, Budapest, 1936.

RUTTER, O.: *The New Baltic States and their Future*, London, 1925.

SETON-WATSON, H.: *Eastern Europe between the Wars (1918-1941)*, Cambridge, 1945.

Survey of International Affairs, 1932, Part IV, Chapter IV: "The Relations between Germany and Lithuania over the Memel Treaty."

Survey of International Affairs, 1932, Part V: "North-Eastern Europe."

TELEKI, P.: The Evolution of Hungary and its Place in European History, New York, 1923.

TEMPERLEY, H. W. V. (ed.): History of the Peace Conference of Paris, 6 vols., London, 1920.

The Vilna Problem, Lithuanian Information Bureau, London, 1922.

TOYNBEE, A. J.: Nationality and the War, London, 1915.

WAMBAUGH, S.: Plebiscites since the World War, Washington, 1933.

WEIGERT, H. W.: Generals and Geographers, New York, 1942.

WHITTLESEY, D.: German Strategy of World Conquest, London, 1944.

5.

The Soviet Experiment in Political Geography

THE WESTERN FRINGE OF IMPERIAL RUSSIA

Although much reduced by losses after the First World War, Russia emerged from that conflict with incomparably the largest, compact area of the world under one government. The lands that were taken from its western flank stretched, end-to-end, nearly all the way from the Arctic to the Black Sea, and contained much of the developed wealth of the Tsarist Empire. They included the forests of the Eastern Baltic, the flax of Estonia and Latvia, the grain of Bessarabia, and the manufactures of the Warsaw-Lodz industrial zone. Almost equally serious to Russia was the loss of all her Baltic ports, save one. Her western window, opened by Peter the Great, was again almost closed, and the other bordering seas were of little use to her. The Black Sea offered no highway to the Mediterranean and the Atlantic, for the Straits of the Dardanelles were closely watched by Powers, formerly allies, but now the most implacable of her foes. The Arctic was, for the Russia of 1918, not a sea but an enormous barrier of ice: whilst the Northern Pacific, on to which the precariously held port of Vladivostok opened, was dominated by her Oriental opponent, Japan.

The industrial development of Russia, in days before the Revolution, had been concentrated in the western provinces of the Empire, and more particularly in those territories which were lost as a result of the First World War. This was not because the economic resources of the western fringe were more abundant than those of other regions. The wealth of the Asiatic lands was a quite unknown factor, although, by the end of the nineteenth century, it was thought likely to prove immense when opportunities for its investigation and exploitation were possible. The absence, however, of an adequate industrial organization in European Russia, and the completely primitive condition of all lands to the east of the Ural Mountains seemed certain to postpone the development of Siberia and Central Asia to a very remote future. These regions, early in the twentieth century, were isolated by the greatest overland distances of the earth and by the backwardness of all means of communication, save only the newly built Trans-Siberian Railway. Thus, until the second decade of this century, the strength of Russia was measured—in the estimation of all other Powers—solely by the resources of the small fraction which was European. Even to-day the possibilities of Russia's vast continental hinterland are but dimly realized by those who think in terms of the Tsarist Empire of 1914.

The Russian Government of the years before the First World War was largely dependent for industrial capital and technique on the advanced countries of Europe.[1] The western provinces, including the non-Slavic Baltic territories, comparatively easily accessible from the west, were geographically the most convenient for foreign enterprise. So it came about that a very high proportion of industry was located in western cities, including the great seaports—Riga and St. Petersburg (renamed Petrograd and, later, Leningrad). Towns clustered most densely near the western fringe of European Russia —a distribution which was significant of the comparative closeness of contacts with Central and Western Europe, rather than a gauge of the superiority of local industrial resources. There was, for example, a general dearth of coal and of other mineral wealth. The only considerable supplies of iron-ore were mined at Krivoi Rog, to the west of the lower Dnieper. On the other hand, the Donetz valley of the Don Basin, rich in coal, was inadequately developed, partly because it lay on the outer edge of the sphere of foreign enterprise in Russia. It was not productive on a considerable scale until the late years of the nineteenth century.

On the basis of its own inadequate resources Western Russia could never have become of first-class industrial importance. Never-

[1] Financial and technical assistance came from several countries of Western Europe—including Belgium, which had a particularly prominent part in the development of the iron and steel industry of Southern Russia.

theless, technical standards and the general level of life were higher in the occidental provinces than elsewhere in the Empire, at the outbreak of the First World War. Moreover, the density of population distribution within the Baltic fringe, Russian Poland and Bessarabia was considerably higher than the average for European Russia as a whole. So that, for the reasons given, the loss by Russia of all her outer European provinces seemed well-nigh irreparable. When these considerations were added to the dislocation caused by the presence of several hostile armies on her best soil,[2] and by the widespread ravages of pestilence and famine, the possibility of Russia retaining its cohesion seemed small indeed.

THE ASIATIC LANDS OF THE TSARIST EMPIRE

The territories lying to the east and south-east of the Ural Mountains were annexed at a comparatively late stage, and some were not fully incorporated within the Empire at the outbreak of the First World War. As a result of the political and economic chaos within European Russia during the period 1917-19, it was fully expected (in Western Europe and America) that they would detach themselves from the political allegiance so recently forced on them, and that the entire Empire would disintegrate. Events flatly contradicted this widely held view, and no achievement of the Soviet Union has excelled the consolidation which it accomplished within a year or two, thereby uniting in a federal State the Russian lands of Europe and the non-Russian territories of North and Central Asia.

Eastward penetration of Russian influence beyond the Urals did not occur until the close of the sixteenth century. In the first place, it was not part of a plan of organized conquest, nor was it evidence of the imperialistic ambitions of the Tsars. It was primarily concerned with trade—in furs particularly—and was organized by Russian merchants of the Urals. Its military aspect was confined to the activities of freebooting Cossacks, who sometimes were hired for the defence of merchant convoys.

The first region to be traversed was the vast plain of Western

---

[2] In 1919-20 the newly created Red Army had to contend against the following anti-Bolshevik forces: the army of Wrangel in the Crimea; of Kolchak in Siberia; of Poland in the Ukraine; of Rumania; of Great Britain at Archangel; of Japan in Eastern Siberia. The Japanese army penetrated as far west as Lake Baikal before it was forced to retreat.

Siberia, half as large as Europe without Russia, and mainly within the drainage area of the Ob-Irtish river-system. Most of the old Siberian towns began as fortified trading posts, and the dates of their foundation illustrate Russian progress across Siberia. Tomsk, in the upper Irtish basin, and close to the ramparts of the lofty plateaux of Central Asia, was founded in 1625. From that time onwards the movement eastwards was rapid. Yakutsk, within the great bend of the River Lena, began its career only seven years later, as the headquarters of further trading expansion as far as the Pacific coast. The territories traversed, though diversified in configuration and of different climates and vegetation, were alike in their scanty populations, so that there was no serious opposition to the advancing traders. The distances involved were enormous. From the Urals to Tomsk is about 1,000 miles by air, and Yakutsk is another 1,600 miles farther. There are 4,500 miles between Moscow and the Pacific coast of Vladivostok (founded 1860), or nearly twice the distance separating the western and eastern extremities of Europe.

Physically, the native inhabitants of Siberia and Central Asia are clearly differentiated from the Russian Slavs. They belong to one or other branches of the great Mongoloid stock, which is widely distributed over Central and Eastern Asia. Many are descendants of the Turki-Tatar communities which provided the armies of Genghiz Khan and Kubla Khan in the thirteenth century. Under a variety of tribal or local names, and despite wide differences of language, they are alike in their principal physical features. They show marked breadth of head, together with straightness of hair, whilst the typical Mongoloid characteristics of yellow skin and slant eyes also occur. The geographical distribution of these widely-scattered communities has not greatly altered since the days of the earliest Slav pioneers in Asia, but in recent time there has been a considerable intrusion of Slav elements, as a result of large-scale colonization from Russia.

In so far as the advance kept approximately to one main route, it passed immediately to the south of the Siberian taiga by way of the restricted zone of good grassland, between the forests of Northern Siberia and the high, semi-arid plateaux of Central Asia. This was the route followed later, for a large part of the way, by the Trans-Siberian Railway. To the east of Lake Baikal the advance diverged along two lines. One went eastwards to the Pacific coast, much of which, north of Korea, was explored during the late seventeenth century; the other led south-eastwards to the Vitim Plateau, which forms the hydrographic divide of the great rivers, Amur and Lena.

On the Vitim Plateau the Russian traders came into contact with Mongol tribesmen, who gave them their first information concerning China. Contact with the outposts of the Chinese Empire (Manchu dynasty) was made in the region of the upper Amur, where it was necessary for the Russians to avoid trespass on lands under Manchu sovereignty.

At Nerchinsk (upper Amur), in 1689, the first treaty negotiated between China and a powerful State was signed. Russia and China defined the limits of their respective empires on the summits of the Vitim Plateau, and from that time onwards the interpenetration of Russian and Chinese civilizations proceeded. Russia's long, unbroken and, on the whole, friendly contacts with China have given her an advantage over other Powers which have entered the Far Eastern sphere. Moreover, the differences of culture between Russia and China are less, by reason of the Central Asiatic elements in both civilizations, than those between China and all occidental Powers. For these reasons it has been suggested by some students of Far Eastern affairs that if any Power can help China to remould its civilization politically, socially, and industrially, along "Western" lines, that Power is Russia.

Until the nineteenth century there was no serious colonization by Russian Slavs of the North Asiatic lands, from the Urals to the Pacific. Moreover, Russian imperialism was little interested in its newly-acquired Oriental dominions, for either strategic or economic reasons, until the middle of last century. Then, largely because of the defeat of Russia's attempt to reach a maritime outlet, by way of the Bosphorus and Dardanelles, the Tsar's Government looked Pacific-wards with a greater ambition than ever before. The pressure of Russia on China—in Manchuria, particularly—was then intensified. Russian colonization of Northern Manchuria became important, though it was never able to affect fundamentally the much more extensive flow of Chinese peasantry into the same region. Defeat in the war of 1904-5, with Japan, excluded Russian influence from Southern, but not from Northern, Manchuria. The Chinese Eastern Railway, completed in 1903, as a short cut across Manchuria from Chita to Vladivostok, remained under Russian ownership until the Japanese "drive" into Manchuria in 1931.

Tsarist imperialism brought about Russian expansion in one further direction during the second half of the nineteenth century. The region formerly known as Russian Turkestan extends from the shores of the Caspian, eastwards to the high mountain country north and west of the Pamirs, where the empires of Russia, China, and British India converge. It comprises two contrasted geographical units: first, the arid grasslands of Turkestan; second, the well-irrigated intermontane valleys, renowned throughout history for their rich sub-tropical agriculture and prosperous trade, and famed also for their cities—Tashkent, Samarkand, Khokand, and others besides.

Around these historic marts of Turkestan were grouped greater concentrations of population than were to be found elsewhere within the Asiatic sphere of Russia. Opportunities for Slavonic colonization were, therefore, smaller than on the grasslands of Southern Siberia, whose tribes were, in general, nomadic. No considerable infiltration of population from Russia accompanied the annexation of territory between the Pamirs and the Caspian, save in the case of the Kazak steppe. The settled life of the agricultural valleys of the upper Oxus and Syr Darya permitted a relatively high standard of civilization. Indeed, there was considerable national development amongst the Turkmens, Uzbeks, and others, which, however, the Tsarist Government attempted to suppress.

In no other part of Asiatic Russia were there, prior to the Soviet régime, wholly or partially developed national communities, except in the confined area of the Caucasus. The Georgians and other non-Slavonic peoples on the flanks of that great mountain system were brought within the Empire of the Tsars early in the nineteenth century. They had already developed, however, a sense of nationality, which the oppression of the Tsars during the nineteenth century failed to obliterate. Such communities were on a definitely higher social and political plane than were the tribesmen of Siberia, as was recognized when Soviet authority extended across Asia.

Concerned primarily as they were with the pressing problems of Slavonic Russia, the revolutionary leaders of 1917 and subsequent years could not have been blamed if the enormous task of restoring the former Russian hegemony over Siberia and Turkestan had proved too great for their strength. Their Asiatic problems were fourfold.

In the main, they were (1), to pacify the vast area and to incorporate it fully within the Soviet Union; (2), to assist the cultural and political development of those peoples who were desirous and capable of autonomous evolution; (3), to survey and exploit, industrially, the vast latent wealth, whose extent was as yet but vaguely conjectured; and (4), to introduce large numbers of European Russians to sparsely populated regions, in order to make such industrial development possible.

In their struggle against disintegrating tendencies, the leaders of Soviet Russia were threatened with the secession of a number of communities. Certain peoples of the vanished Tsarist Empire were uncertain of their political future, but more because of the anti-Bolshevist attitude of the outer world than because of any fear they might have of the principles on which the new Russia was based.

THE GEOGRAPHY OF THE FEDERAL PLAN

By 1921 or 1922 the vast assemblage of European and Asiatic territories and peoples, inherited by the Soviet Union from Tsarist days, was welded into a federation of republics, from which the possibility of internal disruption and external assault steadily receded. It is noteworthy, in view of this triumph of the principle of federalism, that neither history nor geography was favourable to it. There was the greatest possible diversity of race, tradition and custom, language and physical environment. Few outside Russia prophesied the integration and consolidation of the Soviet Union. Many denied the possibility, even when successive years gave evidence of a rapidly increasing measure of success. The triumph of the system, on its cultural and political sides particularly, must be attributed to the power of ideas to surmount the obstacles imposed by geography and tradition.

The Soviet régime was established first over Great Russia and Siberia. The Russian Soviet Federal Socialist Republic (R.S.F.S.R.) came into existence in November 1917, largely as a result of the activities of the Petrograd Soviet of Workers and Soldiers. At that time, Petrograd was not only the capital of the Russian Empire, but easily the greatest industrial centre.[3] Its artisan population was,

---

[3] The population of Petrograd in 1913 was 2,319,000; in 1939 it was 3,191,000. A comparison with Moscow is interesting. The latter—now capital—rose from 1,817,000 in 1913 to 4,137,000 in 1939.

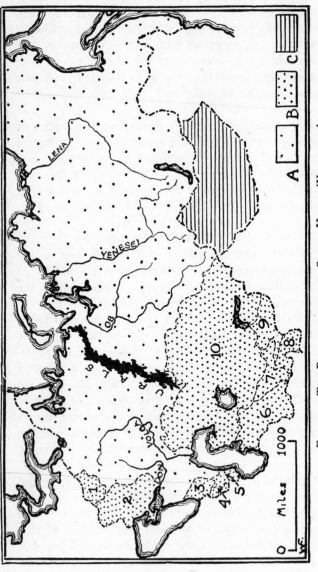

FIG. 22.—THE REPUBLICS OF THE SOVIET UNION (YEAR 1942)

A.—The Russian S.F.S.R.
B.—Other Republics shewn as follows:

1. White Russian S.S.R.
2. Ukrainian S.S.R.
3. Georgian S.S.R.

4. Armenian S.S.R.
5. Azerbaijan S.S.R.
6. Turkmen S.S.R.

7. Uzbek S.S.R.
8. Tadjik S.S.R.
9. Khirghiz S.S.R.

10. Kazak S.S.R.

C.—The Mongol Peoples' Republic, affiliated to the U.S.S.R.

politically, more alert and active than any other community of Russia. In 1918 the First Constitution of the R.S.F.S.R. was adopted, and served as a model for the other Soviet Republics which, within a few years, joined the R.S.F.S.R. to form the Soviet Union.

Despite the subtraction, from time to time, of communities promoted to the status of Soviet Republics, the R.S.F.S.R. still occupies about 90 per cent of the total area of the U.S.S.R. Its population—approximately 120 millions—is Great Russian to the extent of four-fifths. The remaining one-fifth is made up mainly of certain widely-dispersed Asiatic peoples who are backward politically, and some still in the tribal stage of development. The progress of most of the politically-primitive peoples of Soviet Asia has been, however, quite phenomenal during the last two decades. As a community, under encouragement from the Central Government, grows to acquire national consciousness, it is awarded the privilege of enhanced political status. It may graduate from the rank of Autonomous Soviet Socialist Republic to Soviet Socialist Republic, as the Kazak and Kirghiz communities, respectively, have done within recent years.

In 1917 there was widespread illiteracy amongst the nomadic Kazaks ("Freemen") and their kinsmen, the Khirghiz, farther to the east, whilst for long the Tsarist Government had attempted to stamp out any incipient growth of national consciousness amongst them. As late as 1916 there was no registration of births and deaths. Yet in the same year the attempt was made to conscript the tribesmen en masse into the Imperial Army of Russia. Had it succeeded it would have utterly destroyed their corporate life.

Within the Federal system, the Kazak S.S.R. and the Khirghiz S.S.R.[4] have not only been granted cultural autonomy; they have graduated, within the last few years, to full political equality with the more mature communities of the Soviet Union. Such concessions are in advance of local demands, and the loyalty of the more backward Asiatic peoples to the Central Government—on which they are directly represented—may thereby be appreciated. Here there is

[4] The Kazak S.S.R. covers an enormous area—over one million square miles—extending as far westwards as the steppe to the north of the Caspian and, eastwards, beyond Lake Balkash. Its population is, however, only 6,146,000 (1939), so that the density is but 6 per square mile. The Kirghiz S.S.R., with 76,000 square miles and 1½ million inhabitants, occupies part of the high plateau on the Siberian side of the Thian Shan.

evidence that the political structure of Asiatic Russia is in process of unceasing evolution.

In the angle bounded by the Caspian and the northern edge of the Iran Plateau, almost as far eastwards as the Pamirs, there are three Republics, all senior in age to Kazakstan and Khirghizia. The Turkmen S.S.R., considerably larger than Great Britain, but with only one and a quarter million citizens, is passing comparatively quickly from a nomadic stage of civilization, though the sparseness of its population continues to be a measure of the aridity of its grasslands. The dry pastures provide wool, as they have done since the dawn of history, but the coming of the irrigation engineer has enabled the Republic and its neighbour—the Uzbek S.S.R.—to meet all the needs of the Union in respect of raw cotton.

Uzbekistan, like Turkmenistan, received the status of a fully fledged Republic in 1924. Its level of culture is generally higher and Nature is more bountiful than on the Turkmenian steppes, especially as regards water-supply. The Uzbeks, who form a large majority of the population, practised intensive agriculture long before the Revolution, and most notably in the highly fertile district between Tashkent and Samarkand.

As in the case of all other Republics of the Union, the Uzbek S.S.R. is based on its own distinctive nationhood. With only one-third the area of the Turkmen S.S.R. it has five times the population of the latter. Indeed, it is the most densely populated of all Soviet lands to the east of the Caspian, and may be termed the "centre of gravity" of Russian Central Asia. Never since the days of Tamerlane (fourteenth century), who had his capital at Samarkand, has Turkestan contributed so much to the life of Asia. It is at the very heart of the Old World, and certain students of international affairs —Sir Halford Mackinder amongst them—foresee its pivotal position in the world of the future. Tashkent, capital of the Uzbek Republic, is incomparably the greatest industrial and cultural focus of Russian Central Asia. It has shared in the phenomenal growth of most towns of the Soviet Union, and its population,[5] considerably more than half a million, is concerned in an ever-widening range of manufacturing industries, including cotton textiles and agricultural

[5] At the enumeration of 1939 the population of Tashkent stood at 585,000; in 1900 it was barely 100,000. The city ranks eighth in the Soviet Union, and is the only one of Central Asiatic Russia which exceeds half a million inhabitants.

machinery. In Uzbekistan, as elsewhere in Soviet Asia, particularly rapid increase of population has been more marked in urban than in agricultural districts, in consequence of special concentration on mining and manufacturing. In the twenty years from 1914 to 1933 the percentage of urban population in the lands of the U.S.S.R. rose from 18.5 to 24.3 of the total population.

One other Trans-Caspian Republic is to be noted. It is the Tadjik S.S.R., whose parity with its Sister-States of the Union was proclaimed in 1929. Amongst the smallest, in both territory and population (56,000 square miles; population, 1,485,000), it is also one of the most backward. In this case, without doubt, the recognition of nationhood was, to some extent, in advance of the fact, and was intended to stimulate national development. Great wealth of minerals—asbestos, corundum, etc.—lies hidden in the mountain land of the Tadjiks, and it is inevitable that mining enterprise will change the social and economic life of the Republic within a short space of years.

Before leaving the five Trans-Caspian Republics it is noteworthy that most of their nationals are Moslems. One of the outstanding achievements of the Soviet Government has been to propagate its ideas in the Islamic zone of the Union, without offence to the followers of the Prophet.

The chain of Republics distributed along the southern edge of the R.S.F.S.R. is continued across the Caspian into the highland of the Caucasus. Georgia, Armenia, and Azerbaijan were formerly united in a federation within the larger federation of the Soviet Union. They trace the recognition of their independent nationhood, in each case, to the early days (1919-21) of Soviet Russia. The former federation[6] of these three communities, markedly diverse as they are in respect of ethnic origins, language, tradition, and religion, seems to have been instituted temporarily for reasons of administrative convenience. It was unique as a political experiment, and its temporary existence, followed by the recognition and emergence of three separate Republics, is further evidence of the adaptability of the Russian administrative system in the face of ever-changing circumstances. The rigidity of the divisions separating the nations of Western and Central Europe is in striking contrast; yet the European

[6] The Trans-Caucasian Soviet Federal Socialist Republic was established in 1922, by agreement between the three Republics.

nations are no more diverse, racially and culturally, than the communities which make up the Soviet Union.

Of all territories incorporated within the U.S.S.R., Georgia, Armenia, and Azerbaijan seemed the least likely to remain within the Russian orbit at the conclusion of the First World War. Situated between the Turkish and Tsarist Empires, they had long experienced the friction resulting from a clash of imperial interests. Both Empires, however, collapsed within a few months of each other (1917-18), and, in the view of the Western Powers, neither was likely to regain its former authority. France and Britain planned to divide the southern territories of Russia into two spheres of interest. Britain claimed the Caucasus and the Kuban, and proceeded to send in an occupying force. Meanwhile, a French army landed at Odessa, in order to occupy the Ukraine. When both Powers were forced to withdraw, the League of Nations, in complete ignorance—or disregard—of events in Russia, discussed the advisability of placing the entire Caucasus region under a Mandate. It was believed by the Western Powers that local antagonism and the scattered distribution of the Armenians and Tatars made virtually impossible the determination of nationality frontiers. At this juncture, in 1921, Russia moved south into the region and brought all the peoples of the Caucasus within her political embrace.

Whereas the League of Nations concentrated its attention on the difficulties, real or supposed, in the way of the demarcation of the Georgian, Armenian, and Azerbaijan frontiers, Russia was able to reach a speedy and satisfactory settlement without similar embarrassment. It granted autonomy, without sovereign independence, and eliminated the vexed minority question by gaining the loyalty of each community to a super-national State, itself a league of nations of unique design.

To the geographer, certain features distinguish the three Trans-Caucasian Soviet Republics, and provide interesting comparisons with their more immature neighbours, to the east of the Caspian. They are all on a miniature scale—Azerbaijan, the largest, is but 32,700 square miles, which is exceeded even by Tadjikistan, smallest of the Trans-Caspian Republics—but their densities of population are higher than those of any other Asiatic lands of the Union. Moreover, the proportion of urban inhabitants in the population of each Republic is considerably above the average for the U.S.S.R., as a whole.

The *tempo* of industrial development has been particularly lively under Soviet administration, though, even in former days, Baku—capital of Azerbaijan—had become the leading centre of petroleum output in the Old World. This city has experienced an expansion within the last quarter of a century which, if not unprecedented, is hard to parallel, and has placed it amongst the great industrial centres of the world. In 1918, its population was some 250,000, but, by 1939, that figure had increased more than threefold. Even in most of the early years of the Soviet régime, when Russian industry was passing through a particularly difficult phase, and its critics in other lands foretold its imminent collapse, the oil output of the Baku district continued to expand. Within recent years the rise in Russian oil production has been quite extraordinary, and is still due more to the intensive development of the resources around Baku than to the opening-up of new reserves in other parts of the Union—important as the latter are, or will become.

The Georgian centre of Tiflis is the second great focus of urban and industrial life within the Trans-Caucasus. Its growth has been more leisurely than that of Baku—from 327,000 in 1913, to 519,000 in 1939—though in any city of Europe, west of Russia, a percentage increase of sixty within the short space of a quarter-century would be regarded as vigorous enough. No centre of life in Armenia is comparable with Tiflis or Baku, but it is to be remembered that the Armenians are a widely scattered people, who are to be found in many parts of Trans-Caucasia as well as Eastern Anatolia. Indeed, in Georgian Tiflis itself, a high proportion of the townspeople are of Armenian origin.

Outside the eight Soviet Republics, whose distribution and characteristics we have outlined, the remainder of Asiatic Russia is wholly within the frontiers of the R.S.F.S.R. It will be remembered that the R.S.F.S.R. predominates in European as well as in Asiatic Russia; and it is obvious that the conventional division of Europe and Asia along the axis of the Ural Mountains is more arbitrary and unsuitable nowadays than ever it was. To-day, it has no significance in Russian political geography, and is completely disregarded.[7]

The vast territories of the R.S.F.S.R. are divided for purposes of

[7] Far from being a frontier zone, the Central Urals form the heart of an administrative unit—the industrially important Sverdlovsk Area—whose boundaries extend up to one hundred miles or so on either side of the Urals.

administration into a variety of units, differing little in status but widely in their dimensions. Down to the time of Russia's entry into the Second World War, the Asiatic mass of the R.S.F.S.R. was administered in three vast "regions" (*oblasti*)—namely, the Western Siberian, the Eastern Siberian and the Far Eastern—which were in addition to the Yakutsk and Buriat-Mongol Autonomous Republics. Since then, however, the "regions" have been further sub-divided, for they were altogether too unwieldy for purposes of government.

The two Autonomous Republics differ enormously from each other in respect of size. The Buriat-Mongol State lies to the south and east of Lake Baikal, and is of fairly modest proportions, with a population of about half a million. The Yakutsk Autonomous Republic includes the basin of the River Lena and much besides. Perhaps the most convincing way in which to indicate its dimensions is to compare it with India: it is much greater than the combined Provinces, and nearly as large as the entire Indian Empire. Yet its population is but 401,000, and the density per square mile almost insignificant, namely, 0.3. In these two so-called Autonomous Republics the gesture of self-government is offered, but life is still insufficiently organized on a national scale to permit the grant of status equal to that of the Trans-Caspian Republics. At the same time there is a definite nucleus of community life, and the graduation of the population to full national status—as in the case of the Kazaks, for example—may be expected.

All lands to the east of the Urals are in urgent need of population, when it is considered what vast resources of minerals, timber, and soil they are known to contain. They are virtually empty, although in Western Siberia—the Kuznetsk coal-basin, particularly—the position is changing fast, as a result of trends in colonization to which we shall refer later.

To the west of the Urals, a similar division of the R.S.F.S.R. into "regions" and "autonomous republics" holds true. The mass of the population is Great Russian, but here and there occur non-Slavonic communities, whose right to a considerable degree of autonomy is recognized. Full national status is withheld, either because the groups are too small to make self-government efficient, or because national consciousness has not fully developed. In this connexion it may be added that it is against Russian theory and practice to carry the process of territorial sub-division so far as to threaten the efficiency of government. Decentralization of administrative powers for certain recognized ends—e.g., the preservation of what is valuable in the culture of particular regions—is axiomatic in Soviet policy, but it is not allowed to affect the cohesion of the Federation. Solidarity is dependent on unity in matters of defence, foreign policy, and comprehensive planning of the salient aspects of economic life; and no considerations of local interest are permitted to obstruct the grand design. That such a federal plan is acceptable to individual national communities within the U.S.S.R. is no longer denied.

Several Autonomous Republics of the R.S.F.S.R. lie within the basin of the Volga and in the Northern Caucasus. They include Tatar and Ugro-Finnic peoples; and the community of Volga Germans, until 1941, was also numbered amongst them. Down to that year, this, the most easterly of all German groups in Europe, was permitted a considerable measure of cultural autonomy, on Volga lands well below Kuibyshev. In consequence of the deep penetration of the German armies, Kuibyshev—formerly Samara—was chosen as the "reserve" capital of Russia, whereupon the proximity of the Volga Germans became an embarrassment to the Soviet Government. For that reason they were moved *en masse* to Western Siberia.

To the west of the Great Russian zone in Europe, two full Soviet Republics proclaim the nationhood of the Little Russians (Ukrainians) and White Russians (Belorussians),[8] respectively. Along with the R.S.F.S.R. and the Transcaucasian Soviet Federal Socialist Republic (1922-36), they are foundation members of the Soviet Union. Their geographical limits, as national groups, were outlined in Chapter 3, where it was made clear that very large proportions of their lands were annexed by Poland after the First World War. In 1939, when Russia reclaimed all territory occupied by a majority of either White Russians or Ukrainians, Poland again experienced partition. It was then evident that Russia would not tolerate Polish sovereignty over lands farther east than the "Curzon Line."[9] More-

[8] "Belorussian" avoids confusion between two entirely different uses of the term "White Russian." One of these refers to the *émigrés* who opposed the Bolshevist Revolution, and, at various times in various countries, plotted against the Soviet régime. The general use of the term applies to the Slav inhabitants of the district to the north of the Pripet Marshes and to the south of Latvia and Lithuania.

[9] On January 11, 1944, the Soviet Government issued a statement of its intentions regarding the frontier with Poland. It referred to the injustice to Russia

over, now that the facts of nationality, in what used to be known as Eastern Poland, are widely appreciated, there will be no enthusiasm among the United Nations for renewed Polish political expansion at the expense of the White and Little Russians. (v. Appendix B.)

Before the re-annexation of former Eastern Poland by Russia, late in 1939, the White Russian and Ukrainian Soviet Republics numbered about five to six million and thirty-one million inhabitants, respectively. As was mentioned in an earlier chapter, almost as many White Russians, as were included in the original Republic, were left within Poland by the peace settlement which followed the First World War. With the restitution of her lands, White Russia is likely, therefore, to possess a population of more than ten millions, on an area of at least 80,000 square miles, much of it forested. The soils of the White Russian lands are not of exceptional fertility, and the density of population is fairly high in view of agricultural possibilities. Nevertheless, the Soviet Government has planned to raise the farming standards, particularly in those parts of White Russia which were formerly inside the Polish frontier.

Industrial development within the original boundaries of the Belorussian Republic was slower and on a more modest scale than elsewhere in well-populated parts of the Union. Two reasons are suggested for this relative backwardness: first, the scarcity, or complete absence, of coal, petroleum, and other important mineral wealth; secondly, proximity to Poland, by way of which a German invasion was anticipated. Avoidance of the establishment of heavy industries close to the Polish frontier was here, as also in the Ukraine, an article of Soviet policy.

Nevertheless, the industrial development of White Russia between 1919 and 1939 was more energetic than ever it had been in Tsarist days. Evidence for this is provided by the growth of the White Russian capital of Minsk which, if not phenomenal when compared with that of more easterly cities of the Union, was considerable. Between 1913 and 1939 its population almost exactly doubled, and a similar trend was noticeable also in the case of Smolensk—of rather

---

permitted by the Riga Agreement of 1921. That Agreement took Western White Russia and the Western Ukraine from Russia. The Soviet Government, while warning Poland against any attempt to restore the Riga Agreement, proposed the "Curzon Line" of 1919 as the approximate frontier, a frontier accepted at the time by the Western Powers.

smaller size—which, though just within the R.S.F.S.R., has a high proportion of White Russians in its population.[10]

Prior to the Revolution no Russian community ranked higher in civilization than the Little Russian. Ancient and illustrious traditions, largely associated with Kiev, gave it pride of place amongst the Russian Slavs. The rich "black earth" of the Ukrainian steppes has been longer under cultivation than any other Russian soil, and better standards of farming practice than the normal for Russia prevailed there in Tsarist days. Fertility of the chernozem and more expert husbandry combined to explain the highest density of rural population within the old Russia.

In more modern days the Ukraine has retained much of its former supremacy in the cultural life of the Eastern Slavs. Moreover, its contribution, in the realm of ideas as well as in material achievement, to the success of the great Soviet experiment is unlikely to be excelled by any community of comparable size within the Union. To mention but one aspect: the "collectivization" of farming—probably the greatest agricultural reform of its kind known to Europe since the passing of feudalism—though not confined to one part of the Union, depended to a very high degree for its success on the devotion of the Little Russian peasantry.

The intensity of Ukrainian national feeling led the Western Powers, after the First World War, to hope that the "black earth" might easily be detached from the Soviet Union, then in process of earliest growth. Had their ambitions succeeded it is doubtful if the enormous loss resulting to Russia could have been repaired. This the Western Powers fully appreciated. What they did not learn from their expert advisers was the impossibility of finding any considerable support for the secession of the Ukraine from Russia amongst the Little Russians themselves. Such support as there was for this unsavoury project depended almost entirely on non-Russian elements—Poles and Germans, particularly. The abortive attempt to partition Southern Russia was as effective as any other episode in creating that suspicion between Western and Eastern Europe which did much to make the Second World War possible.

In July, 1945, it was reported that the Soviet and Czechoslovak Governments had signed an Agreement, by which Sub-Carpathian

[10] The populations of the two towns rose as follows: Minsk, from 117,000 to 239,000; Smolensk, from 76,000 to 157,000.

Ruthenia, the easternmost Province of Czechoslovakia, was to be transferred to the Soviet Union, and, in particular, to the Ukraine. One clause of the Agreement stated "Sub-Carpathian Russia is again uniting—in conformity with the desire expressed by the population, and on the basis of the amicable agreement reached between the two contracting parties—with its ancient motherland, the Ukraine, and is embodied in the Ukrainian Soviet Socialist Republic." Until the establishment of the "Lublin (later the Warsaw) Government" on a popular basis it seemed likely that Poland would not so easily be persuaded to accept, with good grace, the loss of lands where a majority of the population was Little Russian. However, with the full approval of the first Polish Government established on Polish soil after the Second World War, Eastern Galicia has been merged irrevocably with the Ukrainian Republic. The latter, newly in possession of Galicia and Trans-Carpathian lands, is now raised in population to not less than 38 millions. The entrance of the Soviet Union into the Danubian Basin is one of the most significant developments in the political geography of the New Europe. It must immensely increase the authority and strategic advantages of the Soviet Union in Central Europe.

The balance between agricultural activities, on the one hand, and mining and manufacturing, on the other, is very nicely adjusted within the Ukraine. The western district makes a far larger contribution to the wheat production of the U.S.S.R. than any other zone of comparable area. About two-thirds of the entire Ukraine is intensively farmed, with nearly as much soil under wheat as under all other crops combined. The emphasis on wheat-farming was very marked long before the First World War, and since the Revolution it has not diminished. Yet a very broad basis of agriculture is provided on the "collective farms," with a wide variety of additional crops, including rye, barley, oats, millet, and sugar-beet, in that order of importance. Moreover, stock-rearing—with cattle predominant, despite the semi-aridity of climate—has proved to be one of the most successful ventures of Ukrainian farming. It is a necessary part of Soviet planning to adjust the type of agriculture, with care, to the particular characteristics of climate and soil of each region.

By contrast, the Eastern Ukraine is devoted chiefly to mining and metallurgical industries. The climate is too arid for farming of West Ukrainian standards, but there is compensation in the most abundant coal resources of European Russia. This mineral wealth was developed on but a small scale before the First World War when, though in advance of all other Russian production, the Donetz Basin of the Ukraine produced under twenty-five million tons of coal, or less than the small field of South Lancashire in England. By 1938, Donetz output had risen progressively to eighty-one million tons, which was more than one-third of the production of all British mines in the same year. The blast furnaces of this region, from Kharkov—its industrial and administrative capital—south-east to Stalino, were the leading producers of iron and steel in all Russia.[11] The trend of coal-mining and steel manufacture will inevitably shift the industrial "centre of gravity" of the U.S.S.R. eastwards from the Donetz to the Urals and Western Siberia. That time is not yet due, however, despite the stimulus given to the development of the Asiatic sources of mineral wealth by the enemy's occupation and destruction of Ukrainian industry. It may come within the next twenty-five years.

We have traced the outlines of the Soviet Federal State, as they appear to the political geographer. Its political structure is a subject for the student of politics, but this at least should now be added. Russia is the only State which has succeeded in maintaining its stability and increasing its strength on the basis of, first, the recognition of full cultural autonomy of many varied nationalities, and, second, the efficient centralization and unification of political and economic authority. The adaptability of the Soviet system has already been indicated, and was recently attested by its war-time preparedness for the incorporation, as full Republics, of the communities of Estonia, Latvia, and Lithuania.

These countries were re-occupied by Russia early in the Second World War; and, before the German eastward advance forced the Russians to retreat on Leningrad, elections were held which seemed to indicate the wish of the people concerned to rejoin Russia. Soviet evidence is to the effect that the ballot was secret and that no pressure was exerted to restrict free expression, but no impartial evidence is available.[12] In 1940, the Soviet Republics of Estonia, Latvia, and

[11] By the autumn of 1943 the Russians had cleared the Germans from the Eastern Ukraine, and the rehabilitation of its destroyed industries was begun immediately. Before the German occupation, Ukrainian steel amounted annually to half the total for the U.S.S.R. (9 million out of 18 million tons).

[12] According to a statement issued from Moscow on April 19, 1943 by Professor Vaabel (Tartu University) and two other representatives of the East Baltic peoples, about 90 per cent of the electors voted in each of Estonia, Latvia, and Lithuania, the great majority being for union with Russia.

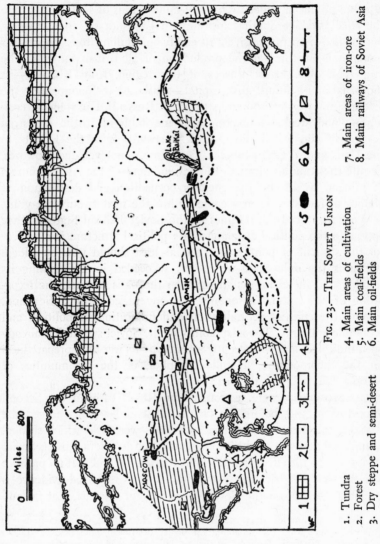

FIG. 23.—THE SOVIET UNION

1. Tundra
2. Forest
3. Dry steppe and semi-desert

4. Main areas of cultivation
5. Main coal-fields
6. Main oil-fields

7. Main areas of iron-ore
8. Main railways of Soviet Asia

Lithuania were proclaimed. As evidence of the loyalty of the East Baltic peoples (other than the Finns) to the Soviet cause, it is reported that, when the invasion of Russia occurred in 1941, many of their citizens fought valiantly against the Germans. A Latvian military division particularly distinguished itself in the defence of Moscow during the winter of that year.

Doubt has long been thrown on the ability of the constituent national bodies within the U.S.S.R. to demand their independence, even to the point of secession, if they should so desire. Certainly, the right of secession is the most critical issue in the history of federations. In the case of the British Commonwealth, it has been granted recently to the several Dominions, though even Eire—hitherto the most separatist of them all in intention—has not availed itself of the right. Less than a century ago, the United States of America waged an exhausting internecine war to decide for, or against, the right of any constituent State to detach itself from the Federation which Washington and Hamilton had founded. The Southern States were defeated in their attempt to maintain what, to them, was of the essence of sovereignty.

The Declaration of Rights of the Peoples (November 1917) proclaimed the equality and sovereign rights of all communities on Russian soil, and their right to self-determination, even if that should result in secession and the setting up of independent States. It must, however, be doubted by friends of Russia if any of the States, which by the Constitution of the U.S.S.R. retain their sovereignty, would ever be permitted to detach themselves from the Union. The men who founded the new Russia were realists, and fully appreciated that the strength of the Soviet Federation would depend on its solidarity. No instance is recorded of a move on the part of any one of the constituent communities to leave the Union or to abandon the tenets of Soviet doctrine. The terrible ordeal of the most cruel of wars has proved that the loyalty of both Slav and non-Slav is not one of compulsion.

Early in 1944, the Soviet Government announced certain constitutional changes in regard to both Foreign Affairs and Defence. At their face value they offer to each constituent Republic some of the rights enjoyed by independent States. "Full power to enter into relations with foreign States and to make treaties with them" is, according to the official statement, extended to each Republic. Yet close observers of the Russian scene regard the change as merely granting to each member-State the right to be directly consulted and represented in matters that concern it. Most of the Republics have frontiers with non-Soviet countries, and it is obviously desirable —not to say necessary—that, in the Union's contacts with neighbouring foreign Powers, the special interests of particular Soviet Republics should be fully considered. On the other hand, it is thought to be inevitable that an All-Union Foreign Commissariat will continue to handle the affairs that affect Soviet Russia as a whole.

There are certain advantages to be gained by Russia in announcing both these constitutional reforms and the right of any Republic to secede from the Union. The Soviet Government has certainly in mind the strength of her moral, as well as material, position in the post-war world. If a large measure of self-government should be acquired by individual Republics, the criticism that Russia augments her strength at the expense of the national development of her varied peoples will be largely silenced. Moreover, if Russia should contemplate the incorporation of certain European countries, which so far have been outside her orbit, the theoretical right to secession, together with devolution of control in both Defence and Foreign Affairs, is well calculated favourably to impress them. Certain countries of Central Europe, whilst wishing to be independent, have come to realize that, as separate sovereign States, they can expect no security in the post-war world.

THE GEOGRAPHY OF ECONOMIC PLANNING

From the beginning, the Soviet leaders were fully aware that the principles on which the new Russia was being founded and built would for long antagonize the great majority, if not all, of the Powers. Hence the realization that, since Russia would be without dependable allies at any crisis of her future, she would need to depend exclusively on her own military and economic strength. A plan to attain economic self-sufficiency naturally followed, and the impulse was strong to investigate and develop the untapped resources of the vast Asiatic territories. It is these lands, well-nigh boundless and of infinite possibilities, which suggest to the geographer that, alone of the Powers, the Soviet Union could, if necessary, long maintain itself in virtual isolation from the rest of the world.

The first requirement was a comprehensive survey of the resources of the State, latent or only superficially developed, together with an investigation of the distribution of population in its relation to the wealth of the land. This was a task primarily for the scientists, and was undertaken in 1920, with characteristic vigour and enthusiasm, under the organization of the State Planning Commission. The latter is a permanent body of scientific experts, and its authority is virtually supreme. Through its activities, within a few years, the vast store-house of inner Asia was opened and, for the first time, its resources were assessed.

Planning followed immediately on the completion of the scientists' reports, and nothing was permitted to delay the beginning of production. Much of the wealth of Siberia and Central Asia is situated in empty or sparsely-inhabited areas. In consequence, new systems of transport had to be devised, whilst labour was required from the nearest available well-settled areas. Much of the inter-regional migration was from European Russia to Western and Central Siberia, where new towns grew up on the basis of immigrants of very mixed origins.

The State Planning Commission began its work with little regard for the interests of particular nationalities within the Union. At that time, Russia observed very critically the shortcomings of the Peace Settlement which followed the First World War. Her leaders were determined that the Soviet Union should not be shackled in its economic development—as was Central Europe—by what appeared to them to be the petty considerations of many mutually-conflicting national sovereignties. They went so far as to underestimate the strength of national sentiment in several communities—White Russia and the Ukraine, among them. Concerned almost exclusively as it was with the problem of land-utilization, the State Planning Commission preferred to employ economic regions rather than national communities as units of administration. Each of these regions (oblasti) was to be defined in terms of economic geography, and was to preserve its distinctive character, especially in regard to the mode of land utilization. In other words, geography was to be allowed to determine the kind of economic specialization which each region should undertake.

In the first sub-division of the U.S.S.R. into economic regions, twenty-one were to be recognized, and were to replace the old Provinces (ninety-three in number) whose boundaries had taken little

FIG. 24.—EUROPEAN RUSSIA

The Economic Regions (*Oblasti*) as proposed by the Soviet Planning Commission, 1920. Administrative centres are shown.

The Regions were named as follows:

1. North-west
2. North-east
3. Western
4. Central-Industrial
5. Vyatka-Vetluga
6. Ural
7. Middle Volga
8. Central Black Earth
9. South-western
10. South-Mining
11. South-east
12. Caucasus

or no account of geographic or economic considerations. Of the twenty-one, twelve were proposed for European Russia and nine for the Asiatic territories. This geographical partition of the Soviet Union was approved in the year 1922, but difficulties at once arose, when it was realized that the new divisions would, in certain instances, cut right across traditional boundaries of old-established national entities.

The Ukraine was divided into the "South-Western Region" (capital—Kiev), whose economic emphasis was to be wheat-farming, to the virtual exclusion of other forms of land development; secondly, the "South Mining Region" (capital Kharkov), which was to be highly industrialized. Two separate administrations would have been adopted for the Ukraine, if the project had been confirmed. The Little Russians, however, expressed in the clearest terms their repudiation of the division of their nation; and the strength of national sentiment, so proclaimed, led to the abandonment of the scheme, in so far as it affected the Ukraine.

Disregard for White Russian national sentiment met with a similar fate. It was proposed to establish a "Western Region," including those parts of White Russia which had not been annexed by Poland, and a considerable area of European Great Russia as well. The entire "Region" was to be controlled, in its economic development, from the administrative centre of Smolensk. White Russian hostility to the scheme was emphatic, largely because it granted Smolensk the status of capital which, in the tradition of White Russia, rightly belongs to the city of Minsk. Consequently the frontiers of the small Republic remained unchanged and the community retained its administrative unity.

The error of disregarding national sentiment was not repeated, and, in the ensuing years, right down to the Second World War, the Soviet Government completely changed its policy. Diversities within the State were not to be obliterated by the adoption of a programme intended to produce cultural uniformity throughout the length and breadth of the U.S.S.R. Rather were they to be encouraged, as contributing to the health and vitality of the State. In pursuance of the new policy, folk traditions of music, dancing, and of culture generally, which were in danger of extinction even before the Revolution, were granted a remarkable revival. Each community was encouraged to appreciate past cultural achievements and to utilize the best that experience had to offer.

In European Great Russia, national sentiment was generally favourable to the projected division of the territory along lines of economic geography. The greater part has been so divided, and each "region" is provided with a detailed and ambitious economic plan, in which the geographical possibilities present are granted their fullest weight. Regional frontiers have been altered from time to time for reasons of administrative convenience, and no local opposition to such changes seems to have been aroused.

In its emphasis on the planning of production, according to principles of physical and economic geography, the Soviet Government indicated at the outset its belief that all peoples, however diverse in ethnic origins and culture, could share equally in the growth of the State's prosperity. Further, it claimed that regional differences in economic development within the Soviet Union were due to environmental conditions, not to the relative superiority or inferiority of the particular communities which made up the U.S.S.R. If the local geographic conditions permitted, there was nothing to prevent a hitherto primitive people from acquiring rapidly the technique of industrial production. Such confidence in so-called "backward" peoples, which has made possible remarkable industrial developments in Siberia and Russian Central Asia, is not, by any means, shared by all the Great Powers. Some accept a classification which distinguishes "advanced" from "backward" peoples, and are all too ready to regard it as both inevitable and unchanging.

The actual, and not merely theoretical, equality of all national communities within the U.S.S.R. suggests the complete absence of any idea of racial superiority on the part of the Russian Slavs, who, at the time of the Revolution, formed the majority as well as the best-equipped (technically) of the Soviet peoples. The inter-mingling of numerous ethnic types, which the Russian experiment has involved, has produced no "colour-bar." It is true that diversities of race within the Soviet Union are not quite as complex as they are, for example, in the British Empire, and that the Negro is absent from Soviet territory: but the ethnic range is still very wide, and could offer full opportunity for racial exclusiveness, if men's minds happened to run in that direction. It is perhaps the greatest possible tribute to the modern Russians to state that the idea of racial supremacy seems never to have occurred to them.

Once the preliminary survey of Russia's economico-geographical resources was complete and the administrative framework of the Plan was ready, both agricultural and industrial production proceeded with almost incredible vigour in an atmosphere of pressing emergency. Russia moved in a hostile world, and the possibility of a combination of Powers in war against her existed for at least a decade and a half.

The more westerly regions, which were already comparatively advanced in economic development, were to continue to carry the main burden of output—agricultural, mining, and manufacturing—for a period, which, however, was to be as brief as possible. At the same time, the unopened regions of Central and Northern Asia were to be brought into immediate production, no matter how great the difficulties of transportation and labour supply proved to be. Wherever resources of fuel, metallic ores, etc., existed, production was to be organized on a scale dependent, not on the condition of a world market or the resources of some prospecting company or other, but solely on the extent of the local resources. Moreover, the Asiatic industries were not to be merely extractive—coal-mining and the like. The economic life of the newly opened regions was to be as self-sufficing and autonomous as possible, concentrating mainly, it is true, on the types of production for which they were naturally endowed, but involving attention also to a wide range of commodities—including foodstuffs—for local consumption. Thereby, it was possible to relieve the inadequate railway system, inherited by the Soviets, from what would have proved to be an insupportable burden of traffic. The Asiatic territories were also freed from that economic subordination to the interests of older-established lands which has been so strongly emphasized in the case of the imperial dependencies of the Western Powers.

Certainly, the imminence of war with Germany, and possibly with Japan also, was a powerful motive in the planning of Soviet Asia. In the event of the two hostile Powers combining against Russia—a contingency which her diplomacy was designed, successfully as it proved, to prevent—the only regions of the Union, which would be relatively secure from land or air attack, lay to the east of the Urals and to the west of Lake Baikal. On them would fall the responsibility of organizing the ultimate defence of Soviet Russia; and, for the purpose, a complete range of primary and secondary industries was essential. For almost everything of a material kind, they would need to be self-sufficing, under conditions of war.

It was hoped by the Russian Government that Japan would be prevented from synchronizing her premeditated attack with that of Germany. The latter was, from the Russian standpoint, the more formidable foe of the two, not only by reason of her greater war potential, but also because a Nazi assault on Russia was, geographically, much more feasible than a Japanese "drive" across Siberia. Seriously embarrassed as she was by the interminable "China incident," and forced to watch with care the attitude of an increasingly hostile America, Japan, in the twenties and thirties of the century, was in no position to begin a Siberian adventure which, to be at all effective, would need to be organized on a colossal scale. Yet Japan was not to be provoked. Russia's Far-Eastern policy seemed to be remarkably complacent in face of the offensiveness of Japanese activities on the Mongolian and Manchurian borders, where the two Powers met. The willingness of Russia to relinquish her sphere of influence in Northern Manchuria, and to sell to Japan the vitally important direct railway connexion between Chita and Vladivostok, was due partly to Russia's need to postpone the day of reckoning with her traditional foe of the Orient, until the offensive power of Germany could be destroyed.

War with Germany would be, as anticipated by the Soviet Government, a defensive campaign, at least in its early stages. The Russian General Staff argued that the Germans would make a grand offensive —according to their own approved formula. This would carry them across the Polish lowland, within a brief space of days, on any realistic calculation of the weakness of the Polish Army. Russia declined to repose confidence in any line of fortifications such as the Maginot defences of France, and was prepared to fall back from White Russia and the Western Ukraine. Her temporary military occupation of Eastern Poland, from the autumn of 1939 until June 1941, effected with the consent of Germany, was a concession, in terms of space and time, which she put to the best advantage in preparing for the expected German onslaught.

In the north of Western Russia, Leningrad stood some fifty miles only from the Estonian frontier. Because of its outstanding capacity for metallurgical and other industrial output, the evacuation of the great city was not to be contemplated. It had to be ensured from

German assault, not only because of its potential of war production, but also because of its intimate association with Kronstadt, the Baltic naval base. The latter could not hold out if Leningrad were reduced, and the loss of the naval base would mean the extinction of the Baltic fleet. Fortunately, the forests and marshes, beyond the suburbs of Leningrad, are well suited to defensive warfare, as the Russian garrison proved in a defence of unmatched heroism and fortitude. The history of warfare has no parallel to the uninterrupted siege for three years of a city of two million inhabitants—a population which succeeded in producing most of the weapons required for its own defence.

Excepting Leningrad, so vital to the industrial and military equipment of Russia, the Government was prepared to abandon a number of highly valuable western districts to the enemy, rather than suffer the annihilation of its armies in over-exposed positions. "Buying time with space" was the current phrase. This might mean the temporary loss of the richest corn-lands of all Russia, as well as industrial centres like Kiev and Odessa, which were amongst the best equipped. Only the most active exploitation of the "new" Asiatic territories could restore the economic balance, which a forced withdrawal from the west would violently disturb. The vast programme of Asiatic developments was concealed from a still-hostile world, and, indeed, will not fully be known until Russia has such confidence as to remove the need for secrecy.

Prepared for the evacuation of the western fringe of the U.S.S.R., the Soviet leaders took the logical, but sacrificial, step of checking even normal industrial development in the areas concerned, so that valuable plant might not fall into the hands of the enemy. The new heavy industries were to be established far from the western frontier, and, save in the special case of Leningrad, such industries as remained in the western towns were to be either of a non-essential nature, or easily movable in an emergency.

As much of the output of industry was necessarily for war, or easily convertible to military purposes, there is no detailed accurate published information concerning production in any part of the U.S.S.R. It is, however, possible to form a fairly clear impression of the extent to which development progressed, prior to 1939, in the "safe" areas of the east, or was retarded purposely—for reasons already mentioned—in the vulnerable western districts. The method

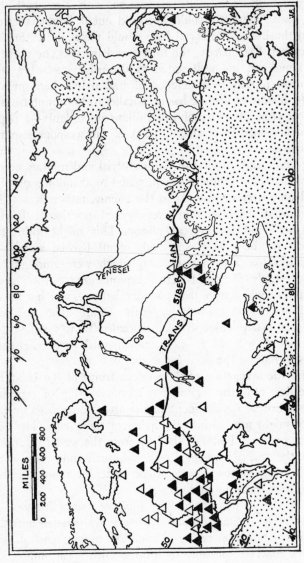

Fig. 25.—The Cities of the Soviet Union

Cities which exceeded 100,000 inhabitants in 1914 are shown by white triangles

Cities which exceeded 100,000 inhabitants subsequent to 1914 are shown by black triangles

is to investigate the growth of population in towns, both those old-established and those founded subsequent to the Revolution. Phenomenal, almost unprecedented, increase of population was true for more than seventy per cent of the towns of the U.S.S.R., as a whole, though in the Asiatic lands of the Union the percentage increase was very much higher than in European Russia. On the other hand, almost without any exception known to the author, the towns which showed a normal or slow growth, or actual decrease of population, between 1912 and 1939, are located within a zone close to the western frontier.

Some instances are particularly striking. As new mining developments are occurring mainly in the Urals and in the upper basins of the Ob-Irtish, Yenisei, and Lena river systems, we may expect to find "mushroom" town-growth throughout these districts. Reference to each important instance of the kind would be tedious to the reader, and for that reason an abbreviated statistical summary is placed below.[13] Sverdlovsk (formerly Ekaterinburg), the great industrial centre and commercial focus of the middle Ural zone, is an excellent example of the revitalization of an old town; whilst Mag-

[13] Trend of Population in certain Russian towns.

Name	Population (approx.) in 1913	Population (approx.) in 1939	Percentage Increase
Moscow	1,817,000	4,137,000	128
Kharkov	248,000	833,000	236
Baku	225,000	809,000	260
Gorky (Nijni Novgorod) .	109,000	644,000	491
Tashkent	272,000	585,000	115
Rostov	200,000	510,000	155
Sverdlovsk (Ekaterinburg) .	75,000	410,000	447
Stalingrad (Tsaritsin) . .	100,000	388,000	288
Stalino (Yuzovka) . .	49,000	286,000	484
Novosibirsk . . .	71,000	278,000	292
Khabarovsk . . .	51,000	199,000	290
Magnitogorsk . . .	Founded 1931	146,000	—
Towns within 150 miles of the Western Frontier:			
Leningrad	2,100,000	3,191,000	52
Kiev	590,000	846,000	43.4
Odessa	630,000	604,000	Decrease
Nikolaiev	120,000	141,000	17.5
Smolensk	71,000	104,000	46.5
Minsk	105,000	180,000	71.4
Vitebsk	104,000	127,000	22.1

nitogorsk, in the south of the Urals, is representative of the cities which began their careers as recently as the post-Revolution period.

The towns of the accompanying list include some, from a zone within 150 miles of the western frontier (1938), which are among the largest and most important of all Russian centres. Without the application of planning to town-growth they might well have been expected, under normal circumstances, to have increased more rapidly than any in Russia. Particularly is this true in the cases of Leningrad and Odessa, the two leading seaports. Under normal circumstances they would have attracted industries more than most towns. It is true also of Kiev which, until the phenomenal rise of industrial Kharkov in very recent years, was incomparably the most prosperous city of the Ukraine.

Odessa is the only considerable town of the Union whose population has diminished during the Soviet régime. Its proximity to the Rumanian frontier, until 1939 only forty miles distant, was a serious disadvantage, and had the effect of retarding industrial and demographic development. The geographical position of Kiev has always been considered by the Soviet authorities to be specially vulnerable, in view of an almost certain German invasion. After the Revolution and the occupation of the Ukraine by hostile foreign armies, the great city was not restored to its status as Little Russian capital until 1934. Up to that time Kharkov, 250 miles farther to the east, served as the Ukrainian seat of government.

To refer once again to Leningrad—that city, the capital of the Tsarist Empire, showed a proportionate increase higher than the average for West Russian towns, though it was not comparable with that of Moscow. Again, there was intention. Because of its foremost position amongst Russian industrial centres at the time of the Revolution, it was the first training-school of a large proportion of Russia's new industrial army, and the supplier of a great part of the machinery, so urgently required for the economic rehabilitation of the country. Nevertheless, it was to lose its metropolitan status, in favour of Moscow, geographically more suited to be capital of the Union, and much less vulnerable to the assaults of a German or other European enemy.

As a result of the Second World War Leningrad may diminish in importance, both absolutely and relatively to other cities of Russia. A new factor, affecting its growth as a seaport, has been introduced since the Soviets gained control of the East Baltic coast, southwards from the Gulf of Finland as far as Königsberg which, with the easterly part of East Prussia, is henceforth to be Soviet territory. A chain of valuable ports—Tallinn, Baltiski, Ventspils, not to speak of Memel, Königsberg and particularly Riga—will now provide Russia's Baltic frontage. Some of these havens have advantages of navigability or commercial and industrial possibilities superior to those of Leningrad, and it is recalled that, in Tsarist days, Riga was one of the busiest ports of the Baltic.

The trend of population-growth in Russian towns, however phenomenal, is not permitted to produce the problem of the unmanageably large city. None compares in size with Moscow, for which a limit of four and a half million citizens was planned. This, not because of any special virtue in that number, but because, in the light of Russian town-planning experience and of local geographical circumstances, within the Moscow district, it is the maximum with which efficient civic administration seemed able to cope.

The growth of towns in Asiatic Russia between 1913 and 1939, which was the more remarkable because of their retarded development or actual non-existence in earlier decades, should not leave the impression that the vast spaces of Siberia and Central Asia were being rapidly filled with settlers. The exodus from European Russia, which was greatly extended and intensified during the late War, has carried several, possibly many, millions into the Urals, Trans-Caspia, and Siberia. Probably not for some years will it be possible to estimate the full extent of the migration. At the end of the conflict, Russia's authority as a European Power will be immeasurably greater than it was formerly, and it will be her Asiatic accession of strength, especially her ability to mobilize the enormous resources of Siberia, which will ensure for her a leading position among the Powers.

Confronted with an extent of material devastation and loss of life, in war, which no other nation has experienced, and with gigantic tasks of Asiatic land development before her, Russia realizes that her own millions are numerically inadequate for the completion of her economic plan.[14] Unless the empty spaces can be filled, their very vastness may prove an embarrassment. Density of population

[14] The Soviet Government, before the end of 1943, had declared her intention of forcing Germany to rebuild by her own labour the areas which she has devastated.

within European Russia shows an average of only fifty persons per square mile, whilst for Asiatic Russia the average descends to ten per square mile. True, that the first of these densities compares favourably with that for the United States of America, namely forty-five per square mile, but it is remembered that the latter figure takes into account the sparsely occupied "Mountain" States of the U.S.A., whereas, counting Russia's European and Asiatic territories together, the density does not exceed twenty-two or twenty-three per square mile.

It may be anticipated that the density of settlement in the Urals and other economically attractive zones of Western Asiatic Russia will approximate to that of the Ukraine (172 per square mile) in little more than a century or so, as a result of planned migration and natural increase. On the other hand, there can be no expectation, even by the most sanguine, that the vast areas of Yakutsk and other territories towards the east of the U.S.S.R. will reach a considerable density—as high, for instance, as fifty to a hundred per square mile—within a century, unless a new stream of colonization should flow there from outside the present frontiers of the Union. The risks of prophecy concerning any phase of development of Soviet civilization are now well known,[15] but, taking into account the low population densities of most Russian lands, it is impossible to expect rapid settlement of the empty Far East of the U.S.S.R.

The Far Eastern and Pacific campaigns of the Second World War contributed to an international situation, highly favourable to the strategic and economic interests of Soviet Russia and of possible advantage to her acute man-power problem. All official declarations, issued by the United Nations with reference to Japan, point to the complete destruction of her imperial system. The teeming millions of Honshiu, Kiushiu, and Shikoku, however, will not diminish as Japan's political power wanes. They will continue to increase and to provide the world with the most serious problem of population congestion which has yet emerged. Sooner or later, the dispersal of a large propor-

[15] Hardly any geographer, or other student, of Russian affairs foresaw the phenomenal town-growth and industrial development of the Soviet Union. Dr. Bowman, Director of the American Geographical Society, writing in 1928, contrasted Russia, with only 20 cities of over 100,000 inhabitants, and U.S.A. with 68 such cities. Within twelve years of the appearance of the 4th edition of his invaluable work, *The New World*, in which the statement appeared, the number of Soviet cities with over 100,000 inhabitants was as high as eighty.

tion of Japan's population over the neighbouring Asiatic mainland to the north of Korea, would seem to the geographer to be inevitable. The regions concerned include the Yakutsk Autonomous Republic and the littoral of Asia, from Vladivostok to the Bering Straits. Eastern China and Korea are ruled out of such calculations by reason of their own high densities, but in the areas mentioned we have already shown that the densities of vast areas descend almost to zero.

The Russia which plans to use German labour, on an enormous scale, to rebuild her devastated towns and villages, is quite capable of a project to invite Japanese peasants and artisans to her territory, as colonists. It seems likely that any revulsion of mood which may turn the Japanese against the régime which has brought them, economically and politically, to ruin would assist the Soviet Union to win their sympathy. On the other hand, those elements within Japan, which might look towards the Soviet Union for purposes of co-operation, are not likely, by reason of their political and social opinions, to recommend themselves to the U.S.A., which, for some years to come, will determine the official policy of defeated Japan.

The prospect, at a time not far distant, of many millions of Japanese becoming Soviet citizens is not by any means extravagant. If, within a very few years, the Soviet Government has been able to establish a political system which is acceptable, not only to Slavs but also to Tatars, Georgians, Armenians, Uzbeks, Mongols, and the rest, it is quite capable of admitting those land-hungry Japanese who choose to settle on the Asiatic mainland. The pseudo-scientific view that, for some undetermined reason, the Japanese are incapable of becoming acclimatized in regions of severe winter cold, never went unchallenged. Since the occupation of Southern Manchuria by some hundreds of thousands of Japanese early this century, not to speak of the settlement of the island of Hokkaido—however sluggish it may have been—and the long-continued operations of the Japanese army in Manchuria, it is evident that the people of Nippon are as adaptable as most to unusual types of climate. Like others, however, they require assistance, both social and economic, in order to make the transfer a successful and permanent one.

It is not pretended that such a possibility as large-scale Japanese colonization of Eastern Siberia, under Russian direction, is a declared intention of the Soviet Union; but it is geographically feasible, and would offer to Russia the only means by which, in measurable time, she would be able to make her Far Eastern regions fully productive. The stoicism, frugality, and technical skill of the Japanese, both peasant and artisan, would prove great assets, both to themselves and to those who would organize their activities in a land of severe winter cold.

There is no other considerable source of population on which Russia could possibly draw. China, reborn, will need her people, for as a whole the country is not over-populated, although certain districts are as congested as any in Japan. Russia cannot count on Chinese labour, highly valuable though it would be to her.

The scale of operations demanded by such a project of colonization in Far Eastern Russia as has been suggested, though formidable, would not exceed that of the migration of Russian Slavs to Siberia and Central Asia which has been going on for long, both before and since the establishment of the Soviet Union. For the Japanese, the economic urge to leave the congested areas of the homeland will be strong, whilst the ties of militant patriotism will be broken for them—perhaps irreparably—as far as can be foreseen. With political considerations favourable, migration to the Asiatic mainland of the U.S.S.R. might well be on the scale of twenty to thirty millions, within half a century or less. Population density in Japan would still be high—even on a reduced basis of fifty millions it would be 350 per square mile—and, if the fertility of the islanders should remain near its present level, a larger exodus than that suggested would be required to keep pace with the overcrowding of Honshiu and the other islands.

In the foregoing discussion of the economic and political geography of the Soviet Union, the Asiatic and the European territories have been combined. Such a treatment is inevitable. The organization of Soviet life and the facts of Soviet geography take no account of a conventional and otherwise meaningless division of the continents. Such contrasts as there were at one time in the life of regions, respectively to the east and west of the Ural Mountains, are being obliterated very rapidly by the processes we have discussed.

In her rôle as a Great Power, Russia of the future will bring the whole of her strength to bear upon those problems of Europe in which she is particularly interested. And, as it is impossible to segregate the problems of Europe regionally—to regard, for example, certain issues as solely Western, Central, or Eastern European, as the case may be—Russia inevitably is involved in all European international questions. At the same time, of course, her undertakings and responsibilities diminish to some extent with geographical distance, as in the case of all other States. Inevitably again, as Russia is incomparably the largest territorial unit of the political world and has by far the longest land frontier of any of her contemporaries, the range of her international interests is more difficult to define and limit than is the case with any other Power, except Great Britain. But British territorial responsibilities in every ocean and continent are as dispersed as those of the Soviet Union are centralized. Geography, as much as political philosophy, determines the contrast in their respective methods of government.

SELECTED BIBLIOGRAPHY

AITOFF, D.: "Peuples et langues de la Russie," Ann. de Géogr., vol. 15, 1909, pp. 92–5.

BERG, L. S.: Landchaftno-geografitcheskie zony S.S.S.R., Vredenie, toundra, lescaia zona/Geographical zones of the U.S.S.R., Introduction, tundra, the forest zone, Leningrad, 1930.

BLANC, ED.: "La colonization et la mise en valeur de la Sibérie et de la steppe asiatique," Annales de Géogr., XXV, 1916, pp. 124–42.

CHANNING, C. G.: Siberia's Untouched Treasure, London, 1924.

CLEINOW, G.: Neu-Sibirien, Berlin, 1928.

COATES, W. P., and COATES, ZELDA K.: The Second Five-Year Plan of Development of the U.S.S.R., London, 1934.

CONOLLY, VIOLET: Soviet Trade from the Pacific to the Levant, London, 1935.

D'ALMEIDA, P. C.: "Etats de la Baltique—Russia," Tome 5, Géographie Universelle, Paris, 1932.

FISCHER, L.: The Soviets in World Affairs, 2 vols., London, 1930.

GILLETT, A. M.: "A Sketch of the Historical Geography of the Black Earth Region of Central Russia," Scott. Geog. Mag., January 1922.

GOUDKOW, P.: "Economic Geography of the Coal Resources of Asiatic Russia," Geogr. Rev., XIII, 1923, pp. 283–93.

GREGORY, J. S., and SHAVE, D. W.: The U.S.S.R.: a Geographical Survey, London, 1944.

GRIERSON, P.: Books on Soviet Russia, 1917–42, London, 1943.

HAUMANT, E.: "Les influences géographiques dans la formation de la Russie," Annales de Géogr., XXVIII, 1919, pp. 360–72.

HAUMANT, E.: Le problème de l'unité russe, Paris, 1922.

HETTNER, A.: Russland, Leipzig, 4e éd., 1921.

JOHNSON, HEWLETT: The Soviet Power, New York, 1940.

KEETON, G. W., and SCHLESINGER, R.: *Russia and Her Western Neighbours,* London, 1942.

KLYUCHEVSKY, V.: *A History of Russia,* trans. Hogarth, 5 vols., 1911–31.

KOVALEVSKY, —.: *La Russie à la fin du XIXe siècle,* 1900.

MAYNARD, J.: *Russia in Flux,* London, 1941.

MIKHAYLOV, N.: *Soviet Geography,* 2nd edition, London, 1937. *Land of the Soviets: a Handbook of the U.S.S.R.,* New York, 1939.

MILIUKOV, PAUL: *Outlines of Russian Culture,* 3 vols., Philadelphia, 1942.

NANSEN, F.: *Through Siberia, the Land of the Future,* London, 1914.

OGANOVSKY, N. P.: *Essays on the Economic Geography of the U.S.S.R.,* Moscow, 1924.

"Russia: Territory and Population, a perspective on the 1926 Census," *Geogr. Rev.,* XVIII, 1928, pp. 616–40.

SKRINE, F. H.: *Expansion of Russia, 1815–1900,* new edition, London, 1915.

SMOLKA, H. P.: *Forty Thousand against the Arctic: Russia's Polar Empire,* London, 1937.

Soviet Union Yearbook, 1931, London, 1932.

TURIN, S. P.: *The U.S.S.R.: an Economic and Social Survey,* London, 1944.

USHER, A. P.: "The History of Population and Settlement in Eurasia" (with maps), *Geogr. Rev.,* January 1930.

U.S.S.R. Handbook, edited by Segal, London, 1936.

WEBB, SIDNEY and BEATRICE: *Soviet Communism: a New Civilization?* 2 vols., new ed., London, 1941.

YARMOLINSKY, A.: *The Jews and other Minor Nationalities under the Soviets,* New York, 1928.

6.

Some Geographical Questions of Peninsular Europe

As the eastern half of Europe is wholly within the frontiers of a single federal State, and the western is divided between more than twenty sovereignties, the contrast in political geography between the "continental" and "peninsular" zones is sharply emphasized. The restoration of full independence to the nations whose lands have been violated by Germany is a responsibility which Britain and the U.S.A. have accepted, believing it to be in the interests, not only of the individual States concerned, but also of Europe as a whole. It is not intended further to discuss frontier problems; but the effects on some of Europe's major territorial questions of devotion to the principle of national sovereignty must now be investigated in the space available.

The recent westward advance of Soviet Russia, ensuring her incorporation of Bessarabia, Bukovina, Sub-Carpathian Ruthenia, western parts of the Ukrainian and Belorussian zones, the eastern tip of East Prussia and the Republics of Lithuania, Latvia and Estonia, not only augments her European influence, but reduces the possibility of the return of Germany to first-class status as a Power. The Soviet gains, all of which have been approved by her war-time allies, represent a very formidable aggregate of territory and population along Russia's entire western frontage, and completely reverse the process of her enforced retreat from Central Europe at the end of the First World War. From the rise of modern Germany onwards a Central European *bloc* has been able to measure up to either a Western or Eastern combination of political power. Now for the first time, it seems that the Eastern and Western Powers of

Europe are determined to make impossible a renewed military challenge from the Centre.

GERMANY IN THE NEW EUROPE

Most critical of all politico-geographical questions affecting Peninsular Europe is the future of the land and people of Germany. As it is now clear that hopes of a federation of European nations are not to be realised, three alternative methods of handling the problem, which the existence of a strong Germany presents to the world, seem possible.

As was the case after her defeat in the First World War, Germany may again return to full sovereignty, within frontiers modified according to the demands of the victorious Powers. A second possibility is the partition of Greater Germany into a number of small sovereign States, with or without the elimination of Prussia. In addition to Austria, whose re-emergence as an independent State is already a fact, there would be Bavaria, Saxony, Württemberg, Baden, if not others of smaller dimensions, much as they were before the days of Prussian hegemony in German political life. The refinement of sub-division could not, in practice, be carried too far, and the former States, above-mentioned, with the exception of Bavaria, would prove unworkable units, because of their small size.[1] On geographical grounds alone, there is no reason to suppose that the re-creation of an independent Bavaria would be less successful than that of an independent Austria. The two States would be approximately equal, as regards both area and population, and their economic resources would be comparable. A suggestion which has already proved popular in certain diplomatic quarters is that a South German Federation should be formed as a counter-weight to Prussia. Such a federation would obviously include Bavaria, and would conceivably be dominated by it. (v. Appendix C.)

The remaining alternative would be the political elimination of Germany, achieved by parcelling-out both territory and people between the Powers which are contiguous. Such a project would not be impossible. A similar fate has been Poland's on repeated occasions.

---

[1] In 1919 the respective areas of the largest States of Germany were as follows: Prussia (114,739 sq. miles), Bavaria (29,500), Württemberg (7,630), Baden (5,817), Saxony (5,789). It will be noted that the disproportion between Prussia and Bavaria was as great as between Bavaria and the next smallest State.

But, as also in the case of Poland, it would not destroy the reality of nationhood, and the reunification of the German State would again become the dominant national objective. A similar aim might, of course, inspire German patriots if the Reich were to be split into the historic, petty kingdoms.

It is clear that one of the objectives of the United Nations will be to reduce the war-making potential of Germany, in one or both of two ways. First, it is settled that the new Germany will be confined to frontiers drawn closer than those she was permitted to retain in 1919. Territorial penalties, paid to Poland, push her eastern boundary right up to the Oder, but such loss of land, to the east of the Oder, cannot greatly affect, except in the case of Upper Silesia, the industrial strength of the Reich. The eastern provinces—East Prussia, Pomerania, and Lower Silesia—are almost destitute of fuel, as of other major industrial resources. Even as farming lands their contribution to the State, though valuable in respect of rye and potatoes, was not essential to the maintenance of Germany's economic standards.

Between Lower Silesia and the Baltic, therefore, frontier rectification in favour of Poland will have little effect in crippling those metallurgical industries on which the material strength of Germany depended, in peace as in war. The main sources of that strength were geographically concentrated, not dispersed throughout the entire country, and were generally closer to the western than to the eastern frontier. They occurred on the coal-fields, of which that of the Ruhr, in Southern Westphalia, was incomparably the richest and most extensive. Other minerals, including iron, usually occur in fairly close proximity to the coal, a geographical advantage which German industry has exploited very thoroughly.

The need to reduce Germany's power to prepare for another war will demand, therefore, some form of control over the main centres of her coal and iron industries. Westphalia must be the headquarters of any such system of control. Although fairly close to the western frontier, it is not strictly a frontier province. It lies wholly to the east of the Rhine, and is too deeply inset within the zone of German nationality to justify its detachment from Germany, however narrowly the frontiers of that country are drawn. The placing of the Ruhr under some form of international control in the interests of world peace is, indeed, likely to prove one of the more difficult questions of the New Europe.

Nevertheless such control will be essential to the preservation of European civilization. Within the Ruhr there was (1939) a greater concentration of both high-grade coal and metallurgical industry than was to be found elsewhere in the world. Some 60 per cent of all German supplies of coal (other than "soft" coal) formerly came from the Ruhr, even before the loss of the greater part of the Upper Silesian coal-field in 1919. The enormous output of 114 million tons was mined in the Ruhr in 1913. For the welfare of Europe, the coal must be mined on a similar scale in the years to come. Indeed, the rehabilitation of Central Europe will depend more on the activity of the Ruhr mines and associated industries than on any other single factor. German miners, German artisans of every type will be required for the work. How to set the Ruhr industries going once again, without, at the same time, providing Germany with the basis for future re-armament, will be one of the supreme problems of international statesmanship. Taking the long view, however, it is incontrovertible that the disarmament of Germany, to be really effective, will be possible only as part of a plan for European settlement, as a whole. Such a plan would embrace the heavy industries of all nations, without exception.

It has already been shown that Germany's pre-war demand for Lebensraum bore little or no relation to the facts of Central European geography. Germany was then by no means crowded—its density of population being only 345 per square mile, as compared with 700 for England and Wales.[2] In fixing the frontiers of their late foe, the United Nations, it is hoped, will avoid reducing the territory within Germany to such an extent as to arouse a German demand for living-space which would be justified. The lands which, prior to Hitler's supremacy in Europe, were recognized by the Powers as being essentially Teutonic, should remain so, if for no other reason than that German rights in them are protected by the Atlantic Charter. The case of East Prussia is in a category different from that of any other German territory, largely by reason of its geographical position as a German "outlier," separated from the main body of the

[2] It is, however, true that, during the last sixty or seventy years, the population of Germany has increased at an impressive rate, when compared with most other Western or Central European nations. As compared with England and Wales, during the same period, the percentage rate of increase was more than half as much again.

nation. Its future has been discussed in an earlier chapter. (v. Appendices B and C.)

The advantages of position formerly possessed by a united Germany in its repeated attempts to dominate Europe will, unfortunately, remain, whatever may be the balance of political power in the future. To underestimate them would be to disregard the influence of geography in the shaping of civilization. Centrality within the long, east-to-west extending peninsula of Europe—however embarrassing to Germany it may prove to be in a world war, when several "fronts" require defence—has greatly assisted that Power to maintain a foremost position in European industry and trade. And it may not be possible permanently to wrest this advantage from Germany, if the latter is permitted to remain a united and highly organized State, on a broad industrial basis.

The pattern of the great trade-routes of Central Europe illustrates the strength of Germany's position. It defies simplification in the short statement which is possible here, but may be said to depend on, and be built around, three or four main arteries. The only highway, which directly links the Atlantic margins of Europe with the continental hinterland of Russia, follows the North European Plain, and, at one point, within Germany, is restricted to a fairly narrow belt of lowland between the Central German highlands and the North Sea. When large parts of the Baltic are frozen for several months each year, this east-to-west overland highway becomes essential to the circulation of traffic between the continental and the peninsular parts of Europe. Equally important as a transcontinental route is the diagonal line from Western Europe to non-Russian Asia, by way of the Paris Basin, the Rhineland, Bavaria (Upper Danubian Basin), the Hungarian Plain, and the Balkan "Quadrilateral." Istanbul, the ultimate European outpost along this highway, marks the position of the Balkan-Anatolian "bridge" between the two continents. This avenue to the Orient has beckoned persistently to Germany. Along it she hoped to extend her influence south-eastwards up to the gates of India, if not farther. The partially fulfilled dream of a "Berlin to Bagdad" railway was to be her route of empire.

In the pattern of Europe's highways, the north-to-south routes serve further to emphasize the nodal position of Germany. Between the northern and southern coasts of the continent the distances are comparatively short, west of a line joining Trieste and Hamburg;

and there are several alternative passage-ways. The shortest of all traverses France, and helps, as it has always done, to fuse, within the "natural" frontiers of that country, peoples and cultures of very different origins. Also short and direct—though, prior to railway tunnelling, interrupted by the great Alpine chains—are the routes, between the North European Plain and the Mediterranean seaboard, which traverse Germany. There are several alternatives, but outstanding is one which negotiates the Brenner Pass (4,110 feet above sea-level), by which the Central Alps are most easily surmounted. The Brenner, normal rendezvous of Italo-German Dictators, in the days of the Axis, marked the corridor along which the armies and munitions of Germany were able to move south swiftly to meet the Anglo-American invasion of Italy. Unfortunately at that time, the nature of the Alpine terrain in the Brenner neighbourhood rendered difficult the obliteration, from the air, of the vital railway of the Pass.

Possessed of so many vital links in the great routes of Europe, Germany, with commendable powers of organization, fashioned, in the years before the Second World War, the best-equipped and most elaborate transport network of Europe, if not of the entire world. The arterial motor-road, the railway, the canal, and the civil air-line —each made its distinctive contribution to a highly centralized system, which was planned to operate as a unit. If her mood had been that of a good European citizen, Germany's genius for transport organization would have proved of immense benefit to the economic well-being of the continent as a whole. Again, had Germany sought the friendship of her neighbours—with whose transport lines her own were continuous—rather than their abject fear, she might well have built a "new order" which would have been irresistible, by reason of its power for good. Under the leadership of Bismarck, Wilhelm II, and Hitler, geographical advantages, which certainly cannot be blamed for determining German aggressiveness, were used to very different ends.

There is one further aspect of the political and economic life of Germany to which the geographer draws attention. Of all the great and highly industrialized Powers of the world, Germany alone, in the years before the Second World War, was without undeveloped territories, held in her exclusive interest. In the industrial history of the other leading States, however, the existence of such "colonial" lands has been taken for granted. During the last half-century, the United States, Russia, Great Britain, Japan, France, Italy, Belgium, and Holland provide the most obvious instances. Each of these Powers has built its industrial and commercial edifice, to a large extent, on the exploitation—employing the best sense of that word! —of territories which are not, or were not in early industrial days, populated mainly by its own nationals.

It will be recalled that in the brief space of three years—1884 to 1886—Germany founded, and completed the frontiers of, an overseas empire, within the African and Pacific Tropics. The agricultural and mining possibilities provided by the Cameroons and German East African Protectorate, in particular, were especially attractive to the Imperial Government. In the short period of thirty years, prior to the First World War, preparation for large production of a wide range of tropical commodities, including rubber, cotton, sisal, and cacao, was vigorously undertaken. The aim was always to free Germany from dependence on other empires for those raw materials of industry and foodstuffs which the vast, yet largely undeveloped, tropical zone was able to supply in great abundance. Given acquiescence in the right of any Power to carve out its own empire—and there had been international agreement, tacit or expressed, on this point in the decades that preceded the First World War—there could be no genuine objection to the German colonial ventures in Africa and the "Territory" of New Guinea.

In consequence of the war guilt, for which, in 1919, Germany was condemned by the victorious Powers, her tropical dependencies in their entirety were confiscated. Shortly after, they were shared out, under little more than nominal League supervision, to Mandatory Powers which accepted—with varying degrees of sincerity—the responsibilities of trusteeship. Whilst admitting the desirability, as well as the difficulties, of placing the ex-German colonies under effective international control, it would have been wise to have prevented any of the victorious Powers from obtaining a leading, not to say exclusive, rôle in their administration. The suspicion that they were virtually prizes of war awarded to Great Britain, France, Belgium, Japan, Australia, the Union of South Africa, and New Zealand, respectively, was never completely dispelled.

After the First World War, Germany's industrial revival came quickly. She was able to re-start her machinery—almost unharmed by war as it was—earlier than most of the other Powers, both the defeated and the victorious. Deprived of colonies, she turned her attention immediately to the manufacture of those "raw materials" (rubber, etc.), without which large-scale imports from the territories of other Powers were unavoidable, if the expansion of German industry was to continue. Self-sufficiency (*Autarkie*) was her objective, but it led inevitably to the coveting of Central European lands, contiguous to Germany yet inaccessible to her old enemies—the naval Powers, Great Britain and the United States. Geography made it possible for Russia alone to intervene, once German aggression moved southwards and eastwards against the Slav countries, but the growing might of the Soviet Union was under-estimated, almost as completely in Germany as in Britain and America.

The years between the wars witnessed no fundamental changes in the characteristics of the colonial systems of the Powers. Each empire guarded its sovereign rights as closely as its military strength permitted, and joint control of tropical dependencies never passed beyond academic discussion. The right of access of every country to the wealth of the Tropics could not be denied by any but the most thorough-going of imperialists, yet to translate this theoretical right into terms of reality is likely to be as difficult in the post-war world as ever it was before. Meanwhile, Germany has provided good reasons why she should not be permitted to return to Africa, or the Pacific, as a colonial Power. The Nazi philosophy has nothing to offer the Negro world, and anything of value, accomplished by Germany in Africa before 1914, is a small matter in comparison.

ITALY'S LAND PROBLEM

So far, Italy has received only incidental attention, in reference to the frontier adjustments, between herself and her neighbours, that were carried out in the Alps and Dalmatia, after the First World War; yet, although the frontier problems of the Trentino and the Adriatic littoral are considered under "Austria" and "Yugoslavia," respectively, they are not regarded wholly from the standpoint of those countries.

However the political situation in Italy may change, the most critical of all national questions—the land-hunger and poverty of the peasantry—are certain to reappear, intensified more than ever, as a result of the war. On an area almost exactly equal to the British

Isles, the Italian population is increasing much faster than our own.[3] The rise in numbers during the past half-century has been associated particularly with the industrialization of the great cities—Milan and Turin within the Po Basin, and Rome and Naples on the western flank of the long, mountainous peninsula. The population of each of these industrial centres exceeds three-quarters of a million, and two have already passed the million.

In the southern and central lands, outside the biggest towns, there has been, however, no marked increase. In several of the provinces— Tuscany, Marches, Umbria, Abruzzi e Molise, especially—the rise in population has been very modest during the past quarter-century. To the south of the highly fertile Po Basin, the soils of the Apennine highlands, which rise above two narrow and discontinuous coastal plains, are, in general, of very indifferent quality. Moreover, the rainfall of the peninsula, though abundant in winter, is not sufficient to compensate for the drought and excessive evaporation of midsummer. For these reasons, agriculture in Central and Southern Italy is generally precarious, though there are certain exceptional lowlands, including the Plain of Naples, which are renowned for their intensive and prosperous farming. In Apulia, and the south-east generally, the deficiency of water is especially acute, and has been alleviated, only to a small extent, by ambitious projects of irrigation.

As a whole, Italy is seriously deficient in mineral wealth, although the extensive use of Alpine water-power compensates for the lack of fuel in the industrial districts of Piedmont and Lombardy. The metal and silk industries, which are concentrated in Turin and Milan, have no counterpart elsewhere; and those peasants of the rural south, who attempt to escape from the harsh conditions of their lives, have hardly any alternative save migration. The industrial north has become a focus for those who, whilst seeking new opportunities, intend to remain on Italian soil.

The Po Basin, where the Italian State had its cradle, and in which occurs the greatest concentration of population in Italy, is likely to remain the geographical focus of the nation. Rome retains its unrivalled prestige, as a heritage from ancient days, but Milan is unique in its own way. It is the industrial and commercial metropolis, and its

[3] The rise of population was from 39,974,000 in 1921 to 41,177,000 in 1931, and to 45,210,000 in 1941. In 1921 the population of England and Wales was closely similar to that of Italy, but by 1931—the last British census-year—the total had been raised to only 39,952,000.

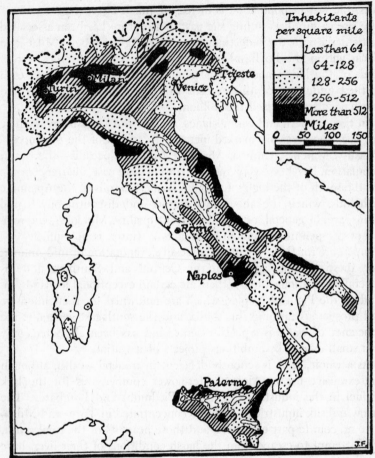

FIG. 26.—ITALY: DISTRIBUTION OF POPULATION DENSITY (1931)

part in the equipping of the nation for both peace and war is unrivalled. In no country of Europe is the contrast between one region
and another sharper than it is between the well-watered, alluvial lowland of the Po, with its rich, varied agriculture and pulsating industrial life, and the dry limestone uplands of the south.

The consequence of a difference of geographical and economic
orientation is the growth of a division between the interests and
outlook of northerners and southerners, respectively. Community
of language and the tenacious hold of Roman Catholicism, in most

parts of the country, cannot compensate altogether for such a divergence. Moreover, racial inheritance emphasizes the contrast between north and south. The "Alpine" ethnic characteristics (of brachycephalism, etc.) are dominant in the Plain of the Po and its mountainous fringe, whilst "Mediterranean" man, notably long-headed, is established in the south of the Peninsula, and in Sicily and Sardinia. The extent to which differences of social and economic outlook, such as those noticeable within Italy, are due to environment or to ancestry, provides a question for which there is yet no satisfactory answer.

It is not suggested that the effect of geography, aided by the shattering effect of the war on Italy, will be to divide the country permanently into two nations. Loyalty to the national ideal is strong throughout, and is deeper than the Fascist régime which it long antedates. Italy is not intended by geography, however, to be a Great Power, and defeat in both Europe and Africa is likely to close the chapter of imperial ambition, at least for some time. There remains the urgent question of the territorial accommodation of the Italian people, so long disregarded by those Western Powers, from which sympathetic appreciation of Italy's necessity might normally be expected.

Migration from region to region within Italy, more particularly from the South to the Po Basin, has been maintained as one of the consequences of the overcrowding which has long occurred, especially on the more infertile soils. The population problem of Central and Southern Italy will be best appreciated by the English reader, when it is shown that semi-arid districts, including some of stony soil, carry densities of rural population which would be considered high— i.e., 180-250 persons per square mile—in the best-farmed counties of Britain. Prior to the passing of legislation (1924)[4] in the United States, which very strictly limited the immigration of settlers from Eastern and Southern Europe, most of the emigrants from provinces as far north as the latitude of Rome (approximately), went to eastern parts of the U.S.A. From the northern half of Italy, prior to 1924, a majority of the emigrants tended to seek new homes, either in the

[4] Under the U.S.A. Immigration Law of 1924, the annual admission of Europeans was reduced to 2 per cent of the number of any given nationality residing in the United States in 1890. As by that date the big influx of Italians into the United States had hardly begun, the restriction was particularly severe on Italian immigrants.

prosperous industrial cities, or, across the frontier, in France or
Switzerland. Many of these represented a seasonal movement of
artisans and mechanics, for the spring and summer only. On the
other hand, a considerable minority of emigrants from the North left
Italy, by the great port of Genoa, to join the stream of westward
migration, going, mainly from Southern Italy, to North and South
America.[5]

By the year 1924 there were, in America as a whole, nearly eight
and a half million Italian-born settlers, whilst in Europe (outside
Italy) the corresponding figure was 1,303,000, of whom the great
majority were in France. In addition, there were about 190,000
Italians in Africa, though mainly outside the Italian Empire and
within French-protected Tunisia.[6]

From the standpoint of the Italian Government, the loss to the
nation, which these figures represented, was of the utmost gravity. It
so happened, however, that the widest doorway open to the Italian
colonist, namely the harbour of New York, was virtually closed at almost exactly the same time that the Fascist régime, on coming to
power, forbade further large-scale overseas emigration outside the
Italian Empire. Mussolini's policy was designed, first, to augment
Italian territory both in Europe and in Africa, particularly at the expense of France and Abyssinia; secondly, to intensify the settlement
of Italian North-East Africa, and, at the same time, to increase the
potentialities of the soil of Central and Southern Italy, by grandiose
schemes of land reclamation and irrigation. Such reclamation of soil,
however, as the Italian Government achieved in the years before the
Second World War, touched only the fringe of the country's population problem. Throughout the Fascist period the density of population on the poorer soils remained too high in relation to the available
resources, and the number living on the margin of subsistence was not
appreciably lessened by the land projects undertaken.

It is not widely appreciated that the colonial dependencies of
Italy, despite their vast extent—nearly one million square miles in
North-East Africa—were, for the greater part, merely desert wastes,

[5] Throughout the greater part of the nineteenth century the majority of the
Italians who crossed the Atlantic entered South America—Brazil, Uruguay, and
Argentina, in particular. At the end of the century, and down to 1914, the main
westward stream entered the United States.

[6] These statistics were obtained from the usually reliable *Commissariato dell'
Emigrazione*, which published them in 1927.

which no other Power coveted. Libya, taken from Turkey as a prize
of war in 1912, seemed to offer greater possibilities for colonization
than Eritrea and Italian Somaliland, combined. Yet Libya is part of
the Sahara, with a narrow fringe of relative fertility along the Mediterranean littoral, in Cyrenaica and Tripolitania. In the year 1938, there
were in the Empire as a whole (excluding Ethiopia) some 95,000
Italians, and, of these, 89,000 were settled in Cyrenaica and in the
neighbourhood of Tripoli. These numbers were not in themselves impressive, yet they represented, in view of the widespread aridity, a
notable success in the taming of the North African wilderness. No
other territory of comparable size and poverty in any continent could
show so populous a colony of white men.

The short-lived Italian conquest of Abyssinia in 1935-6 was an act
of aggression, largely condoned by the same Powers which were
allied to Italy in the First World War. France and Great Britain
had jointly refused Italy's claim to a share in mandatory responsibilities for the ex-German and ex-Turkish dependencies, in Africa
and Asia, respectively; but, from the final decade of the nineteenth
century onwards, they had recognized the special interests of Italy
in those parts of Abyssinia which were contiguous to Eritrea and
Italian Somaliland.

From the Italian point of view, Abyssinia offered unrivalled opportunities for colonial settlement. Its lofty, well-watered plateau of
savanna and forest was but sparsely occupied by a primitive people,
who, moreover, were outside the protection of any Power. The agricultural possibilities were recognized to be immense, and it was believed that residence in virtually equatorial latitudes would not be
inimical to the health of Italian colonists, who, at home, had acquired
some experience of excessive summer temperatures.[7] Italian settlement proceeded apace between 1936 and 1939, and, by the middle of
the latter year, numbered over 30,000, which was greater than the
white population of the British East African Colony of Kenya, after
half a century of colonization. Whether or not the Italians could
withstand successfully the physiological consequences of settlement in
high altitudes seems not to have been proved, one way or the other,
by their brief Abyssinian venture; but it is certain that, in those parts

[7] The summer heat of Southern Italy is almost African. Naples is not the
hottest place in Italy in July, but its mean temperature for that month (76° F.)
virtually equals that of Algiers (77° F.).

of North Africa where altitude is normal, they are not unduly troubled by torrid conditions or by excessive sunlight, and are able to undertake and depend on their own manual labour.

Tunisia has been, for over half a century, the chief African outlet for the South Italian emigrant, whose labour has been mainly responsible for the agricultural prosperity of the French Protectorate. Under French law the Tunisian Italians received a generous measure of autonomy, but their mother-country laid claim to full rights of sovereignty, largely because of a supposed numerical superiority of Italians over French in the non-native population. For this reason the Protectorate Government felt the necessity to close the door to further Italian immigration.

The events of the Second World War are not likely to improve Italian opportunities for colonization outside Italy, nor are they likely to produce the quiet atmosphere in which to consider the needs of the Italian peasantry for new outlets. Despite Italy's part in the war, it seems very likely, at the time of writing, that some portions of Italy's former territories in Africa will be restored. Yet were Italian sovereignty in North-East Africa to be again as extensive as ever it was, the effect in reducing congestion in Italy would certainly be as insignificant as in former days. Moreover, unless there should be an international settlement more far-reaching than any that may now be foreseen, Italian overseas migration is not again likely to compare with the large-scale exodus to the Americas, which preceded the First World War.

Italy must depend on a more intensive development of her own resources—for which, however, the guidance and tangible help of the Great Powers will be required—and on a changed social outlook, which will help to adjust the size of families to the area of available agricultural land. The territorial needs of her peasants may, some time in the future, receive consideration within a new European order, which will have less regard for the immutability of frontiers and the exclusiveness of nationalism than had the European system of 1919-39. In the immediate future, however, there can be little expectation of the extension of Italy's frontiers beyond the limits of 1939.

France is the only neighbour which could concede, from its vast wealth of agricultural land, sufficient space to ease materially the overcrowding of the poorer lands of Central and Southern Italy.

Since the beginning of the twentieth century, the number of Italians residing on French soil—more particularly the rural districts of Southern France—has been high. In 1911 it was nearly half a million, or nearly as many as all other foreign contingents within France added together. By 1931 the number had risen to about one million, which was easily the greatest colony of Italians throughout the Old World. The largest concentration was in the south-eastern angle of France, to the east of the lower Rhône, where the demand for agricultural labour could not adequately be met from a slowly dwindling French population. Before the Second World War, there were certain areas where Italian immigrants outnumbered the French natives, as Fascist propaganda was quick to proclaim. Moreover, history could easily be invoked to establish a claim to French lands, notably Savoy and Nice, which, as late as 1859, were part of Piedmont, the nucleus of the then evolving Italian State.

France and Italy are nations between which there is no natural antagonism. The Roman tradition in law and religion is still strong in France, and the Western democratic way of life, with its emphasis on the rights of the individual, is common to both. An *entente* between them is a not unlikely outcome of the war, partly for reasons already suggested, and partly because of the suffering which both have endured at the hands of Germany. Fear of the re-birth of a militant Germany would be, in itself, sufficient to draw the two principal Latin nations of Europe together.

It may, however, be safely contended that mutual sympathy between France and Italy will be enduring, only if France, from her abundance of rich territory in both Europe and North Africa, concedes, to her geographically unfortunate neighbour, room for expansion, sufficient to relieve the extreme pressure on the overcrowded lands of the Italian peninsula. Tunisia and South-Eastern France are suggested because of their proximity to Italy. Each already has a considerable Italian population: neither has been part of France for as long as a century, and an appeal to history would not necessarily confirm, beyond question, the French title to possession, in either case. Such territorial concessions would be acts of grace, which would abundantly repay the nation that made the sacrifice.

For her part, Italy must be prepared to relinquish her hold on parts of the Dalmatian coast which she obtained, with dubious right, as a result of her participation in the First World War. The basis of her claim to Trieste, Istria, Fiume, Zara, and certain Dalmatian islands was examined earlier, in the light of the distribution of Italian and Slav communities on the eastern shores of the Adriatic Sea. Although decisions regarding the Italo-Yugoslav frontier in the neighbourhood of Trieste are still (October, 1945) deferred, it is clear that Italy's claims require much more substantiation than was the case in 1919. Justice to the Yugoslavs demands that their natural outlets to the sea should be restored to them. Yet, even if Italy were permitted to retain its Dalmatian outposts, no relief to her population problem would ensue. The Dalmatian coast is a narrow, much-broken shelf, shut off from the Balkan interior, and its geographically confined settlements cannot expand.

We have outlined very briefly the geographical problem that confronts the statesmen of Italy. It is a problem whose demands will affect the planning of national policy, as much in its domestic as in its international aspects. As already shown by her participation in two World Wars, Italy will attach herself to any group of Powers which is sympathetic to her aspirations—that is, unless Peninsular Europe should learn to handle its territorial questions in ways which the federal experience of the United States and Soviet Russia, respectively, have proved possible.

FRANCE AS A GREAT POWER

Until the national disaster of 1940, the claim of France to a place among the Great Powers of the world was unquestioned in diplomatic circles. Her contributions to civilization for nearly one thousand years, and an unrivalled military tradition were the guarantees of her prominence in the social and political affairs of mankind. No nation in this world of ruthless competition may depend for long, however, on past glory and achievements. Authority goes to the Power whose territorial resources and population—vast in their scale—are highly organized, with the aid of the most modern technical equipment; and, judged by the standards of her rivals, France, even before the First World War, failed to qualify for the rôle which she demanded as her right.

In two respects France falls short of the modern standard of a Great Power. She is deficient in population; secondly, her mining and manufacturing basis is inadequate.

Reference to Italy has already emphasized the great numerical surge of her population in recent time. In dealing with France the first consideration is a population which is virtually stationary at the small total of approximately forty-two millions. Allowing for the accession of Alsace and Lorraine in 1919 and for a very large colony of foreigners, the total of French inhabitants was lower in 1936 than it was thirty years earlier.[8] A very grave position was revealed by the census of 1921, when, despite the inclusion of the populations of both Alsace and Lorraine, the total was considerably less than it had been in 1911.

Even when her military victory is taken into account, the First World War was more disastrous to the welfare of France than to any other Power that was engaged. The death-roll of her finest manhood mounted to nearly one and a half millions, a figure which far exceeded the total for the entire British Empire. To this were added enormous lists of wounded casualties, and the devastation of the principal industrial zone of the country. From the grievous loss of blood France has not yet recovered, indeed may never fully recover. She entered the Second World War in no mood for the renewed slaughter of her manhood in a struggle with her old enemy; and the mood was a virtual admission of her physical inability to fulfil any longer her commitments as a first-class Power.

The depopulation of the French countryside is not compensated, as it is in many other countries—the British Isles provide an instance —by increased crowding in the towns. Birth-rates are low for both town and country, and such increases in urban population as have occurred are due mainly to the settlement of foreign workers— Belgians and Poles in the north-eastern mining and manufacturing centres, and Italians in the south-eastern towns, especially Marseilles and Nice. The great Mediterranean port is almost exceptional amongst French cities in that it has experienced a lively growth during the last quarter-century. Its population rose from 551,000

[8] The population of France during the early part of the twentieth century is shown in the following table:

Year	Area in sq. miles	Population	Inhabitants per sq. mile
1906	207,000	39,252,000	189
1911	207,000	39,602,000	191
1921	212,660	39,210,000	184
1931	212,660	41,835,000	196
1936	212,660	41,907,000	197

in 1911 to 914,000 in 1936, whereas Bordeaux, the senior Atlantic port, diminished from 262,000 to 258,000, in the same period. Lyons and Lille, the textile capitals, were normal, in that they showed either slight increase or actual decline. Paris has the rare distinction, amongst the great capitals of the world, of failing to maintain an upward trend of population.[9]

The welfare of France depends less than that of Britain on the prosperity of its cities. This is testified by a comparison between the two nations, as regards both the number of large towns in each country and the respective ratios of urban to rural population. France still depends for her social stability on a peasantry, which numbers one-half the nation and is in owner-occupation of three-quarters of the land of the country, distributed in more than five million holdings.

Examination of the geography of France discloses the high fertility of its wide river-basins—those of the Seine, Rhône, Garonne-Dordogne, in particular. In no country of Europe is the combination of climate and soils more favourable to a varied and abundant husbandry. The physical environment of rural life is, therefore, widely different from that of Italy. There is no geographical reason why there should be movement away from the richer farm-lands, and, in general, there is no such trend. Excepting the mountain regions, notably the *Massif Central* and the French Alps, from which there has been for long a slow migration, the depopulation of the countryside is due almost entirely to a conscious restriction of the birth-rate, which is common even in the prosperous land of Aquitaine. There, and elsewhere, the practice of keeping families down to one child is intended to avoid excessive sub-division of the tiny farms.[10]

None can tell how France, confronted by the changed Europe to which she is restored, will adjust her national and imperial policy. With self-respect and dignity regained, it is certain, however, that she will wish to reassert herself as one of the leaders of Western civilization. Experience in her latest struggle for national independence and solidarity is likely, in the long run, to strengthen, rather than to weaken her spirit. Fortunately, her casualties were but a small

[9] Paris: 1911—2,888,000; 1936—2,829,000
Lyons: 1911— 524,000; 1936— 571,000
Lille: 1911— 218,000; 1936— 201,000

[10] v. A. Demangeon et M. Matruchot: "Les Variations de la population de la France, de 1881 à 1921," *Ann. de Géogr.*, vol. 35, 1926.

fraction of those of the earlier war, and vast numbers of her manhood returned from German prison-camps. The restoration of the 1939 frontiers is not questioned, and whether or not, on international

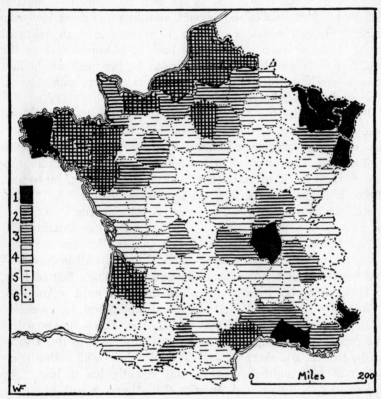

FIG. 27.—FRANCE: DISTRIBUTION OF POPULATION DENSITY (1931)
(BY DEPARTMENTS)

1. Over 256 persons per square mile   4. 128–154 persons per square mile
2. 180–256   ”   ”   ”   ”   5. 100–128   ”   ”   ”   ”
3. 154–180   ”   ”   ”   ”   6. Under 100 ”   ”   ”   ”

grounds, the re-annexation of Alsace and Lorraine is defensible, in respect of economic geography these two rich provinces are vitally important to her.

Limiting our view to the France of Europe, it seems that her prosperity is guaranteed by geography, particularly as regards agricultural output. In mining and large-scale manufacturing she has never been able to rival either Germany or Great Britain, and it is doubtful if she has ever seriously attempted to do so. Coal, upon which every Great Power has so far built its industrial edifice, is deficient in both quality and amount, and the vast field of low-grade *minette* ore in Lorraine is not able to compensate as an industrial asset. Without either an adequate basis of industrial fuel or the tradition of large-scale industry possessed by her great neighbours, it is extremely doubtful if France could ever compare with them in magnitude of metallurgical output.

But France has the advantage, rare in Western Europe, of possessing in her own fertile and varied soils the means of complete agricultural self-sufficiency. In a way that is surprising to the English visitor, who is accustomed to foodstuffs imported from every continent, the French are satisfied to depend on their own husbandry. There is no problem of food supply, and no demand for "living-space," which is one reason why France is not a menace to the peace of Europe. Wheat, the staple of diet, is grown to an extent which demonstrates the wealth of the French granary. Between 1924 and 1938, the average annual output—more than 350 million bushels—was twice that of Germany, and one and a half times that of Italy.

There is another France with which the world must reckon—the France of Algeria and of the tropical and sub-tropical dependencies. For a long period of the Second World War, Algiers functioned as the capital of France. There the national resistance to the invader was organized, and there General de Gaulle spoke with authority on behalf of his countrymen. Only very recently has it been fully appreciated in Britain and America that Algeria is part of metropolitan France, and that its *départements* are on precisely the same footing as all others of France, with direct representation in the National Assembly in Paris.

Algeria is part of the well-watered Mediterranean rim of Africa, and its environment offers to French and other Latin settlers geographical conditions which closely resemble those of the Midi. The climate and vegetation—both wild and cultivated—of Mediterranean France are repeated, with no fundamental differences; and Algeria, apart from its contribution of high-grade iron-ore, sends big supplies of wine and wheat to the French market.

The political importance of Algeria, which greatly increased as soon as European France was overwhelmed by Germany in 1940, originated in the attempt of France, from 1871 onwards, to recover in North Africa the prestige which it had lost in its first war with Germany. Unfortunately, however, the attempt to make Algeria strong by the "planting" of French peasants was hindered, almost from the outset, by the decline in the French birth-rate, which became pronounced from 1871 onwards. The urgency which characterized Italian emigration from 1880 onwards was generally absent from the French settlement of North Africa. Even in Algeria, to which the main stream of emigrants was directed, there was doubt for some time if the French would exceed the combined numbers of Italian and Spanish settlers. Until the beginning of the twentieth century, Spaniards were as numerous as French in Western Algeria, whilst, farther east, an Italian influx from Tunisia was considerable. In the period between the World Wars French migration to Algeria diminished to insignificance.

Nevertheless, the aggregate of the French population of Algeria is impressive enough, when compared with other "white" colonies in Africa. At about 850,000 it is, excepting the solitary case of Dutch settlement of South Africa, the largest, and probably the most successfully acclimatized, "white" colony within the African continent.

With a disregard for a "colour-bar" which is entirely at variance with British colonial policy, the French have approved the intermarriage of colonists and natives (Berbers and Arabs). The "mixed" Algerian type which is evolving, and for which a successful future is foretold, demonstrates its ability to fit into French civilization and to withstand the difficulties of the North African climate. The present signs are that, ultimately, the entire French colony will merge with the native population, to form a distinctive Euro-African community.

Although Morocco and Tunisia, as Protectorates of France, are different in status from Algeria, all three fall within the same major geographical region, and serve as bases not only for French agricultural and industrial enterprise, but also for French settlement.[11] In an entirely different category are the vast tropical territories administered by the French Republic in Africa and South-Eastern Asia. French West and Equatorial Africa, together, cover a compact

[11] In 1936 the European population of the Protectorates was: Tunisia, 213,000 (including 108,000 French); Morocco, 237,000 (including 177,000 French).

area of some three million square miles, or one-quarter of the African continent. France, indeed, possesses the largest, compact domain of any Power within the tropical zone of the world. The Sahara is included, and considerably reduces the French Empire's economic importance, but the lands outside the limits of the Great Desert are still enormous. whilst their potential value is beyond estimate.

It is obvious that the magnitude of the French dependencies, in Africa alone—where they are nearest and most accessible—constitutes an imperial responsibility capable of fulfilment by a first-class Power only. And here it is necessary to question seriously if metropolitan France, with the evidence of its population trend before us, will be able to maintain a burden of empire, which was proving excessive in the period between the World Wars.

Greatly differing between themselves in geographical character and in civilization, the majority of the tropical dependencies of France are yet alike in their climatic hostility to the settlement of French or other European colonists. The Republic has no considerable holdings in the temperate zones—except the North-West African littoral—which are comparable with the British Dominions. But, in all parts of her Empire, France extends to native peoples, irrespective of colour, the possibility of citizenship, involving social, economic, and political equality with Europeans.

The declared aim is to "assimilate" native peoples to French civilization. It is realized that the process is likely to be prolonged, but in its logical, ultimate result it will sweep away native laws, customs, and the tribal or other indigenous organization of community life. In time, it is hoped that the difference between *la France métropole* and *la France d'outremer* will be merely one of geographical position. One consequence of the extension to African Natives of the privileges and duties of French citizenship is that, in her European wars, France has called freely on the services of the Senegalese and other regiments. In itself, this is a tacit admission of the inability of the French to complete from their own numbers the manning of their frontiers.

On its economic side the development of the French tropical dependencies has contributed comparatively little to the welfare of either Africa or Asia. In French Africa, outside the Mediterranean littoral, there is no indigenous agricultural activity comparable in scale with the cultivation of cocoa and cotton in the Gold Coast and Uganda, respectively. French Equatorial Africa, immense in its latent resources of forest and savanna, has virtually stagnated, in an economic sense, since it was incorporated, towards the close of last century. Active pioneering, supported by capital, has been lacking in the French Empire as a whole,[12] and the conclusion is inevitable that France—both the Nation and the State—has not the resources for extensive empire-building.

It was not until the First World War that France was aroused to its paradoxical position—a great colonial Power, still failing to supply more than a very small fraction of its requirements of tropical food-stuffs and raw materials from its overseas dependencies. Products such as rubber, cotton, and cabinet-woods—all of which French Africa and Indo-China should be able to furnish in quantities far exceeding French demands—were imported into France, mainly from the territories of other Powers. Even after the First World War, economic development was desultory, in general.

Like Great Britain, the French Republic obtained, under the mandate system of the League of Nations, a large share in the administration of the ex-German and ex-Turkish territories. Syria, without Palestine, together with much the greater parts of the Cameroons and Togoland were allotted to her. Without investigating the feasibility of the mandate system as a method of international administration of backward communities, it is indisputable that France found it difficult in the extreme—largely because of her other imperial burdens—to improve, or even maintain, the standards of administration in Syria and the Cameroons.

So highly centralized was the Empire before the collapse of France in 1940 that, when Paris was captured by the enemy, there was little hope that any territories, with the possible exception of Algeria, would be able to function in isolation from the metropolis. But for the military assistance of Great Britain and the U.S.A. the conquest of French Africa by Germany and Italy would have been inevitable. At the same time, within even the most distant parts of French Africa, there was real enthusiasm on the part of the Natives for the

[12] In 1930 it was estimated that France had by then invested 7,200 million francs in all her overseas territories, and that of this total 70 per cent was concentrated in Mediterranean Africa, particularly Algeria. By contrast, the Netherlands had invested about 20,000 million francs in Java and Sumatra alone.

cause of France. Such loyalty was a consequence of the wisdom and humanity of a policy which extended opportunities for the enjoyment of French citizenship to backward peoples within the Empire.

France has to answer much criticism for the shortcomings of her imperial system. No doubt, sweeping reforms will be necessary, and the Republic will dangerously embarrass its future if it insists— as seems certain—on regaining all colonial territories which were within the Empire of 1939. Because of remoteness and of the attitude of the new China to the imperialism of the Western Powers, Indo-China will be a particularly difficult region for the French to administer. It would be a wise economy to relinquish exclusive authority over Tong-king, Annam, and Cochin-China, at least.

The future safety of France, especially in the immediate, post-war period, will depend on the close co-operation of powerful friends. Fear of a revival of German militarism may be expected to remain a dominant consideration, and adequate defence demands more than the protection of a line of frontier fortifications, such as that devised by General Maginot.

After the First World War, but before the emergence of Soviet Russia as a Great Power, France attempted to ensure her safety, in the face of a hostile Germany, by arranging a series of alliances with those States which, on Germany's eastern and south-eastern frontiers, had equal reason to fear renewed Teutonic aggression. Hence the defensive treaties with Poland and Czecho-Slovakia. These diplomatic instruments, however, proved useless for their purpose when they were required, in the crises of 1938 and 1939. They were useless, for the reason that the Soviet Union, the only European Power with a war-potential comparable with that of Germany, was not associated with France and Great Britain, in their plans. If the defence of France rests on the timely aid of a great army, Soviet Russia, for geographical reasons, is the only Power which is able to provide that military insurance. Russia is equally concerned to curb German aggression, and the organization of her vast resources in Asia will have the effect of reducing the relative importance of Germany as a military Power. On the other hand, with the passage of time, the military strength of France, insecurely based on a diminishing population, is likely to compare less and less favourably with that of Germany.

The influence of Great Britain cannot be omitted from these

considerations, and we turn to her special place in the political geography of Europe.

GREAT BRITAIN, IN ITS EUROPEAN ASSOCIATIONS

On many occasions, when Britain has been moved to intervene energetically in the affairs of continental Europe, her geographical detachment has been a disadvantage. This has been most obvious when a great army has had to be transported to the mainland of Europe. Yet the natural defences of the English Channel remain Britain's outstanding geographical asset in time of war, so long as the threat of invasion remains. The war-making possibilities of Hitlerite Germany, as of Napoleonic France, were shown in the continental scale of its land operations. Yet neither made adequate preparation for that stage in the conquest of Europe which required the projection across the Channel of an army, able to overwhelm the island garrison of Britain, and so well escorted as to be safe from naval assault. From both Germany and the France of Napoleon the naval arm received, inevitably perhaps, less attention than the military; and, in offensive operations against the foremost maritime Power, an inadequate estimate of naval possibilities proved ultimately decisive.

Although the evolution of air-power, fundamentally disturbing as it is to old conceptions of naval and military strategy and tactics, has not eliminated the function of the sea-moat between continental Europe and Britain, it has recently prevented the latter Power from deploying her full naval strength in the narrow seas. During 1940 and 1941, when Germany held air superiority over Western Europe, the heaviest and most vulnerable units of the British Fleet could not afford to move within easy bombing range of the continental coast. Conversely, owing to the collapse of France and a mounting air strength, Germany, in the second and third years of the war, was able to use the French Channel ports with considerable immunity, and even with local command of the sea, despite the marked inferiority of her fleet.

In this connexion, significant of the influence of air-power is the recent German occupation of the Channel Islands. This small archipelago, which was attached to the Crown of England continuously from the days of the Norman Conquest until 1940, is, at its nearest point, within twenty miles of the Normandy coast, but not less than sixty miles from Southern England. During the Napoleonic

Wars, when France was hostile, the British defence of the islands rested securely on naval supremacy. An advantage over her enemy at sea was retained by Britain, in her two continental wars of the twentieth century; but, in the second of these, Germany's air strength over the Channel Islands was temporarily overwhelming.

In time of peace, Britain's insular detachment engenders a mood of aloofness, which is frequently manifest in her political and social relations with continental countries. Because of her naturally drawn and hitherto unassailable frontiers, Britain's economic, social, and political traditions appear to her citizens to be distinct from those of any other nation. On the other hand, insularity sometimes makes it difficult for Britons to appreciate, with understanding, the problems which determine the inter-relations of continental peoples. These problems, in their political aspects, are, as we have seen, of a complexity and a gravity which have no parallel within Britain. Yet this small island, by dint of its international authority and its own war-time exertions, has inevitably played a leading rôle in the peace settlements which have terminated successive continental convulsions. In the settlement which ended the First World War, Britain's sanction was required for every important alteration of frontier, no matter how geographically remote from Britain the region affected might be. Yet, once its part in the last peace settlement was completed, Britain, following its tradition, reduced its European commitments to the minimum, and withdrew into comparative isolation.

Acknowledging membership of the European community, as both history and geography demand, Britain, by virtue of her position off the Atlantic coast of the continent, is yet obliged, as no other European country is to the same degree, to prevent European commitments from outweighing those which link her to the continents where her imperial interests lie. It is not always fully appreciated—though the political map of the world makes it obvious—that Britain, with the largest overseas empire which any Power has yet acquired, holds hardly any territory on the mainland of the continent of which she is a leading member-state.[13] Her African, Asiatic, and American interests divert her from concentration on the special problems of Europe. It has never been claimed, even by those most hostile to Britain's imperialism, that she has territorial ambitions on

[13] The naval base of Gibraltar—area under two square miles—has been part of the British Empire since 1713, and is a Crown Colony.

the continent of Europe. Since the loss of the French dominions of the English kings, in the sixteenth century, there has been a clear realization that occupation of a country in the face of its aroused nationalism has no future save disaster.

Largely determining Britain's European policy, at all times, is the desire to prevent any one Power from acquiring hegemony over the continent. If any State, hostile to British interests, should gain the mastery of the mainland, and particularly of that part lying adjacent to the narrow seas, it would be impelled to invade these islands. So runs the argument. Britain's defence requires, on this reckoning, a policy devised to ensure, as far as possible, a balance of military strength between the leading States of Europe. On the other hand, the disastrous events of this century have driven home the lesson that such an international balance is incapable of safeguarding peace, except for very limited periods.

Until 1939, the only Powers which had gone far to achieve European hegemony were Germany and France (prior to 1815). Each offered, in its period of aggression, a direct threat to Britain, by reason of its control of all, or part, of the mainland littoral facing the narrow seas. After the Napoleonic Wars, Britain was party to the plan to "neutralize" the Low Countries, from which, as a military base, the challenge to her security might, most easily, be renewed. The achievement of Belgian sovereignty in 1831 coincided with international recognition of the new State, as one which was to be "perpetually neutral." The interposition of Belgium as a "buffer" served its purpose for the remainder of the nineteenth century; but its neutrality counted for little, when, early the following century, the interests of these same Powers clashed in war.

Along the western seaboard of continental Europe extends a continuous belt of States, all of them—with the exception of France —"small," as political power is reckoned nowadays. In each case association with Great Britain has for long been close and friendly, and, although she does not pose as their protector, their welfare is very much Britain's concern. Indeed, enemy occupation of their territories at once introduces a threat to the defence of Britain herself.

Four of these small Powers—namely, Norway, Denmark, the Netherlands, and Portugal—though diminutive in population in every case,[14] possess illustrious records of maritime enterprise. They have

---

[14] Of these Powers, the most populous does not exceed eight million inhabitants, whilst Norway possesses fewer than three millions.

carried their influence across every ocean, and their overseas associations of empire or of commerce match, or exceed, in importance
the links with their continental neighbours. Yet, although the influence of these small maritime Powers on the course of European
affairs is greater than their actual physical size of area and of population would suggest, it is still modest, in aggregate, by comparison
with that of a single first-class Power. This is the more true because
they have never yet co-operated in the formulation of a common
foreign policy. Indeed, their respective national interests are frequently divergent, if not competitive, as shown, for example, by
the differences that recently divided Belgium and the Netherlands,
in regard to the control of the navigable channel of the River Scheldt.

In the Europe of to-morrow the future of the little States is likely
to remain uncertain, even precarious. No longer is it possible, if it
was ever so, for countries of a few million inhabitants and modest
resources to seek security on the basis of national independence and
a strictly neutral attitude to the disputes which divide the Great
Powers. It is, without question, a time of enormous concentrations
of economic and political power within a few Super States. They
alone can plan their industrial and agricultural development on the
basis of adequate resources and, at the same time, employ their
wealth to build formidable weapons of offence and defence. In a
better world than ours the small nation would be able, on the basis of
a modest, yet efficient, economy to maintain a high cultural standard,
without the ever-present fear of the aggression of powerful neighbours. As it is, the Norways and Denmarks of to-day realize that
their cherished neutrality is no longer an adequate guarantee of their
survival as States or as Nations.

It seems inevitable that the small maritime States of Western
Europe, if they are to survive, should associate themselves more
closely than ever before with some Great Power, within whose
geographical range they are situated and for whose cultural standards
and tradition they have respect. Norway, in so far as it has been
able to express the national will, wishes the protection of Great
Britain, and of the United States also. Some small nations of the
western fringe have not made their wishes so clear, but it is reasonable
to suppose that Portugal, Belgium, the Netherlands, and Denmark,
for at least some years to come, will welcome a British guarantee
of their integrity as nation-states. If they do so, it will be partly

because Britain's particular kind of democratic ideal has close ideological contacts with their own,[15] and partly because Britain, as the principal sea-and-air Power of Western Europe, is in a specially favourable geographical position to act as guarantor.

The permanence of any such British "system" within Western Europe will necessarily depend on Britain's authority in its relations with the other Great Powers of the world. The question, whether or not Britain will be able to increase its commitments as a European Power—not to speak of its wide-ranging responsibilities in other continents—can be answered only by an investigation of its sources of strength. A lengthy analysis is not possible here, but the relation of Britain's European and Imperial undertakings to its resources of man-power and material must be kept in mind.

As the Empire is, in a geographical sense, the most dispersed group of politically-associated territories which the world has known, the problem of defence is particularly difficult. In war, the maintenance of extended supply-lines is a matter of constant concern, whilst Great Britain, the heart of the Empire, requires for its protection so great a concentration of all arms of defence that the weakening of outlying and—strategically—less important territories may become inevitable.[16]

Until 1939, the Navy, the mainstay of Imperial defence, possessed an armament equal to that of the United States Fleet, according to a ratio settled by the Washington Treaty, shortly after the First World War. The arrangement between the two leading naval Powers involved no necessary diminution of the absolute strength of the Empire at sea, but its maritime supremacy was at an end. Not many years before, Britain had been able to maintain a "two-Power standard" at sea, and at that time Germany was her most serious competitor.

The defence of the United States' coastline requires two separate ocean fleets, whilst scattered islands demand the maintenance of supply lines as far west as the Philippines. Even so, the geographical range of the American Navy in 1939 was small in comparison with

[15] This is true in the case of every small nation of Western Europe, with the exception of Portugal, whose national ideal is not yet clearly expressed.

[16] In 1939, apart from Britain, no part of the Empire was in a position to undertake its own defence. The weakness of the Dominions and Dependencies was especially notable at sea. Australia alone had a more than negligible fleet, yet its heaviest unit was a cruiser of 10,000 tons.

that of the British. In the Indian and South Atlantic Oceans, the United States had no special responsibilities. Taking into account the wide dispersal of the British Fleet, it was, therefore, not possible, at short notice, to concentrate in home waters a weight of armament equal to that which the U.S.A., or Japan, could concentrate for the defence of its own shores.

In order that the small maritime nations of Western Europe should receive protection, equivalent to that extended by Great Britain to the Dominions and Dependencies, not only would a considerable expansion of the British Navy in European waters be required. It would also be necessary for Britain to possess naval and air bases on the European mainland, at such points as Bergen (Norway), Esbjerg (Denmark), and Antwerp (Belgium). Each of these possible developments would be open to strong objection; the first, mainly on the ground of economy; the second, because the sovereignty of the small States would be infringed—a matter of concern not only to the States directly affected, but also to all the Powers of continental Europe. The possibility of the co-operation of the French Navy may also be considered, but there can be no certainty that post-war France, in deciding between alternatives, will prefer to be more closely associated with the first naval Power of Europe than with the greatest military Power, namely, Soviet Russia.

There is a further consideration which would strengthen opposition within Britain to a plan for extending naval, as well as air, protection to the small maritime Powers of Western Europe. In the modern world the widening of the "sphere of influence" of one Great Power inevitably restricts the "sphere" of another. From such causes wars originate, as Britain, with long experience and a tradition of extreme caution in European affairs behind her, has never been slow to realize.

The maintenance by Great Britain of naval and air fleets, with bases on the mainland of Western Europe, would involve principles of policy which are absent from her naval undertakings within the Mediterranean Sea. The function of Gibraltar and Malta, her only European naval bases outside Britain itself, is not to promote British interests in Spain and Italy, respectively; neither is it to protect these countries, but to ensure the safe passage of British shipping between the Atlantic and the Indian Oceans. For the same purpose, the naval base at Alexandria and the Suez Canal are parts of Britain's imperial defences.[17] The strength of the Mediterranean Fleet, to be effective, has to be commensurate with any possible hostile combination that may be brought against it. In the years between the wars, when Fascist imperialism threatened, the Italian Navy, with a geographical range limited to the Mediterranean and East African Seas, was in a position to threaten British supply lines between Gibraltar and Alexandria. When the collapse of resistance in France involved her fleet also, the balance of naval power in the Mediterranean was, for a time, violently disturbed in favour of Italy, and even the defence of Malta then became problematical.

Within Eastern Atlantic—including Mediterranean—waters, the supremacy of Great Britain, in combined sea-and-air power, was as complete immediately after the Second World War as it was after the defeat of Germany in 1918. The naval establishments of France and Italy respectively will, however, inevitably expand once again, and a new challenge to Britain's Mediterranean security will not be postponed indefinitely. Such a challenge will not necessarily be restricted to France or Italy, for developments in aviation may enable some Power without a coast on the Mediterranean to exert influence over its waters. It may even be necessary to take into account once again the view, formerly held by Fascist Italy, if not also by Spain, that Britain has a doubtful right to maintain a patrol of Mediterranean waters, so formidable in strength as to constitute a challenge to the sovereignty of Mediterranean States.

From this brief summary of certain aspects of Britain's relations with the European continent, we pass to an estimate of its resources in territory and population. Of the Great Powers likely to survive the war, Britain is remarkable for high density of settlement on a very limited area. Yet the aggregate population is less than one-third of that of the U.S.A. or of European Russia. Contrast with the latter Powers is important, for they alone, in company with Britain, are likely to be of the first magnitude.[18]

Will Britain be able to maintain its authority in Europe and

[17] By the terms of the Anglo-Egyptian Treaty of 1936, Egypt authorizes, without prejudice to her sovereign rights, the maintenance of British forces in the vicinity of the Canal.

[18] The defeat in the Second World War of Germany, Italy, and Japan has proved to be so comprehensive and devastating that their recovery must be long delayed; whilst China, enormous in bulk and population, cannot command authority as a Great Power until the process of national consolidation has proceeded much farther than at present.

elsewhere on the basis of a population, less than fifty millions strong, and increasing very slowly to a "peak," which is likely to be reached before the close of the present century? The labour required to handle the industrial and military equipment of a Great Power at war, already greatly exceeds the standards set by the First World War. Both the United States and the Soviet Union are able to mobilize a citizen population far in excess of 100 millions, and mass-organization for national ends is likely to involve much bigger totals in the future. In respect of numbers of citizens, Great Britain ranks with France and Italy, rather than with Russia or the United States.

Unlike other Great Powers which have known vigorous expansion of population, Britain has sent all her emigrants to distant continents.[19] In the nineteenth century, the population of these islands, increasing apace, sought outlets, mainly in the temperate latitudes of America, where new nations were in process of growth. The United States received a very large proportion of the stream of British colonists, and the ensuing loss to the motherland was not one of numbers only. It was the more serious in that the proportion of the young and virile amongst the emigrants was inevitably high. Other lands of British settlement are even more distant than North America. There is, however, the compensation that, although migration to South Africa, Australia, and New Zealand has involved loss to Britain, no foreign Power has gained at Britain's expense.

Within the Dominions of the Commonwealth the sum total of citizens of British stock reaches a bare twenty millions, and of this number nearly one-half are within Canada. By reason of geographical position, the settlers of the most distant Dominions are unable to devote themselves to the complicated questions which concern Europe, however sympathetic they may be. More and more they become preoccupied with the problems of their respective regions, all remote from Europe. Menaced as Australia and New Zealand have been for half a century by a predatory Japan, concentration upon the defence of their shores, even to the neglect of European issues, is appreciated with understanding by ourselves. As is everywhere true, the international questions in which any country is most

[19] In this connexion, consider the westward expansion of the United States to the Pacific coast in the nineteenth century; the contemporary Asiatic expansion of Russia; the German colonization of certain lands in Central and Eastern Europe; the Italian settlement of the Dalmatian coast and Tunisia; the French occupation of Algeria, etc.

intimately involved are those which affect the welfare of the region in which it is situated. No nation is free from narrowness of geographical outlook. It is an unavoidable conclusion that, owing to their wide geographical dispersal and to their comparatively small numerical strength, the Dominions are unable to exert, either separately or jointly, a powerful influence on the course of European affairs.

As compensation for its diminutive area and comparatively small population—when measured against the massive proportions of some other Powers—Britain has the notable advantage of a highly compact organization. Linking the industrial regions, each with its particular specialization of craft and product, is a dense network of transport lines, including a railway system remarkable for the number of alternative routes available between the main centres of population and industry. Inter-regional co-operation is easily possible, and could be more effective than in any other country of the world, if the re-planning of local government units, according to geographical principles, were seriously undertaken.

Moreover, in general it is true that the population of this "old" industrial country is so distributed as to be immediately available for industrial expansion. In the Soviet Union and United States, the opening-up of new industrial areas has caused large-scale transfers of labour, with consequent dislocation—however temporary. By contrast, Britain's population, situated mainly in and around the great ports and on the coal-fields, has experienced no fundamental change in geographical distribution for a century or more. Such recent changes as have occurred have, in the main, further emphasized the vast concentrations around London, Manchester, Birmingham, and two or three other centres, which were already developing by the end of the eighteenth century.[20]

The close proximity of most industrial districts to tidal water is an advantage of economic geography, for which there is no parallel in any other country, with the exception of Japan. In import and export trades, by which industrial Britain lives, charges for overland haulage, to and from the ports, are lower than in countries whose geographical situation is essentially continental. The advantage is

[20] Between 1921 and 1931 the total population of Great Britain increased by 4.7 per cent, whilst that of the seven largest cities, combined, increased by 6.5 per cent.

perhaps most in evidence in the export of coal—a particularly bulky commodity—whose influence on the overseas commerce of Britain has been pre-eminent. The South Wales and Durham coal-fields, which have played a particularly prominent rôle in the export of high-grade fuel, are closer to tidal water than any big "fields" of Europe or America.

As in British commerce, so also in our industry, the importance of coal is fundamental. Apart from the convenience of position already discussed, industrial Britain has no great geographical advantage, save an abundance of accessible coal. At the present rate of output the supply is considered likely to last for at least four centuries to come. No other mineral resource of industrial importance exists in such abundance, however, and of industrial metals—including iron—there is a scarcity. As a factor in her international authority, the ultimate dependence of Britain on coal has, unfortunately, received inadequate attention from both the statesman and the citizen. This is shown by repeated crises in the organization of the mining industry.

With hardly an exception, all raw materials of industry must be brought from overseas, and, for the maintenance of the traditional diet of the Englishman, great imports of foodstuffs are also necessary. Moreover, the overseas markets are more important to Britain's principal manufacturing industries than the demands of home consumption. At the same time, the skill and organization of foreign industry exert ever greater competition, and Britain cannot hope to regain all her former markets. The urgency of the need to find new customers in all parts of the world should be a spur to British enterprise, and openings in Europe—with its vast population of comparatively high material standards—should be investigated more closely than ever before. Such enterprise will be frustrated, however, by any rigid partition of the post-war world between a multitude of States, each determined to retain its economic sovereignty. More than any Great Power, because of the extreme sensitiveness of her industry and commerce to the condition of international relations, Britain, in her own interest, if for no higher motive, should strive for a new order, and particularly for a federated Europe.

SELECTED BIBLIOGRAPHY

AHLMANN, H. W.: "La Libye Septentrionale," *Geografiska Annaler*, Nos. 1 and 2, 1928.

ALMAGIA, —.: "The Repopulation of the Roman Campagna," *Geog. Rev.*, October, 1929.

ATSATT, MARJORY: "Population Estimates for England and Wales from the Eleventh to the Nineteenth Century," *Document 1459*, Washington, American Documentation Institute, Offices of Science Service, 1941.

CHARLES, ENID: "The Effect of Present Trends in Fertility and Mortality upon the Future Population of England and Wales and upon its Age Composition," *London and Cambridge Economic Series, Special Memorandum No. 40*, August 1935.

CIPPICO, COUNT A.: "Italy: the Central Problem of the Mediterranean," *Institute of Politics*, New Haven, 1926.

DAINELLI, G.: *Atlante Fisico Economico d'Italia*, Milano, 1939.

DEMANGEON, A., and MATINCHOT, M.: "Les variations de la population de la France de 1881 à 1921," *Ann. de Géogr.*, vol. 35, 1926, pp. 499–510.

EINZIG, P.: *Hitler's "New Order" in Europe*, London, 1941.

FOERSTER, F. W.: *Europe and the German Question*, London, 1941.

FOERSTER, R. F.: *The Italian Emigration of our Times*, Cambridge, 1919.

GALLOIS, L.: "Alsace-Lorraine and Europe," *Geogr. Rev.*, vol. 6, 1918, pp. 89–115.

GLASS, D. V.: *Population Policies and Movements in Europe*, Oxford, 1940.

HARROD, R. F.: "Britain's Future Population," *Oxford Pamphlets on Home Affairs*, No. H.4, London, 1943.

HUBER, M., etc.: *La Population de la France, son évolution et ses perspectives*, Paris, 1937.

KOLNAI, AUREL: *The War against the West*, London, 1938.

LONGOBARDI, C.: *Land Reclamation in Italy*, London, 1936.

MARINELLI, O. (ed.): *La Cirenaica: Geografica-economicapolitica*, Milan, 1923.

MARTONNE, E. DE: *Europe Centrale*, Tome IV, Première Partie: Généralités-Allemagne', Paris, 1930.

McGUIRE, C. E.: *Italy's International Economic Position*, New York, 1927.

NEWBIGIN, M. I.: *Southern Europe*, London, 1932.

ROBERTS, S. H.: *French Colonial Policy*, 2 vols., London, 1929.

United Kingdom, Royal Commission on the Distribution of the Industrial Population, Report . . . Command 6153, London, H.M. Stationery Office, 1940.

ZIMMERMAN, M.: "La Population de la France d'après le recensement de 7 mars, 1926," *Ann. de Géogr.*, vol. 36, 1927, pp. 328–35.

7.

Europe—In Its World Relations

In this final chapter we leave the interior of
Europe in order to place some major problems of the continent in
their world setting.

The disastrous effects of two World Wars on the social and
economic welfare of mankind cannot yet be measured. Destruction
of life and material on an unprecedented scale has been greater in
Europe than in the other continents, with grievous consequences for
the physical and moral health of the nations.[1] At the end of the
First World War it was widely held that European civilization would
not survive another such conflict. Yet the victorious Powers, without
exception, failed to appreciate the perilous condition of a world in
which they were the acknowledged leaders: and the ensuing war,
fought out on issues closely resembling those of 1914-18, outdid its
predecessor in destructiveness and ferocity. It is not surprising that
standards of European civilization are no longer accepted, without
searching question, by the citizens of other continents.

THE EMPIRES OF THE MARITIME POWERS

The hostilities of the European Powers have inevitably involved
those distant regions of the world where their empires extend.
During the present century, no fewer than twelve European nations
have possessed—in most cases, still retain—colonial domains in
other continents.[2] The downfall of Germany and Turkey in the

[1] Apart from other casualties, the death-roll in Europe, taking both Great Wars
together, is not less than 25 millions of their finest manhood.
[2] The colonial territories of Britain, France, Spain, Portugal, Belgium, the
Netherlands, Italy, and Russia, respectively, will be obvious to the reader, but
those recently held by Germany, Turkey, Denmark (the Virgin Islands), and
Greece (Western Anatolia) should not be overlooked.

First World War brought extensive additions to the empires of the Western Powers, though under the guise of Mandated Territories; and the defeat of both Japan and Italy in the Second World War has brought a further concentration of territories in the hands of a small group of States, all but one of which is based in Europe.

The process of eliminating the weaker contestants in the struggle for empire thus goes on, and nowhere is it more apparent than in Africa. Britain's influence in that continent, already predominant before the Second World War, has become overwhelming as a result of the defeat of Italy and of the heavy blow from which France will require Britain's help to recover. Not only France, however, but Britain, Belgium, and the Netherlands also, which between them in 1939 controlled much the greater part of the immensely rich tropical zone, have been weakened, as never before, by the dreadful attrition of war. Their own resources will be inadequate to meet, unaided, the needs of economic reconstruction, when their lost colonies in the Far East are restored. The material assistance, which the one Great Power of the American continent lavishly extended to its European allies in two World Wars, will be still urgently required in the years of peace.

Three of the smallest European Powers possess distant empires of enormous, though largely undeveloped, resources. In Africa alone, Portuguese territories are, in aggregate, more than 800,000 square miles, and even larger areas of at least equal economic possibilities comprise the dependencies of the Netherlands and Belgium, respectively. Burdened with heavy imperial responsibilities, each of these three small States finds itself at the mercy of an international situation which is dominated by the Great Powers. Moreover, their national reserves of capital for colonial development are modest in comparison with those of the Great Powers.

In possession of the oldest of all overseas empires, Portugal has yet been unable to initiate extensive and enduring economic development in Angola, Mozambique, or elsewhere. Except on their margins, these territories are to-day little more important to the commerce and industry of the world than they were a century ago. The Netherlands Empire of the East Indies is, however, of different calibre, as shown remarkably by the agricultural development achieved in Java. This island alone—some 50,000 square miles—makes an incomparably greater contribution to the markets of the world than the entire Portuguese Empire. But, apart from Java and the neighbouring part of Sumatra, the Dutch East Indies, after three centuries of occupation, are still at the threshold of their agricultural and commercial development.

From her vigorous population, considerably larger than that of Portugal, Holland, in the seventeenth and eighteenth centuries, sent out considerable colonies, to South Africa and Java. It is probable, however, that not more than 300,000 persons, all told, were involved, and the much bigger proportions of the modern Dutch population in South Africa—now numbering about one and a half millions—are due to natural increase, almost unaided.

Imperial responsibilities were thrust upon the Kingdom of the Belgians as recently as 1908. In that year the greater part of the Congo Basin was inherited, but the occurrence of the First World War postponed active colonial development until 1920. Since then the record of Belgian administration has been on the whole progressive, while much has been done to discover and use the vast wealth of Central Africa, of which copper is now an outstanding item. The Congo is not, however, and is unlikely ever to be, suitable country for White settlement; and the tiny Belgian, and other European, population—in all, about 35,000—is not composed of permanent settlers.

Even the briefest reference to the smaller imperial Powers of Europe leads to the conclusion that none is able, on the basis of its own human and material resources, to provide adequately for colonial defence, or to develop latent industrial and commercial possibilities as they could be developed in the hands of a great Power. Appreciating the impossibility of their armed forces proving sufficient in a war in which they might be involved, Belgium, the Netherlands, and Portugal maintain abroad naval and military contingents which are little more than are required for policing. The Dutch, despite an illustrious maritime record, station in the East Indies a fleet composed of units which are mostly old and unserviceable, according to modern naval standards. It is regarded as fortunate by Portugal and Belgium that their colonial territories, in the one case mainly and in the other wholly, lie in Africa, where Britain, their traditional friend, has proved in effect to be a protecting Power also. On the other hand, the Netherlands Indies, before the Second World War, lay so close to a threatening Japan that Britain's naval and military assistance was much uncertain.

The further question is unavoidable: whether or not any Power has the moral right to retain exclusive control over land which it fails, over a long period, effectively to occupy and to use. The world needs urgently, in an ever-increasing degree, the agricultural and mineral wealth which the undeveloped lands of the Tropics are known to possess. From time to time, the land-hungry nations, such as Japan, turn their gaze towards Central Africa, Amazonian South America, the East Indies, and Northern Australia, each of which (for the greater part) continues to lie fallow. Lack of economic development is by no means entirely due to the backwardness of the native civilizations: a very important factor is the policy of the suzerain Power concerned, in each case. Yet it has been a persistent argument of certain European nations that their control of tropical lands is necessary, in order to ensure not only the welfare of the native peoples, but also the active exploitation of undeveloped territories, in the interests of mankind, as a whole.

There is no civilized defence for the outrages committed by the Japanese war-lords; but the success of their appeal for national solidarity, in the face of what they termed the aggression of the Western Powers, has been due in part to the obvious discrepancy between the proclaimed intentions and the performance of those Powers in their colonial enterprises. As they have contrived to dominate so much of the undeveloped territory of the world the European nations have a special responsibility to civilization. Unfortunately, the need for fulfilling the trust which they have accepted becomes particularly urgent at a time when certain of them, gravely weakened by recurrent and wholesale war, are no longer in a position to bear, unaided, the full responsibilities of their trust.

AMERICAN PENETRATION OF THE OLD WORLD

So far, the U.S.A. has refrained from territorial commitments on the mainland of any other continent. True to tradition in this respect, its Government was preparing to raise the political status of the Philippine Islands from autonomy to independence, just before the threatening attitude of Japan forced it to revise its entire Pacific policy. At the close of the nineteenth century, the U.S.A. had occupied the Philippines in the process of eliminating Spain's authority in all seas where American interests were jeopardized by that Power; but it had no desire to maintain its suzerainty over territories so distant from its own shores, and so difficult to defend.[3]

The "isolationism" of the U.S.A. was, however, an intelligible and possible policy only so long as domestic problems—including the settlement of its empty spaces west of the Mississippi—demanded attention, almost to the neglect of its place in the world at large. Once the nation had expanded to the Pacific coast of the continent and its final frontiers had been reached, it became increasingly involved in questions whose scope extended beyond the North American continent. Possession of a coastline on each of two widely separated oceans stimulated the Panama Canal undertaking, which, however, at the beginning of this century, was a matter of concern almost as much to Great Britain—then easily foremost in ocean commerce—as to the United States. In the European War of 1914 the original issues had little to do with the U.S.A., but as the war went on, the German threat to dominate, not only Europe, but the North Atlantic Ocean also, inevitably roused the United States to action.

Several factors may co-operate to induce the United States to extend their "sphere of influence" farther east than the Caribbean and farther west than the Philippines, apart altogether from the need to participate very actively in the political and economic resettlement of Europe and Asia. One such factor is the increasing demand of American industrialists for access to supplies of certain minerals and agricultural products, which are either not available within the frontiers of the U.S.A., or, if available, are in process of becoming exhausted. Included amongst such commodities are petroleum and natural rubber. In the first case, there is an abundant, but rapidly wasting, supply: in the second, the absence of suitable climatic conditions renders production virtually impossible.

For about half a century the petroleum output of the U.S.A. has been greater than that of all other countries combined, and the quantity produced (mainly from California and Texas) is still on the increase. But demands on North American petroleum have increased

[3] Lest American policy in the Philippines be regarded as dictated solely by self-interest, it should be widely known that, in its care for the welfare of the Filipinos, the U.S.A. Government showed more enlightenment than has ever been shown by an imperial Power in its treatment of backward peoples of the tropical zone. Expenditure on the education of the Filipinos is a useful guide in any comparison.

faster than the growth of output, and in the years before the Second World War it was widely held by American oil geologists that the reserves would be well on the way to depletion by 1960. The phenomenal development of the oil wells of countries on the south side of the Caribbean Sea—Venezuela, in particular—has somewhat allayed anxiety regarding the future of supplies within the American continent. Nevertheless, the American oil companies look eastward to the Old World, being reasonably certain that the "centre of gravity" of production in the near future will move to Southern Asia. Two zones stand out with special prominence: one extends from Arabia to Iraq and Iran, and the other from Burma to the East Indies. Already American interests hold oil concessions on the western flank of the Persian Gulf, in a region where Britain's influence has hitherto been more evident than that of any Power. Other concessions, obtained recently in Saudi Arabia, help to confirm the impression that the United States will proceed to "protect" the Asiatic oil interests of her nationals. The only machinery for such "protection" has long been employed, in one guise or another, by European imperialist Powers with interests in Asia and Africa. It is either a "sphere of interest" or a "protectorate."

If the U.S.A. were to establish commercial bases in South-West Asia their immediate neighbours would be two other great Powers—Britain and Soviet Russia—each with a "sphere of influence" of its own. To the Soviet Union the Caspian Basin, rich in oil, has become indispensable, and for this, as well as for military reasons, Russia allows no interference with her special interests in Northern Iran. To Britain, the oil of South-Western Iran and of Eastern Iraq is equally vital, and both territories fall well within her scheme of imperial defence. Neither Power would observe without anxiety the entrance of the U.S.A. into the political geography of South-Western Asia.

However conveniently, from the geographical standpoint, the three Great Powers may arrange between themselves a partition of interests in Asia, the history of economic exploitation in backward countries gives no grounds for supposing that international competition has ceased with the defeat of Japan. The latter's evacuation of the Far Eastern Tropics has been followed by armed occupation on the part of the United States, Britain, France, and the Netherlands, in their respective areas; whilst, throughout the Japanese Empire—as it was in 1939—the Government of the U.S.A. demands the right of exclusive occupation for an indefinite period. There is no doubt of the intention of the victors of the Pacific War to restore exclusive sovereign authority within their colonial territories, temporarily lost to Japan: this irrespective of the wishes of the native communities of Annam, Java, and Burma who have demanded their independence.

The economic attractiveness of certain lands of the Old World to American industrialists depends on much more than the available resources of oil. This commodity has been selected for special mention merely because the geography of its development illustrates particularly well the tendency for American industrial interests to expand beyond the frontiers of North America. The conventional limits of a continent—even as well defined as those of America are—cannot always segregate its society from the rest of the world. A dynamic, expanding nation, such as the U.S.A. has been from its earliest, colonial days, is likely to range far in its activities, until at last the urge to extend its horizon has subsided. This may well occur without the least suggestion of conscious aggressiveness in the attitude of its people. The Old World, whose more backward countries are likely to experience the penetration of American ideas and ways of life, has not the power, because of its political disunity, to resist such penetration, even if it would. One effect of the Second World War will be to enlarge the influence of the U.S.A. in every continent. In respect of area, of size of population, and of political cohesion, only one Power, namely Soviet Russia, will be able to treat with the U.S.A. on equal terms.[4]

On the other hand, the influence of the Old World on the New can never be negligible. Yet it is well to bear in mind that the "Monroe Doctrine" still lives: it has no equivalent in the Old World save the abortive attempt of Japan, under its policy of a "Co-prosperity Sphere," to exclude the interests of all non-Asiatic Powers from the Far East. No non-American Power may establish new bases, or extend existing ones within the Americas, without incurring the hostility of the United States.

[4] The British Commonwealth is composed of States which are able, as the member States of the U.S.A. or of Soviet Russia are not, to act independently of each other if they should so wish. At times of international crisis the cohesion of the Commonwealth may thus be threatened, as occurred when Eire declined to enter the Second World War.

EUROPEAN SETTLEMENT OF THE TROPICS

Turning from the industrial and political interests of European and other States in the tropical and sub-tropical zones of the Old World, we devote brief attention to the degree of success which has attended the colonization of the Europeans in low latitudes.

Within a belt, extending to twenty degrees on either side of the equator, the only considerable settlement of Europeans has been at altitudes exceeding 3,000 feet. The East African Highlands, particularly of Kenya and Tanganyika Territory, offer some of the most attractive terrain. In these latitudes, the reduction of temperature on account of high altitude makes residence for the white man tolerable, so long as there is protection from the sun's rays. Even so, there is a notable absence of a marked seasonal rhythm of temperature, such as is characteristic of Western Europe, from which the majority of White colonists of the Tropics are derived: and it is generally agreed that the monotony of the seasons is detrimental to the sustained vigour of mind and body of the settler.

Europeans, save those of Latin countries, have certainly not proved their capacity for successful acclimatization within the Tropics. Complete acclimatization demands the fulfilment of certain tests, including the ability of the colonist to preserve his virility, without impairment due to climate or other circumstance of the physical environment. The population of the colony should be able to maintain its numbers by natural increase alone; whilst a further test demands that, as regards manual work, the colony should be independent of the native population.

Most Europeans whose families have lived for several generations in very low latitudes bear the evidence of physical and mental deterioration. Tropical climates are particularly severe on women and children, and it is not unusual for them to seek relief from the strain of tropical residence by fairly regular holidays in temperate latitudes. There are relatively few instances of British families remaining in tropical residence for several successive generations, whilst it is extremely rare for such colonists to undertake the heavy work of agriculture or of manufacturing and mining industries.

Queensland is renowned as providing the only considerable instance of a colony of British origin, able to undertake agricultural work well within the Tropics. The sugar-cane plantations, established along the coast to the north of Brisbane, have prospered without the necessity to recruit coloured labour. Yet it has been shown conclusively that the plantation workers are carefully selected for their superior physique, that their ages range usually between twenty and forty, that the percentage of women in the population of Eastern Queensland is lower than the average for Australia as a whole, and that many workers, in their years of retirement, choose to reside in the more temperate parts of the continent. Other factors in white acclimatization include, in addition to high rates of wage, severe tariff restrictions on imported sugar, which virtually exclude such sugar from the Australian market.

The field labourers of Eastern Queensland cannot, therefore, be cited as evidence of successful white acclimatization in a tropical environment; whilst, throughout the remainder of the hot, humid belt of Australia, there is no other case of considerable European settlement. Moreover, in no other tropical part of the British Empire is there a serious attempt on the part of Europeans to undertake the heavy manual work required by agriculture or other industry. Only the very limited areas of British Tropical Africa, which exceed an elevation of about 4,000 feet, are used for permanent European occupation; and, beyond the frontiers of the Union of South Africa, the total British population of the continent is but 100,000, or very little more.

Not only the climatic factor, however, militates against British or other West European colonization within the African and Asiatic Tropics. There, unlike Australia, the native population has proved its capacity to adjust itself to the various régimes which European Powers have established. The labour of the African Negro, of the Indian and other peoples of colour, has, from the outset, proved indispensable to the maintenance of the white man's own standards of civilization. Throughout the Orient and Africa, south of the Mediterranean border, there is no place for the unskilled or semi-skilled European worker, who, in Europe, to the number of many millions, was unemployed in the years before the Second World War. In British Africa, the density of the white population is low almost everywhere, when measured by the densities prevailing in Europe. Yet for one reason or another—the menace of climate; the presence of a virile native population fully capable of meeting demands for unskilled, and some branches of skilled, labour; or the established tradition that the white man should not engage in manual toil—it has been virtually impossible for British citizens, other than the wealthy or the highly skilled, to settle in Africa.

No doubt, the Dominions offer climatic advantages which are not found in other parts of the Empire. It is also true that in Canada, Australia, and New Zealand there is no considerable population of backward natives. Nevertheless, the colonization of the Dominions by British citizens was virtually at a standstill in the period before the war. No more urgent problem confronts Britain, and the Dominions also, than the adjustment of the economic organization of the Empire to make possible the colonization of the comparatively empty but highly desirable lands of Canada, Australia, and New Zealand by British citizens.

To the emigrant, New Zealand has proved to be one of the most attractive of the Dominions in respect of its physical endowment. Of an area and climate which bear close comparison with those of Great Britain, its population—like that of Australia also—is largely of British origin. For these and other reasons it offers a standard of life closer to the British than that of any part of the Empire, despite the extreme distance of its position. It seems clear that these affinities of a mother-country and its colony, at opposite sides of the world to each other, are strengthened as much by similarity of climate as by any other factor.

If ever large-scale emigration from Britain should be regarded as necessary for the economic health of our country, or in order to strengthen the white population of the sparsely settled lands of the Empire, there can be no doubt that a large proportion of the intending colonists will choose New Zealand. The factor of extreme distance which hitherto has hindered settlement, by raising unduly the time and cost of overseas travel and by threatening the home-loving colonist with almost inevitable exile, will cease to operate in days of cheap air travel and fast ocean liner services. Moreover, New Zealand will cease to be a mere outpost of white civilization when its population-density is raised—as well it may within a century or more!—to a figure comparable with that of a European country. With only fifteen persons per square mile at present, its density is less than one-fortieth that of England and Wales.

Unlike the white colonists of tropical and sub-tropical lands who have migrated from North-Western Europe, Southern Europeans have proved their capacity, not only for residence in similar latitudes, but also for vigorous and sustained labour. The successful record of the French, Spanish, and Italian settlers in Algeria has no parallel in Africa, south of the Sahara. There are those who believe that the Italian peasant has proved indispensable to the development of Tunisia, Libya, and Abyssinia, and that, when the future of the fallen Italian Empire is decided, the contribution, both actual and potential, which Italian labour has made to African civilization, must be taken into account.

It is not overlooked that the climate of the Mediterranean rim of Africa is hardly more severe than that of Southern Italy, Provence, and South-Eastern Spain, from which a majority of the Latin colonists of Africa have come. The summer temperature of Tunis (a mean of 78°F. for July) is not markedly in excess of that of Palermo (77°), and is actually deficient when compared with 85°F. for Seville in the same month. Obviously, the problem of acclimatization is rendered easier for the Southern European in North Africa than it would be for the Englishman in the same region.

South of the Sahara there is no considerable settlement of Latin peoples, and the record of Portuguese colonization in the African tropics is complicated by a readiness to marry Negro women. Most of those who are counted as European in the population estimates of Angola and Mozambique are "coloured," and would so rank if the census standards of the neighbouring Union of South Africa were to be applied. Miscegenation on the part of the Portuguese is no new development, and seems to have been accepted as inevitable policy by the colonists who followed in the wake of Bartolemeu Diaz and Vasco da Gama.

THE ANTICIPATED DECLINE OF POPULATION IN EUROPE

Emigration from Europe to North America has not been considerable since severe restrictions were imposed by the Immigration Laws of the United States, shortly after the First World War. To other continents also—apart from Russian migration across Northern Asia—there has been no considerable flow of European settlers for many years. The last large exodus across the Atlantic was mainly from Eastern and Southern Europe, and had little effect on the congestion of industrialized Western Europe. The high densities of Britain, Belgium, the Netherlands, and Western Germany, all approaching—if not exceeding—700 inhabitants to the square mile, are a response to the expansion of their commerce and industry; but such high densities depend on continued industrial expansion.

Emigration from Western Europe is no longer necessary—if it ever was!—as a relief to congestion; for the entire continent, excepting certain areas in the east and south-east, is moving towards a decline in population. Indeed, such a decline has already been marked for several decades in the case of France, though concealed in the census by the immigration of Italians and Poles in large numbers. A fully maintained birth-rate in Europe is limited to the Slavonic East and to certain southern countries, notably Italy; and even there, as the standard of civilization rises, there is a corresponding tendency for births to decline. Thus, although in Soviet Russia as a whole, the fertility of the inhabitants is very satisfactory, it has shown a slight decline in the Ukraine, the most "advanced" of all the Soviet Republics.

The considerable fall of natural increase in Western and Central Europe during the late nineteenth and early twentieth centuries, and the contemporary rise in the birth-rates of certain Slavonic peoples, have shifted the "centre of gravity" of European population slowly eastwards. The "centre" is estimated to have been in Central Austria about the year 1820, and some 120 miles farther east by 1930.[5]

The continuance of this tendency cannot help but affect the balance of economic and political forces on the continent. Moreover, if the mineral and agricultural resources of Eastern and South-Eastern Europe should be greatly developed in the post-war years—as, for example, the Eastern Ukraine was developed in the period between the wars—the eastward shift of the "centre of gravity" would likely be accelerated.

In Asia also the "centre of gravity" of population is on the move towards the east, as a result of two main causes. The first is the fecundity of the Indian, Chinese, and Japanese, which rises superior to their depressed economic condition: all three peoples—numbering together more than 900 millions[6]—lie to the east of the arid and sparsely inhabited lands of South-Western and Central Asia. The

[5] See a paper by J. Haliczer in the Proceedings of the International Congress of Geography, Warsaw, 1934.

[6] This figure approaches one-half of the world's population.

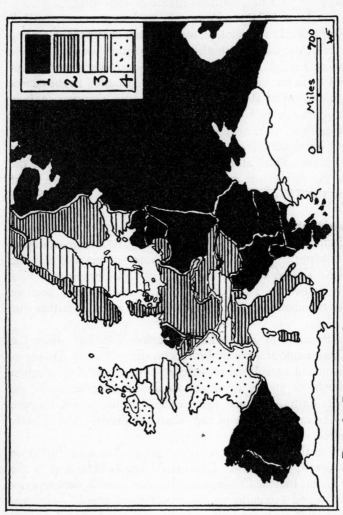

FIG. 28.—PERCENTAGE INCREASE OF NATIVE POPULATIONS IN EUROPEAN
COUNTRIES, 1920–1930

1. Countries with increase of over 10 per cent
2.   ,,   ,,   ,,   6–9.9   ,,   ,,

3. Countries with increase of 2–5.9 per cent
4.   ,,   ,,   ,,   under 2   ,,   ,,

second is the colonization of Soviet Asia, the ultimate effect of which will be to establish the headquarters of Russian power well to the east of the Urals. Within North America, on the other hand, the shift of the "centre" is westwards, as population continues to fill the vast Mississippi Basin and the lands of the Pacific slope.

A great, though slowly evolving change is, therefore, taking place in the distribution of the world's population, and nothing that can be foreseen will disturb its progress during the twentieth century. The cumulative effect will be to increase the proportion of the world's population which is distributed on the flanks of the North Pacific ocean, and so to diminish the relative importance of the North Atlantic focus of population. Increasingly, the international issues that arise in the Pacific zone will claim the attention of the Powers. All the Great Powers, save Germany, were directly concerned in the recent war of the Pacific.

Whether or not the European Powers, which, through their several empires, control the political destinies of about one-half of mankind, will be able effectively to populate those of their dependencies which are now undeveloped and virtually empty, the trend of population in Europe suggests that the continent will be able to house its many nations, without the necessity for further emigration. Re-distribution of population within Europe, so as to relieve the congestion of certain crowded areas, or to reunite "minorities" with parent nations, is needed, but could be effected without involving any other continent.

The attractiveness of Europe as the main residence of the white peoples is likely to remain, when its war-wounds have healed. Abundant fertility and variety of soils, together with the highest farming standards in the world, are assets which will endure. Moreover, from the standpoint of climate, Europe has marked advantages. Severity of temperature and exposure to lengthy drought are not so characteristic as they are of Asia, the Americas, and Africa. In respect of habitability the closest comparison is with North America which, though larger, has a much greater proportion of virtual desert. The cold-desert lands of Northern Canada are of vast extent, and so far have severely restricted the settlement and development of the Dominion. As in North America (excluding Mexico, usually classified as a Central American land) there is no climate of Europe which is of definitely tropical standard, though, in each of these continents, the southern districts approach the tropical in summer.

The natural endowment of the continent is, therefore, exceptionally favourable. Moreover, there is geographical advantage in Europe's ease of access to the vast continental areas of the Old World. For more than two centuries this advantage has been utilized in the economic development of Asia and Africa. The invasion of the Balkans and Central Europe by the Ottoman Turks in the fifteenth century was the last of the series of Great Migrations from the heart of Asia; and, after the withdrawal of the Turks from the gates of Vienna, there was no serious obstacle to wide expansion of European interests across the world, until the emergence of the United States and Japan as Great Powers. The momentum of that expansion is now almost exhausted, except in the case of the continued advance of Russia beyond the Urals.

Ellsworth Huntington, notable American climatologist and geographer, has proclaimed the doctrine—widely accepted, though not by the "coloured" nations—that equable, yet stimulating climates serve to explain the superiority of Western Europeans and Eastern Americans, in respect of energetic vitality, over all other peoples. It is a comforting theory to those who accept it, and is based on the historico-geographic view that all the "advanced" civilizations of the world have evolved within what may be described as the North Atlantic temperate zone. Climatic determinism, such as that of Huntington, regards the extreme seasonal range of temperature and the excessive aridity of the Euro-Asiatic steppes as inimical to sustained human effort. Before the Russian Revolution, the comparatively primitive standards of life within the Tsarist Empire seemed to support the theory. A climate as rigorous as that of Russia certainly offers difficulties to economic development, in such ways as the freezing of soil and water throughout a long winter. But may not the toughness and powers of endurance of the Russian Slavs be a response to a climate which is much more favourable to human energy than Huntington has thought possible? Such a suggestion is made here in order to advise caution to those who would, over confidently, explain human energy in terms of climate.

EUROPEAN CONTACTS WITH BACKWARD PEOPLES

Although the imperial burdens of certain States of Europe sorely tax their political capacity, so far there has been no serious proposal that such Powers should abandon any part of their colonial territories. On the contrary, it is held that the responsibilities of colonial government are inevitable, if the Powers concerned are to develop the colonial resources on which their standards of life, to a considerable degree, depend. Undoubtedly, the political ascendancy of Europe throughout the greater part of the Tropics—almost unquestioned as it has been until very recent years—has brought it abundant wealth. Since the First World War, however, the emphasis in the colonial policy of the more important Powers has shifted—avowedly at all events—from economic development in their own interest to the responsibilities of trusteeship in the treatment of backward peoples.

Concern for the welfare of the natives of certain tropical and sub-tropical lands was formally expressed in the Treaty Settlement with Germany in 1919. Then, with sanction derived from the Covenant of the League of Nations, Mandates for the administration of the ex-Turkish and ex-German Dependencies were shared between Great Britain, three Dominions of the British Empire, France, Belgium, and Japan.

In the clearest possible terms of which the legal draftsmen were capable, the respective Mandates left no doubt that the intention was to guide and generally assist the peoples of the Mandated Territories concerned, until they should be ready and able to lead an autonomous existence in reasonable security. It was appreciated that the peoples concerned were not all to be on exactly the same footing. For example, the inhabitants of the ex-Turkish Dependencies were regarded as approaching a stage in their political evolution, in which they would be able to accept the opportunities for self-government; whereas, in the case of the natives of the ex-German Cameroons, East Africa, South-West Africa and Togoland, it was claimed that a much more backward stage of political development necessitated an almost indefinite postponement of the withdrawal of the Mandatory's protection. Most important of all, the terms of most of the Mandates left no doubt that the interests of the native inhabitants should prevail if ever they should conflict with those of the Mandatory, or its nationals.

When reviewing the Mandates experiment of the period 1919-39 its success or failure should be judged by its positive achievements for the welfare of the native inhabitants. It is recalled that the latter were not invited to choose the particular Mandatory Power under whose authority they were placed, much less to express at any time an opinion on the operation of the Mandates system. The verdict of the brief history of the Mandates seems to be that the Mandated Territories have been administered very much as if they had been formally annexed by the Powers concerned.

Each Mandatory favoured a type of government which had already proved successful in its own colonial Dependencies. Japan treated the Caroline and Marshall Islands as annexed territory, and proceeded to fortify them in defiance of her agreements: France, in the case of the Cameroons and Togoland, assimilated both people and territory to her own imperial system: Belgium's action was similar in the Ruanda-Urundi Province: whilst Britain in Tanganyika introduced principles of government, which were generally enlightened and had previously proved their worth in British West Africa. Although the interests of its white settlers were by no means neglected, Tanganyika under Mandate was one of the brighter features of a system which, as a whole, was not conspicuously different in principle from ordinary standards of colonial government.

In the history of imperial rule the cause of backward, subject-peoples has never been without its champions. Considerations of a less altruistic nature have, however, influenced most colonial Powers to improve native standards of life. They know that the social and economic misery of subject-peoples reacts sharply and very unfavourably on the material interests of the suzerain Power.

The Union of South Africa is but slowly advancing to this realization. In that Dominion a wide, deep, and virtually unbridged gulf separates the white settlers and natives. Economic and social segregation is there more rigid than in any other colonial territory, and matches even the caste system of India. It demands, in order that it may endure, a continuous frustration of energy and achievement on the part of the Negro population; and grave tension in the community as a whole is the inevitable result. The quality of native labour is kept low, in order to reserve all skilled occupations to the white settlers, even though expert advice has not failed in its warning that such a policy is a hindrance to industrial and agricultural prosperity and social health.

Although the Government of the Union of South Africa is more repressive in its native policy than any in Africa, it is by no means alone in regarding the interests of European settlers as paramount. The reservation of the most fertile and healthy lands of Kenya

Colony and Southern Rhodesia to Europeans indicates all too clearly that, wherever in British Africa the territorial interests of white men and Africans are in competition, there is little chance of equitable compromise.

The greater part of the tropical world is, however, untenanted by European colonists. Even so, the economic possibilities tend to be regarded largely—one may say primarily!—from the standpoint of the industrial and commercial needs of the colonial Power concerned. This is normal, even where policy is, in general, benevolent to the natives. Black and brown men, willingly or under duress, provide labour for plantation agriculture, for mines, as well as for roads and other constructional work essential to the controlling Power. Their own economic advantage has sometimes been considerable, but usually only incidental to the enrichment of their employers. Who can deny that, since the African coasts were first charted by Portuguese mariners in the fifteenth century, the great continent has been treated as an economic and political appendage of Europe?

The white man's medical science is his greatest contribution to the welfare of backward peoples. Endemic and epidemic disease are in retreat, whilst equatorial swamp and jungle are reclaimed for healthy settlement. Yet, incidental to the establishment of an industrial order, new perils for native peoples emerge. Every European-built town in Africa has its slum where disease is introduced, along with intemperate habits of the more irresponsible settlers. The health of Africa's finest manhood is gravely threatened. In Western Europe industrialism developed without a plan, and so it has been in Africa also. The urban slum is a result, and an African slum beggars description for its squalor.

To what political future are the backward peoples moving under European guidance? The trusteeship of the Western Powers is, admittedly, a temporary phase only. Britain, in Africa, expects to build a civilization, essentially African, but equipped with the advantages of "Western" science. She tries, by "indirect rule" in Nigeria and elsewhere, to interfere as little as possible with native law and institutions, intent to preserve the best in native civilization. This is her compromise, and it may work well for a time; but it is without a clear vision of the place of the African in the future world. Moreover, there is some inconsistency in an attempt to preserve the ancient foundations of native society, whilst introducing the revolutionary ideas which are inseparable from the scientific apparatus and technique of the Europeans.

For the native policy of French imperialism in Africa, there is, as we have seen, one goal only. It is the bestowal of both the privileges and the duties of French citizenship upon all French subjects. Assimilation to the French way of life is regarded as the greatest possible contribution to the progress of African civilization. In consequence, "indirect rule," as understood and operated by the British, is not generally in favour. There is no intention of preserving the traditional basis of native law and custom. The tropical empires of certain other European Powers show in their native policies variations on the *motifs* of British and French rule, respectively. Britain and France, owing to the enormous geographical range of their empires, and to their long experience of the government of "coloured" peoples, are accepted by some less experienced Powers as setting standards of colonial government.

The emergence of Soviet Russia as the greatest Asiatic Power has set, however, an altogether new standard in the treatment of backward "colonial" peoples. It is not the policy of the Soviet Union to assimilate the non-Slav peoples to a dominant Slav civilization; neither is it the intention, by "indirect rule," to postpone the planning of the future, or to discard scientifically prepared "blue prints." Regional diversities of culture are fostered, but, at the same time, the Plan, which determines the contribution of every community, must cover all.

Varied as are the policies and the methods of the European States in their handling of backward peoples, their wealth of experience in such matters is unmatched by the rest of the world. The territory of Europe may, in the future, occupy a less important place in the world than it has done in the past, but the contribution of European genius to the solution of human problems will not thereby be diminished.

SELECTED BIBLIOGRAPHY

BANSE, E.: *Raum und Volk im Weltkriege*, Oldenburg, 1932.

CARR-SAUNDERS, A. M.: *World Population: Past Growth and Present Trends*, Oxford, 1936.

CASTELLANI, A.: *Climate and Acclimatization*, London, 1938.

CLARK, COLIN: The Economics of 1960, New York, 1942.

CLOSE, C.: "Population and Migration," Geography, vol. 14, 1927, pp. 1–24.

DEMANGEON, A.: L'Empire britannique: Étude de géographie coloniale, Paris, 1923.

FAWCETT, C. B.: A Political Geography of the British Empire, London, 1933.

FAWCETT, C. B.: The Bases of a World Commonwealth, London, 1941.

FORSYTH, WILLIAM D.: The Myth of Open Spaces: Australian, British, and World Trends of Population and Migration, Melbourne, 1943.

HUNTINGTON, E.: Civilization and Climate, 2nd ed., New Haven, 1924.

HAUSHOFER, KARL: Geopolitik des Pazifischen Ozean, Berlin, 1924.

ISHII, RYOICHI: Population Pressure and Economic Life in Japan, London, 1937.

KAT ANGELINO, DE: Colonial Policy, 2 vols., The Hague, 1931.

KNIBBS, GEORGE H.: The Shadow of the World's Future, or the Earth's Population Possibilities and the Consequences of the Present Rate of Increase of the Earth's Inhabitants, London, 1928.

LIPPMANN, W.: U.S.A. Foreign Policy, London, 1944.

MAURETTE, F.: "Le Petrole: Étude de géographie économique," Ann. de Géogr., vol. 35, 1926, pp. 1–26.

NOTESTEIN, F. W., etc.: The Future Population of Europe and the Soviet Union, Geneva, 1944.

OBST, E.: England, Europa, und die Welt, Berlin, 1927.

POLLARD, A. F.: The British Empire: its Past, its Present, and its Future, London, 1909.

"Poor White Problem in South Africa," Report of the Carnegie Commission, Stellenbosch, 1932.

PRICE, A. GRENFELL: White Settlers in the Tropics, New York, 1939.

SAUER, C. O.: "The Prospect for Redistribution of Population," Limits of Land Settlement (Council on Foreign Relations), 1937.

STRAUSZ-HUPÉ, R.: The Balance of Tomorrow, New York, 1945.

UYEDA, TEIJIRO: "Future of the Japanese Population," Japanese Council, Institute of Pacific Relations 1933, Tokyo, 1933.

WELLES, SUMNER: The Time for Decision, London, 1944.

ZIMMERN, A.: The Third British Empire, London, 1926.

Appendix A

Extracts from the Decree of the Polish National Council, Setting up the Polish Committee of National Liberation, July 21st, 1944.

"The fundamental principles of the Constitution of March 17, 1921, will be binding until the convocation of a Constituent Sejm elected on the basis of universal, direct and equal suffrage by secret ballot, which, as the body expressing the will of the people, will adopt a new Constitution."

"Poles! Rise to the struggle for Poland's greatness, for return to the motherland of old Polish Pomorze and Opolskie Silesia, for East Prussia, for a wide access to the sea, for Polish frontier posts on the Oder!"

"History and the experience of the present war show that only the building up of a great Slav dam, founded on Polish-Soviet-Czechoslovakian accord, can serve as a safeguard against the pressure of German imperialism."

"For 400 years, constant conflicts between Poles and Ukrainians, Poles and Belorussians, Poles and Russians have been the rule—to the detriment of both sides. Now a historic change has taken place in these relations. Conflicts are giving way to friendship and co-operation dictated by the mutual vital interests of these peoples. The friendship and fighting co-operation inaugurated by the brotherhood-in-arms of the Polish Army and the Red Army must be converted into a lasting alliance and neighbourly co-operation after the war."

"The Polish Committee of National Liberation recognizes that the question of the Polish-Soviet frontiers should be settled by mutual agreement. The eastern frontier must not be a barrier between ourselves and our neighbours, but a line of friendly neighbourship. It must be settled in accordance with the principle: Polish lands to Poland: Ukrainian, Belorussian and Lithuanian lands to Soviet Ukraine, Soviet Belorussia and Soviet Lithuania. An enduring alliance with our immediate neighbours—the Soviet Union and Czechoslovakia—will be the fundamental principle of Polish foreign policy."

"In order to expedite the rehabilitation of the country and to satisfy the age-old desire of the Polish peasantry for land, the Polish Committee of National Liberation will immediately proceed to carry out a broad agrarian reform in the liberated territories."

"For this purpose a Land Fund will be inaugurated, which will be under the charge of the Department of Agriculture and Agrarian Reform. Besides farm implements, machinery, buildings and livestock, this fund will include the land of Germans, the land of traitors to the people, as well as landed estates of over 50 hectares. The land of Germans and of traitors to the people will be confiscated. The owners of estates turned over to the Land Fund will be provided for, but no compensation will be paid depending on the size of the estates. Estate owners who have rendered service to the country in the fight against the Germans will receive more generous provision. The land gathered into the Land Fund, with the exception of such areas as are set aside for model farms, will be divided up among the small and medium peasants, small tenant farmers with large families, and agricultural labourers. The land which is distributed by the Land Fund at a minimum price, like the land previously belonging to individuals, will constitute their private property. The Land Fund will set up new farms or increase the holdings of small farms, taking as a basis five hectares of arable land of average quality for an average-sized family. Families which are unable to obtain this quota in their own districts will have the right to re-settle with government assistance in areas where land is available, chiefly in territories recovered from Germany."

Appendix B. The Boundaries of Poland

Excerpt from Speech by Mr. Churchill (Prime Minister) on December 15th, 1944.

"I cannot accept the view that the arrangements which have been proposed about the frontiers of the new Poland are not solid and satisfactory, or that they would not give to Poland that abiding home of which I spoke to the House in February. If Poland concedes Lwow and the surrounding regions in the south on the line known as the Curzon Line, if Poland makes this concession and those lands are joined to the Ukraine, Poland will gain the whole of East Prussia, west and south of the fortress of Königsberg, including the great city and port of Danzig, one of the most important cities and harbours in the whole world, and famous for centuries as a great gathering-place of the trade of the Baltic, and indeed, of the world.

"Instead of the artificial corridor which was built so laboriously after the last war, Poland would stretch broadly along the Baltic on a front of over 200 miles. The Poles are free, so far as Russia and Great Britain are concerned, to extend their territory at the expense of Germany to the west. I do not propose to go into the exact details, but the extensions in which they will be supported by Britain and Russia, bound together as they are by the twenty years' alliance, those extensions are of high importance. They gain in the west and the north territories more important and more highly developed than they lose in the east. We hear of a third of Poland to be conceded, but that third includes vast tracts of the Pripet Marshes, a most desolate region, which, though it swells the acreage, does not add to the wealth of those who own it.

"Thus, I have set before the House what is in outline the offer which the Russians, on whom the main burden of liberation still falls, make to the Polish people. I cannot believe that such an offer should be rejected by Poland. It would, of course, have to be accompanied by the disentanglement of populations in the west and in the north. The transference of several millions of people would have to be effected from the east to the west or to the north, and the expulsion of the Germans, because that is what is proposed—the total expulsion of the Germans from the area to be acquired by Poland in the west and in the north, for expulsion is a method which, so far as we have been able to see, will be the most satisfactory and lasting. There will be no mixture of populations causing endless trouble as in Alsace-Lorraine. A clean sweep will be made.

"I am not alarmed at the prospect of the disentanglement of the population, nor even am I alarmed at these large transferences, which are more possible than they ever were before, through modern conditions. The disentanglement of the population which took place between Greece and Turkey after the last war was in many ways successful and has produced friendly relations between Greece and Turkey ever since. That disentanglement which at first seemed impossible to achieve and about which it was said it would strip Turkish life in Anatolia of so many extra services and population and could never be assimilated and sustained by Greece— I say that disentanglement solved problems which had before been the cause of immense friction, of wars, and of rumours of wars.

"Nor do I see why there should not be room in Germany for the German population of East Prussia and the other territories I have mentioned. After all, six or seven millions of Germans have been killed already in this dreadful war, into which they did not hesitate for a second time in a generation to plunge all Europe and the world. At the present time, we are told, there are another ten or twelve million prisoners or foreigners used as slaves who will, we hope, be restored to their homes and lands when victory is gained, and we must expect that many more Germans will be killed in the fighting which will occupy the spring and summer, and which will involve the largest and fiercest battles fought in this war."

Excerpt from Speech by the Foreign Secretary (Mr. Eden) on December 15th, 1944.

Referring to the Curzon Line, Mr. Eden pointed out that this line was originally drawn up by a Commission on Polish affairs of the Paris Supreme Council, and that they drew it up to mark the eastern limit of what was indisputably Polish territory so that the Polish Government could immediately take over the administration in that area without question, even while relations with Russia were obscure. That was in 1919. The proposal became associated with Lord Curzon only a year later when it was put before the two parties as an attempt to bring hostilities to an end. Then it was called the Curzon Line. It was from the outset only intended to show the minimum amount of territory which should be assigned to Poland in the east.

It was true to say that the British delegates at the Peace Conference consistently maintained that any further eastward extension of Polish territory beyond the Curzon Line would be highly dangerous to Poland, and, before the Treaty of Riga was signed in 1921, we several times warned the Polish Government against such an extension. In August, 1920, the opposite happened. At an earlier date the Curzon Line was proposed by us to the Soviet Government with the approval of the Polish Government. At a later stage the Soviet Government in their turn approached the Polish Government with a proposal which was approximately the Curzon Line. The Polish Government asked our opinion, and we told them that we considered that such terms would leave her ethnographical position unimpaired, and we urged the Polish Government not to refuse it.

Mr. Eden said two alternatives were proposed to the Supreme Commission on Polish affairs. One proposal was Line A, which the Soviet Government now claimed as the basis of a frontier settlement. That line was then proposed as the boundary between Poland proper and an autonomous Eastern Galicia, which it was hoped to set up under the general suzerainty of Poland. Line B, farther to the east, which left Lwow to Poland, was recommended if the bulk of Eastern Galicia was excluded from Poland and the autonomous State was not created.

"Our Delegation did favour Line A in any case, the line which the Soviet Government are now asking," he added. "It was eventually adopted by the Supreme Commission and embodied in the draft treaty. Several reasons actuated our decisions at that time. One was the necessity to keep this economic area of Eastern Galicia as a whole. There was also the possibility that there might be a larger independent State, perhaps as part of the Greater Ukraine. A final reason was the population problem. At that time between Line A and Line B the population was about one and a half millions, of which rather more than half were Ukrainians, a quarter Poles, and the rest Jews."

Looking at the population problem generally between the Riga frontier and the Curzon Line, Mr. Eden quoted from the 1931 Polish census, the latest available. There were likely to have been very considerable changes since then. The population in that area was approximately 10,700,000. Of that total 3,900,000 were Polish-speaking and 3,200,000 were Roman Catholics. Those who were authorities on these matters said that the religious figures were usually rather nearer the mark than the language-speaking figures. He thought it was fair to say that while there were no later figures than 1931, the Poles had never constituted more than a third of the total population of that area. In his view there was certainly a Polish majority in Lwow itself.

"Before the Treaty of Riga was signed we advised Poland not to go so far east as the frontiers given by the Treaty of Riga." It was perfectly true that the Russians accepted the Treaty of Riga, but Mr. Eden did not think any one could say that that was the one place where they took their stand and refused to look back over the pages of history.

The Frontier of the Soviet Union and Poland, 1945

Following conferences held in Moscow during August, 1945, the Soviet Union and Poland agreed on their new frontier. The text of the Agreement shows that, in addition to several small deviations from the Curzon Line to the advantage of Poland, Russia has ceded two larger districts, one about 50 miles north-east of Lwow and the other between Brest-Litovsk and the Lithuanian frontier. The text gave the alignment of the new frontier as follows:

"From a point approximately 600 yards south-west of the source of the River San, towards the north-east and down the middle of the River to a point south of Solina, then east of Przemysl and west of Nova Russka to the River Soloki. From there to Nemirov Jarovlsev, and to the frontier of the Soviet Republic of Lithuania, the Polish Republic and Eastern Prussia, leaving Grodno on the side of the U.S.S.R. The part of the frontier adjacent to the Baltic Sea is only provisionally defined until the final settlement of the territorial questions by the Peace Treaties.

"The area of pre-war Poland which has passed to the Soviet Union is 77,703 square miles, with a pre-war population of 12,775,000."

Appendix C. A Proposed Partition of Germany

In his book—The Time for Decision (Hamish Hamilton), London, 1944—Mr. Sumner Welles outlines a plan for the partition of Germany. It includes the following points:

He believes that German unity is a threat to the peace of the world and that partition is the only way of off-setting the German menace. A number of plans have been devised, varying from the reconstitution of the old German Federation, as it existed prior to 1848, to the inclusion within a federation of Western Europe, as an autonomous State, of the industrial regions west of the Rhine, leaving the remainder of Germany much as it was prior to 1936.

It is Welles' opinion that, exclusive of East Prussia, Germany should be divided at the time of the armistice into the following three separate States, the boundaries being determined primarily by cultural, historic and economic factors:

A new State of Southern Germany, comprising the former sovereign nations of Bavaria, Wuerttemberg, Baden, and Hesse-Darmstadt, together with those regions which may roughly be defined as the Rhineland and the Saar. The populations which would be comprised within this division are predominantly Catholic:

A State consisting of the following old German subdivisions together with the smaller subdivisions contiguous to them: Upper Hesse, Thuringia, Westphalia, Hanover, Oldenburg, and Hamburg:

A State composed of Prussia (exclusive of East Prussia), Mecklenburg and Saxony.

In the second and third States the populations are predominantly Protestant. In each of these three new States, the historical, as well as the religious and cultural, divisions which existed during the centuries prior to the creation of the Third Reich have been maintained.

By this suggested division a complete economic balance, both agricultural and industrial, would be established within each of the three States, and the proportionate relationship within each State of the prime economic factors, such as agricultural and industrial production, and mineral resources, would be roughly equivalent to that in each of the two others. If the end of the war sees the lowering of customs barriers within Europe, and the creation of customs unions, the new German States should be afforded free opportunity to take part in such customs unions.

The capacity for economic development in each one of the proposed States is almost unlimited. What would vanish would be the giant combines which could be used again as a means of military penetration in other countries.

The problem of the disposition of East Prussia affects world security not only with regard to Germany, but with regard to Eastern Europe as well. There are four main points to consider:

First, it is generally recognized that the Polish Corridor, far from providing a permanent solution of Poland's need for an outlet to the sea, was, on the contrary, a major source of danger to her. The Corridor was an alien sovereignty separating one portion of Germany from the other. No statesman familiar with European history and politics should have regarded the Corridor as anything but a makeshift. The solution was repugnant to the Polish as well as to German nationalistic forces. It left Poland at the mercy of Germany whenever Germany felt strong enough to close the gap which the Corridor created.

Second, the legitimate requirements of the future Polish State include unimpeded access to the sea, without the complications resulting from such artificial arrangements as those involved in the international control of Danzig.

Third, to be taken into account is the insistence of the Soviet Union that the eastern frontier of Poland, as it existed in 1939, should be rectified, to include within Russian territory the regions inhabited by non-Polish populations living to the east of the Curzon Line.

Fourth, inasmuch as these boundary changes would deprive Poland of a considerable portion of her eastern territories, some equivalent restoration must be made if she is to become that "strong and independent Poland" which not only the United States and Great Britain are pledged to see reconstituted, but which likewise has been proclaimed officially by the Soviet Government as an objective of its own policy.

The only solution of these four questions is to give Poland the province of East Prussia, at the same time readjusting the frontier between Western Prussia and the old Polish Corridor so as to give the new German State, of which Western Prussia will form a part, an area of the old Corridor. This will leave the seaports of Danzig, and Gdynia in Polish hands. The exact frontier between the new State of Eastern Germany and the western flank of Poland can be determined only after an actual survey in which the question of populations and availability of land for agricultural purposes should be deciding factors.

It is estimated that one-third of the population of East Prussia consists of individuals who are either Polish nationals or of Polish descent. The human problem involved in a transfer of populations on so vast a scale is very great. However, in the only instance in recent times—the exchange of populations between Turkey and Greece, after the First World War— the transfer was not only humanely and successfully carried out, but is to-day recognized by both Greece and Turkey as having been beneficial to both.

Index

291

Date Due

	May29		